# Serving the Church and the Nation

*JDV Philosophy Series - 14*

# Serving the Church and the Nation

Gratefully and Faithfully

*Editors*
**Kuruvilla Pandikattu SJ**
**Sebastian Vazhapilly SJ**
**Prasad Lankapalli SJ**

**Jnana-Deepa Vidyapeeth**

&

**Christian World Imprints**

First Published in 2020 by

**Jnana-Deepa Vidyapeeth**
Ramwadi, Nagar Road, **Pune-411014**
jdvoffice@jdv.edu.in
www.jdv.edu.in
Phone: +91 20 41036111

&

**Christian World Imprints**
*Christian Publishing & Books from India*
C-3, Wazirpur Industrial Area
**Delhi-110052**
cwidelhi2017@gmail.com
www.ChristianWorldImprints.com
Phone: +91 11 41526079

ISBN: 978-93-5148-496-7

"Published with the help of the Institute of Missiology – Germany"



Printed in India.

# CONTENTS

# JDV PHILOSOPHY SERIES - 14

Since 1893 Jnana-Deepa Vidyapeeth has been pioneering philosophy discussion and debate inspired by prominent personalities like Richard De Smet, Jean de Marneffe, Salvino Azzopardi, Cyril Desbruslais, Noel Sheth, John Vattanky, etc. It has been in the forefront of promoting Indian philosophy and making philosophical thinking relevant for contemporary times. In its effort to reach out to like-minded scholars, JDV Philosophy Series has been visualized as a catalyst for interdisciplinary thinking and contemporary exploration on social issues fostering holistic liberation, integral development and creative engagement.

**Chris Baglow,** Notre Dame Seminary, New Orleans LA USA

**Rubén Herce,** University of Navarra, Spain

**Maribel Nonato,** University of St. Thomas, Manila, Philippines

**Raul Melendez,** Nacional Universidad, Bogota, Colombia

**Donald Frohlich,** University of St. Thomas, Houston TX, USA

**Louis Caruana,** Dean of Philosophy, Gregorian University, Rome, Italy

**Chae-Yong Kim,** President (2014-16), Korean Association for Religious Studies

**George Pattery,** Vice-Chancellor, Jnana-Deepa Vidyapeeth, Pune

## JDV Philosophy Series

1. Salvino Azzopardi: **Epistemology and Phenomenology of Religions** (2018)
2. Kuruvilla Pandikattu & Thomas Karimundackal (eds): **Melodies from the Flute: For Prof Noel Sheth SJ** (2018)
3. Kurien Kunnumpuram: **Freedom and Joy** (2018)
4. Cyril Desbruslais SJ: **Postmodernity: An Indian Christian Philosophical Appraisal** (2019)
5. Cyril Desbruslais SJ: **Metaphysics: Philosophy of Be-ing for Today** (2019)
6. John Peter Vallabadoss: **Indian Thinkers: Modern and Contemporary Period** (2019)
7. Thomas Karimundackal & Kuruvilla Pandikattu (eds): **Logic and Love: For Prof John Vattanky SJ** (2019)
8. Fabian Jose UMI: **Relevance of Thomas Merton's Spirituality for the Consecrated Life in India** (2019)
9. Kuruvilla Pandikattu & PT Mathew (eds): **Committed to the Church and the Country: For Prof Kurien Kunnumpuam SJ** (2019)
10. Cyril Desbruslais SJ: **The Philosophy of God: Faith and Traditions** (2019)
11. Thomas Karimundackal & Kuruvilla Pandikattu (eds): **Fully Spiritual, Fully Human: For Dr Stephen Chundamthadam SJ** (2019)
12. Kuruvilla Pandikattu (ed) Fully Human and Fully Alive: **Essays on Being Human Today in Honour of Dr Cyril Desbruslais SJ** (2020)
13. Thomas Karimundackal SJ & Dolichan Kollareth SJ (eds) Reason: **Faithful and True: For Dr. George Karuvelil SJ** (2020)
14. Kuruvilla Pandikattu SJ, Sebastian Vazhapilly SJ & Prasad Lankapilly SJ (eds) **Serving the Church and the Nation: Gratefully and Faithfully**
15. Kuruvilla Pandikattu (ed) **Befriending the Other: Diversity as Sustaining**
16. Gargi Mukherjee: **Emancipation for the Wretched of the Earth**

# MESSAGE FROM POSA

It is nice to write to Papalites as a Papalite. I have plenty of memories to revisit, since I was myself a Papalite from 1969 to 1979. I don't think any of the student has superseded that experience of being here for 10 years at a stretch. In those days we had many friends around and it is pleasant to back to those friends and to acquire new ones as Papalite. To see their faces together is an enriching and refreshing experience.

During my stay at Papal Seminary, there are many memories that are pleasant, joyful and inspiring ones.

I recall vividly my first meeting with late Fr. Lionel Mascarenhas, SJ the then Rector of Papal Seminary, way back in 1969. As a young seminarian, in my broken English, with fear and trembling, I tried to greet him. On his part Lionel said: you are most welcome to this 'Home of Love.' Here in Papal Seminary, you may strive to be holy! But above all, try and become more human! That was Lionel – utterly human and fully true. He makes you feel great in being who you are and at the same time invite you to become 'more.'

Years later, on my occasional visits to Papal Seminary, I would chat with Lionel. Sitting in his wheelchair, Lionel would enquire about all past students. One of his favourites was now retired Professor Virginius Xaxa. He would ask all details about him, his work, and his family. Papal Seminary Family included for him everyone who has been through the seminary. He was fond of keeping 'night vigil' with the sick. One could say: Lionel kept vigil with all Papalites; and continues to do so from his heavenly abode!

In a sense Lionel defines in himself who a Papalite should be: utterly human, deeply caring and always available. In the larger JDV Campus, 'Papalites' stood for certain bonding that is at once palpable and growing. For the church in South Asia, a 'Papalite' is a dependable and learned priest. No wonder then that 'Papalites' are a species known and appreciated among the clergy across the country.

I am happy to know that Papal Seminary is publishing this book with the collected papers of the Seminar conducted during the Jubilee days. I hope that Papal Seminary will continue to serve the Church and the Nation creatively and joyfully.

**Rev George Pattery SJ**
President
South Asian Assistancy (POSA) of the Society of Jesus

# MESSAGE FROM RECTOR

The Papal Seminary, Pune, India, launched its 125th Jubilee Year celebrations in June 2018. What is Papal Seminary celebrating? It is celebrating the presence of God. It is celebrating God's accompaniment and care of every Papalite (present and past). It is celebrating God's graciousness in making Papal Seminary a Home of Love. We believe that in God we move, and grow and have our being. We therefore celebrate God every day of our life, praising and thanking Him for His loving presence and accompaniment. Papal Seminary in the span of 125 years, through its committed services has moulded thousands of Priests. It has formed them not only as messengers of good news, but they have become God's message to the world. It has formed them not only as prophets, but as prophetic witnesses in the world.

Celebrating the grace-filled Jubilee culmination event in November 2018, Papal Seminary, together with its sister-institute Jnana-Deepa Vidyapeeth, joyfully and gratefully recalled God's unwavering fidelity and the generous giving of so many persons who have supported this Formation Mission. The celebration was truly memorable and meaningful. Coming together with 274 former Papalites and seven Archbishops and Bishops, we celebrated our life-giving roots, our journey in love, and our companionship in mission.

Leafing through our albums and archived documents rekindled memories of the history of Papal Seminary from its very inception when, on his electionin 1878, the idea first struck Pope Leo XIII. Pope Leo XIII shared his dream of starting a national Seminary for the whole of India, in his encyclical *Ad extremas* (1893) on Seminaries for native Clergy. He then wrote to Bishops all over the world, announcing his intention of founding a new national Seminary for India, and appealed to the generosity of Catholics for support. With deep gratitude, we acknowledge the generous contribution and the prayers of innumerable faithful in establishing the Papal Seminary. We continue to be blessed by the support of institutions and persons across the world who contribute to the well-being, growth and development of the Papal Seminary.

Remembering our history urged us to revisit our motto: *Filiitui, India, administritibisalutis!* (Your own sons, O India, will be the heralds of your salvation!) These words, inscribed on the Sacerdotal Jubilee medal of Pope Leo XIII, are inscribed on the hearts of every Papalite. Spurred to do something concrete and more for religious harmony in India, Papal Seminary together with Jnana-Deepa Vidyapeeth, organized a seminar: "Ministering to Contemporary Indian Church: Challenges, Opportunities." We are grateful to the JDV President, teaching and non-teaching staff for their support and collaboration for organizing this seminar. We are publishing the scholarly and thought-provoking seminar presentations in a book edited by three of our Papal Seminary staff members: Frs. Kuruvilla Pandikattu, Prasad Lankapalli & Sebastian Vazhapilly. I thank and appreciate them for their hard work.

The vision of Pope Leo XIII was realized in 1893 under the able leadership of Archbishop Ladislaus Miachael Zaleski, when the Papal Seminary started in Kandy (Sri Lanka, then Ceylon, which was a colony of the British Crown). The administration and management of Papal Seminary was entrusted to the Society of Jesus, since its inception.

After independence, it was found impractical to have the national Seminary of India in Sri Lanka. Hence, after due discernment, it was decided to shift the Seminary to India. Of the many prominent cities of India, Pune - the hub of education and abode of saints - was chosen as home for the Papal Seminary. In 1955, under the leadership of the Jesuit Mission Superior of Pune, Fr. Pius Geisel, the Papal Seminary and Pontifical Athenaeum were shifted to Pune. Fr. Pius Geisel purchased the land and the Jesuit Brothers were given charge to build the Papal Seminary and Pontifical Athenaeum. The practical design of architecture and layout, and the rock-solid building are the fruit of their labour of love and commitment.

So also, the thousands of Priests formed in Papal Seminary are solid in their faith and strong in their commitment. Most are serving in the country with great zeal and pioneering spirit. A few are missionaries serving across the globe. Every Papalite is special in the eyes of God; and the Church has chosen about 4 Cardinals and 75 Bishops and Archbishops from among the Papalites for servant leadership of the people. During the inaugural Jubilee seminar, former Papalites were offered an opportunity to share their sentiments about their Alma Mater.

Many expressed deep gratitude to their formators, narrating how they were spiritually accompanied and how they benefited from the gospel and human values practiced by their formators. Their sharing and the theme chosen for the Jubilee celebration: *Looking Back with Gratitude, Looking Forward with Trust* inspires and challenges us, as we recall the marvelous works done by the Lord in and through us. We are presently 193 (174 seminarians and 19 staff), from 62 dioceses and four religious congregations.

The inaugural Jubilee celebrations were a time of grace and spiritual consolation, as also of solidarity with those struck down by natural calamities. We are deeply grateful to the Dioceses and Religious Congregations who joined us, with prayers, presence and support, in the celebrations. I thank every member of Papal Seminary community for sacrificing personal interests and time to prepare for the Jubilee celebrations.

While expressing sincere thanks to each one in Papal Seminary, I am especially grateful to Fr. Kuruvilla Pandikattu, Fr. Vincent Crasta and Fr. Joe Francis for planning and coordinating the inaugural celebrations, right from the preparations to their culmination – a truly spiritual and meaningful experience. I praise and thank God for blessing our staff and seminarians with multiple talents and gifts. We owe our deep gratitude to DNC, JDV and PG communities for their support and collaboration. We thank the campus Rectors and Superiors and Sisters from Women's Study Center for their cheerful help. I sincerely acknowledge, appreciate and thank our support staff for their hard work and efforts for the success of celebrations. Treasuring this spiritual experience of the inaugural Jubilee celebrations, the book is titled: *Serving the Church and the Nation: Gratefully and Faithfully*.

**Rev BhausahebSansare SJ**
Rector
Papal Seminary

Lovingly dedicated to **Rev Dr Prasad Lankapalli SJ** (October 6, 1966 - January 27, 2020), who left us unexpectedly. May he live forever in and through us. RIP. He was one of the organisers of the seminar, which has birthed this book.

# FOREWORD

Ministering is serving with love. As Christians, redeemed by the blood of Christ, it is our bounden duty to offer ourselves in service to the Church in India. Improvising the words of the American President, Mr. J. F. Kennedy, we have to say "Ask not what the church can do for you, but ask what you can do for the church."

The Church needs our voice to speak for the voiceless. The Church needs our eyes to see the injustice going on around us… and the ears to listen to the cry of the poor. What about our hands? They could be of so much use to do good. And our legs to walk the extra mile to help someone in need.

Jesus' assertion of his mission in Lk 4:18-19 "The Spirit of the Lord is upon me, because he has anointed me to bring good news to the poor. He has sent me to proclaim release to the captives and recovery of sight to the blind, to let the oppressed go free, to proclaim the year of the Lord's favour" is a clarion call with Jesus to join Him in the work of proclamation, liberation and redemption. Today is our day and now is the time. May God find us worthy to be His ministers in His vineyard. I wish the readers of the book a fruitful and grace-filled time!

**+ Peter Machado**
Archbishop of Bangalore

# EDITORIAL

How can we serve the Church and Nation creatively and meaningfully? As we know that Papal Seminary was established to enable the Christians and Indians to lead lives that are gratefully, faithful and so joyful.

Drawing from the vision of its founder, Pope Leo XIII, *"Filii tui India, administri tibi salutis!"* (Your own sons, O India, will be the heralds of your salvation!) Indian Christians in general and Jnana-Deepa Vidyapeeth (JDV) students, including Papal Seminarians, in particular, are called to reflect on the role of priests and Christian leaders in promoting an Indian Church at the service of God. By the initiative of Pope Leo XIII a National Seminary was established in Kandy, Sri Lanka, in 1893.

We have just completed 125 years of its existence and so we thought it proper to reflect on the role of the Christian leaders in promoting a Church that is both genuinely Christian and truly India. So, an academic was held on November 8, 2018 to reflect on the challenges that the present church in India faces, as well as the opportunities offered to her. Being a general topic, we have dealt with the various dimensions affecting the Indian Church in a creative way and offer solutions and possibilities for committed action and prophetic vision.

- Church in India Today: Historical Perspectives
- Rooted and Grounded: The Churches in South India and Opportunities
- Firm and Flexible: Church in North India and its Richness
- Embracing the Dalits: The Church as fostering Human Dignity (Reaching out to the peripheries)
- With Roots and Wings: Church in North East India
- Dialogue as a way of life for the Indian Church Today
- Ecologically and Economically Sensitive: The Tribal Church
- The Future Vision of the Church in India
- Inculturation and Enculturation: The Challenge for Christian Minsters

- The Joy of the Gospel: Being ministers of Joy in India, inspired by Pope Francis
- The Church and the Intellectual Apostolate: Role of Higher Education in fostering an Inclusive Church
- Poets, Prophets and Mystics: The Role of Christian ministers in promoting Harmony and Peace
- Mother Teresa: The Merciful and Maternal (Feminine) Face of the Indian Church
- Being Ministers of the Church in India: Challenges
- Leaven in the Dough: The Indian Church responding to the invitations of a Multicultural, Multireligious Context
- "A Diocesan Response to the Present Indian Realities"
- Missives of Pope Francis: i.e., Pastors with the Smell of Sheep; A Church "Going Forth"; A Church like a Battlefield Hospital; A Church Interested in the Peripheries, etc.
- "Spirituality through Science" or Science-Religion Dialogue
- Creating Space for Sacramental Equality in the Church
- Diocesan Spirituality for Today
- Crisis of Credibility of Contemporary Indian Church
- "Prophetic Mysticism in Consecrated Life of India."
- Sexual Abuse: Crisis, Challenges and Response of the Church
- The Challenge of Formation in the Contemporary Church
- Reading the Parish as *Sacra Pagina*
- Public Theology

The 28 papers in this volume, we are happy to say, came out of this interactive and enriching seminar which was actively participated by almost 1200 participants, including the students of Jnana-Deepa Vidyapeeth and about 300 alumni of Papal Seminary who came for the celebration.

Part One gives an overview of serving the Church and the Nation. Rt Rev Bishop Jacob Manathodath, the Chief Guest of the Seminar and Rt Rev Bishop Thomas Dabre, the Bishop of Poona and Dr Francis Gonsalves SJ, Dean, Faculty of Theology, situate the seminar in the present context of both India and the Indian Church.

The next part focuses on some of the challenges and corresponding promises that the Church in India faces in terms of dialogue, mediation, ecumenism, Hindutva politics, women, mentally handicapped and the poor. The need for intellectual reflection is also emphasised.

The Third Part focuses on spiritual openness and mystical depth, which is essential to deal with the challenges the Church and the Nation today faces. The seven articles in this part focuses on topics related to spirituality, mysticism and pastoral life which will help us to be open to the contemporary promises offered by our society.

The last part takes up the Indian roots both of our challenges and opportunities. It deals with the need to find local and specific issues facing the Church and the Nation. The eight articles in this section takes up the care and concerns of the diverse local churches. The final article speaks of the audacity of the impossible, made possible by deep faith in the Divine, in ourselves and in life.

We are grateful to the Rev Fr Bhausaheb Sansare SJ, Rector, Papal Seminary and Rev Fr Vincent Crasta, SJ, Minister Papal Seminary and the staff and students of Papal Seminary for making this seminar and the publication possible. We acknowledge the support and encouragement given by Fr Joe Francis Manickam (Diocese of Aizhol), who was the Principal Coordinator of the Jubilee Programme. While acknowledging God's abundant blessings for 125 years, we wish that the Seminary continues to cater to the spiritual and intellectual needs of young men, who are called to be leaders of the church. We are also grateful to Jnana-Deepa Vidaypeeth, who has co-sponsored the seminar and who is closely related to Papal Seminary. Rev Fr Selva Rathinam SJ, Rector, Rev Fr Jose Thayil SJ, Minister and Rev Fr Alex G, Treasurer, Jnana-Deepa Vidyapeeth deserves our special thanks. Finally, the participants from Papal Seminary and Jnana-Deepa Vidyapeth and their alumni as well as the resource persons deserve our special gratitude.

It is our modest wish that this volume will contribute to the making of a Church and Nation, which takes care of the concerns of the least and those of the periphery. The message of the Father of our Nation, which is deeply resonated by the present Pope and the present Superior General of the Society of Jesus, is apt here: "I will give you a talisman. Whenever you are in doubt, or when the self becomes too much with you, apply the following test. Recall the face of the poorest and the weakest man [woman] whom you may have seen, and ask yourself, if the step you contemplate is going to be of any use to him [her]. Will he [she] gain anything by it? Will it restore him [her] to a control over his [her] own life and destiny? In other words, will it lead to *swaraj* [freedom] for the hungry and spiritually starving millions? Then you will find your doubts and your self melt away." (One of the last notes left behind by Gandhi in 1948, expressing his deepest social thought. Source: Mahatma Gandhi, *Last Phase*, Vol. II (1958), p. 6.)

May this volume help us to serve the Church and India, by wiping away the tears of the hungry and helping all Indians to be truly joyful and free!

**The Editors**

PART ONE

# SERVING JOYFULLY: THE CHURCH AND THE NATION

# 1

# Ministering to the Contemporary Church in India

**Rt Rev Bishop Jacob Manathodath**

The contemporary Church is facing a lot of crises and challenges. The Indian Church is no exception. Reports of scandals of various sorts, accusations, litigations, internal conflicts and strife, counter witness especially by the consecrated people, etc. frequently appear in the media. The entire church is affected in different ways by these sad events and developments. Such crises scandalize the faithful, demoralize the innocent people and put the church leadership into task. These scandals may be characterized in the words of St. Paul, as acts of the flesh (Gal 5:19-21). They are, according to his list, idolatry, adultery, fornication, uncleanness, hatred, variance, emulations, wrath, strife, seditions and drunkenness. Apart from the internal crises, the church is challenged also by the threats, planned or otherwise, from outside, namely, politicized moves, hate-talks, aggressive media attacks against the church personnel, etc.

The allegations against the church create at least three grave spiritual challenges. First, the name of God is dishonored among the non-believers. In the words of St. Paul: "God's name is blasphemed among the Gentiles because of you" (Rom 2:24). Second, the credibility of the church is seriously shaken. There is no correspondence between what is preached and what is practiced. Third, the faithful get scandalized. These are serious consequences. What is imperative is that we make a realistic analysis of the crisis. Only then will the crisis help produce sustainable and heroic Christian fruits. It is good to recall what St. Paul told the strife-ridden Corinthian communities: "But, of course, there must be divisions among you so that you who have God's approval will be recognized!" (1Cor 11:19). The present crisis will serve as a touchstone to test the real faith of the people.

The saintly Archbishop Fulton J Sheen used to state in his retreats: 'I like to live in a suffering and turbulent church, rather than in a peaceful church. For, it is the time for worthy men and women to rise up.' The way we understand and address a crisis is very critical. For instance, in the sixteenth century, the church faced a host of moral crises and ecclesiastical challenges. But Martin Luther reduced the whole issue to one question, namely, how can an unworthy Pope be the head of the Church? Had Luther addressed this issue from another angle, the history of the church would have been quite different. In what follows, I propose first, some basic convictions we should hold firm in this period of crisis and then some practical steps towards a solution.

## 1. Basic Convictions in a Challenged Church

a. For a Christian, faith in the church is concomitant to faith in the Trinitarian God. In the Credo we affirm our faith in the Church which cannot be forgotten when she is despised and her image is tarnished. The Church in which we believe is holy and at the same time tends to go unholy. The church is holy because of its divine elements such as the Trinitarian presence, Holy Eucharist, sacraments, Word of God, Mother Mary, communion of saints and a host of saintly people around us. The unholy elements emerge because numerous men and women in the church are sinful. To admit it does not mean excuse to condone unholy practices in the church; they need to be fought against. Those who defile the Church are not condemned or despised people. They are sinners who await conversion. They continue to be members of the church. Those who cause scandals in the church too belong to the church. That is why the CCC (827) qualifies the church as one that is sanctified and at the same time that needs sanctification. Vatican II made it clear that the church which embraces sinners is at the same time holy (LG 8).

b. The reason why we believe in the Church is Jesus Christ. The crucified and risen Jesus is the head of the Church. We believe in the Church not because of its leaders; they are also believers of Christ in the Church. They take a leading role and minister to the Church and the world. In principle, failures of leadership shall not shatter the faith of the faithful. The failure of the church leaders however, often challenges the faith of people.

The thirteenth century Italian church faced plenty of scandals and damages. That Church, according to the gospel-standards, was to a great extent rotten. St. Francis of Assisi took upon himself the task of renewing it. He with his confreres started a heroic life in their religious community. Once a member of his community asked Francis, "Suppose that you come to know that the concubines of the celebrant priest are also attending the Holy Mass, what would you do?" Francis answered, "Without any hesitation I would receive Holy Communion from his anointed hands". With this answer, he was making it clear that the effectiveness of the ministries of the Church does not essentially depend on the sanctity of its ministers. It does not however mean that the ministers can therefore choose a wayward life.

c. If the Church belongs to God, He shall take care of its ultimate survival and victory. The Church grew to the present state and stature continually facing challenges. They include schisms, heresies, strife, failure of its leaders, attacks from outside, religious persecution, political opposition, etc. The wellbeing or growth of the church is a work of God; He will ensure it in His own ways. In that process individuals may however fail and falter. The fall of a few Church leaders does not just lead to the end of the Church.

Arianism for example divided the Church of the fourth century. Divinity of Jesus along with God the Father was the point of contention which was settled in the Nicene Council in 325. During the heresy, many bishops and priests drifted away from true faith. The holy Spirit however led the church along the path of true faith.

Prophet Elijah during the reign of Ahab complained to the Lord, "All people have deserted you except myself. But the Lord replied, "I have reserved seven thousand in Israel, all whose knees have not bowed to Baal, and every mouth that has not kissed him" (1 Kings 19:18). That is the remnant chosen by grace, according to St Paul (Rome 11:4-5). The Lord leads the Church forward through the community of people chosen and led by grace. Our task during the time of crisis is to belong to this holy remnant which can revitalize the church and thereby the world.

## 2. Practical Steps Towards a Solution

a. The first and foremost response to any crisis in the church is the holy life of its members. We cannot fight evil with evil; we cannot eradicate sin with sinful acts. We cannot regain the glory of the church through immoral or undesirable ways. The Church cannot challenge anybody except through evangelical means. The holy life is the best way of confronting any crisis in the church. This suggestion may look like a kind of spiritualization. This however is how saintly people faced challenges in the church, which in return resulted in the renewal of the faith-community.

The present crisis in the church is a loud call to holy life. Responding to the crisis, many men and women should resolve to lead a holy life and strive for the renewal of the church; They must renew the church internally; The obesity of the church in structural matters should be burnt out; All anti-gospel fascinations existing in the church must be discarded. Some may suspect that only the reverse may happen in a crisis-ridden church. This suspicion carries some weight. Only when genuinely motivated pastors inspire the communities with their holy lives the crisis will be overcome.

Church history proves that after every serious crisis or during it there emerged holy people with brilliant caliber and character who were able to revive and reform the church. For example, Peter Damian, a saint and doctor of the church, could rebuild the Church of the tenth century; similar role was played by Francis of Assisi in the thirteenth century. St. Ignatius Loyola healed the wounds of the Church divided after Reformation and regained its vitality. The same period also witnessed the saintly archbishop Charles Borromeo in Italy. The Lord brought forth St. Francis de Sales to lead the church wounded in the wake of Calvinism.

b. When a controversy brews up, there shall be factions and divisions within the Church. Everybody tends to stand by a position which he or she thinks is right. Nobody in good conscience would love to stand by evil. That is how different factions emerge in the church on the account of the same issue. Every group would believe that their position is true. They may get deceived. St. Augustine acknowledges his intellectual delusions, especially in his attitude to Manichaeism. He says, "I believed what they told was true. I did so, not because I understood the truth of what they professed, but because I decided them to be true".

We must be intelligent enough to know that often what the media provide is not unadulterated truth. Rather than factual description and exact facts and figures, the media offers partial news or partisan analysis. Prudence demands that until we know the truth at least in a morally convincing way, we shall not take sides in a row. And once we know the truth, we have to abide by it. The following maxim is often attributed to Aristotle, *"Amicus Plato, sed magis arnica veritas"* which can be translated as "Plato is my friend, but better friend is truth". Aristotle meant that he would value truth more than Plato, his mentor and friend.

If issues in the family or the church are not dealt with prudence, it may result in greater disputes. Crisis management can create greater crisis. We should seek first and foremost the Kingdom of God and His justice. Otherwise we may be led astray. St. Francis de Sales was asked once: how do you look at the scandals among priests? He replied in a succinct way, "Those who give scandals are guilty of spiritual murder (because they kill the faith of others); those who are scandalized are guilty of spiritual suicide (because they allow their faith to be killed)".

To regain the purity and strength of the church, its members, as members of the same body, must make reparations through prayer and fasting. The simple reason is that behind every serious scandal and often in the way it is handled, there is sin, and selfishness. Sin requires reparations. St. Paul writes: "And, apart from other things, there is the daily pressure upon me of my anxiety for all the churches. Who is weak, and I am not weak? Who is made to fall, and I am not indignant?" (2 Cor 11:28-29). In a similar way, he says, "Now I rejoice in what I am suffering for you, and I fill up in my flesh what is still lacking in regard to Christ's afflictions, for the sake of his body, which is the church" (Col 1:24). It is the duty of faithful Christians to suffer for and make reparations for the church.

You may think that I am spiritualizing issues rather than addressing them. It may seem so. All issues and scandals must be settled first and foremost in a spiritually acceptable manner; we should listen to what the Spirit of the Lord tells the churches. So whatever be the solutions proposed, they must be spirit inspired and gospel-friendly. The supreme law is the glory of God and the salvation of souls.

Any crisis must be solved keeping in mind truth and justice. St. James says, "Peacemakers who sow in peace reap a harvest of righteousness" (Jam 3:18). What is desired is a peaceful establishment of justice. That would naturally include admission of wrongdoings, forgiveness of the offender, reconciliation between parties, modification of structures, if required, etc. We need however to reiterate; no evil means can bring about a right solution to a problem.

In solving any problem in the church, space must be given also for mercy and forgiveness. In other words, the verdicts of the church must transcend secular jurisprudence. Mercy should supersede justice.

## Conclusion

In conclusion, two short notes of caution: First, we have to keep a realistic perception of the crises in the Church. Secondly, some of the so-called crises or scandals about which fake. They may be products of the media or creations of people who are ill-motivated. premises because they are fabricated for ulterior purposes. I don't mean that all scandals are such. Similarly, some of the scandals may not really affect the whole church. They might be upsetting the church leadership or people who are involved in its administration. The ordinary faithful may live least concerned about such issues, as far as their faith life is concerned. On the other hand, certain crises might do enormous harm to the church. So my point of caution is this: we shall not exaggerate crises in the Church to undue proportions; in the same way, we shall not underestimate real issues.

Secondly, handling a crisis reveals the mettle of the church. The way in which internal or external issues are sorted out would reveal the maturity and faith of the community. In this process, confirming the line of thought I have been following, I must say, all anti-gospel means adopted by us should be thrown into the trash bin of church history. Those structures and individuals who do not follow the spirit of the Gospel of Jesus have no lasting value in the Church which is the sign and signboard of the kingdom of God. Those however who advocate gospel- means to address crisis in the Church will be held dear for generations to come, as light of the world and salt of the earth. We are not to become causes of any crisis in the church, but people who solve crisis in keeping with the spirit of the Gospel and the mind of Christ.

I conclude on a positive note quoting American Roman Catholic religious sister, artist and educator Corita Kent: "Love the moment. Flowers grow out of dark moments. Therefore, each moment is vital. It affects the whole. Life is a succession of such moments, and to live each is to succeed."

# 2

# Serving the Indian Church Some Challenges and More Opportunities

**Rt Rev Thomas Dabre**

The Papal Seminary has served India for the last 125 years with success stories at various levels. As we celebrate with joy and gratitude this event, it is quite appropriate to consider how we have to serve the Church in India and our country in the contemporary world which has seen so many upheavals and undergone unexpected changes and has faced and faces formidable challenges. Understandably therefore, we cannot exercise our mission to continue as in the past but in a manner relevant and intelligible to the people of our times. Such a vision has been opened to us by the spirit of the Second Vatican Council, the new evangelization and the post-Vatican Council *Magisterium.*

I would consider some of the urgent issues we face today are: a unity in diversity, culture and multiculturalism in the Church and the country, unity in the Church, faith-formation and small Christian Communities and removal of poverty, Relations among the three rites, the Religious and the Diocese, the promotion of the Dalit Christians and the tribals are also areas of concern.

## 1. Humans as Cultural Beings

As anthropologists remind us, living as members of community/society we not create our own way of life, language, values, life style from the beginning of life. We inherit and adopt an already existing culture of his community/society. Thus all human beings receive their culture and live according to it. Nobody can live without any culture. Certainly culture is formed and fashioned by human beings by their world vision, genius, creativity and activity. However, culture is guided by divine light. The God we believed in rules, guides and leads all people's of the world with His light, wisdom and justice. He has created all people in His image and likeness (Ps. 67, Gen 1: 27 ).

Anthropologist Edward B. Taylor has offered us a broad definition of culture: "It is that complex whole including beliefs, art, region, values, norms, ideas, law, taught, knowledge, custom and other capabilities acquired by a person as a member of a society." Thus culture is the totality of human experience acquired during transmission of heritage from one generation to another and to learn the ways of learning, eating, drinking, behaving, walking, dressing, and working is the culture of man.

## 2. Multiculturalism as a Lived Reality in India

In India people speak 122 major languages and 1599 other languages. Unity in diversity is the dominant feature of India.

According to the 2011 census, 79.8% of the population of India belong to Hinduism and 14.2% to Islam, while the remaining 6% to other religions (Christianity, Sikhism, Buddhism, Jainism and various indigenous ethnically-bound faiths).

The various religious communities, though they are categorized under one common title, belong to different sects, denominations and divisions within their common religion be it Hindu, Jains, Sikh, Christians, Buddhists, etc.

In some cases their differences are quite striking affecting their relationships and dispositions towards one another, e.g. Dalit Hindus and higher caste Hindus. These too have their own specific cultural way of life. There are also atheists, agnostics and rationalists etc, who constitute our large Indian family.

Thus ours is truly a multicultural society. There is wide-spread appreciation for India's tradition of tolerance and religious harmony across the world. People of all religions and cultures have contributed significantly to India's nationhood and stature.

In this context, we may recall that Christians in India are known for their patriotism. The contribution of the Christian community in the fields of education, health and social services and, charitable and humanitarian activities has been acknowledged by all, so much so that people of other religions fight for admission to the Church's various social services! Therefore, we have always been fostering openness to other religious traditions and multiculturalism.

## 3. Erosion of Unity, Pluralism and Diversity Today

There is, however, now growing intolerance, tension ,violence, distrust and division among people, e.g.. clashes between Naxalites and security forces, Kashmir turmoil and communal riots, political rivalry, atrocities against women and minorities, intolerance of dissent etc. Discontent, resentment and protests have also been growing.

Present-day manifestations of such a situation are as follows:

- Intellectuals, scholars, artistes and activists have protested against intolerance of the beliefs, traditions, practices and customs of minorities and against secular- minded liberals like Dabholkar, Pansare, Kalburgi and Gauri Lankesh who were all killed. Though they were Hindus they worked for reform of the Indian society.
- Insistence on Hindu practices and religious texts for non-Hindus.
- Anti-conversion laws in the name of freedom of religion have been passed or proposed restricting the free practice of religion and evangelization.
- Some extremist elements constantly accuse Christians of conversion by fraud, force and enticement. Important national leaders too always see conversion motive in all social, charitable and humanitarian activities of the Church.
- There have also been attempts in different paces to impose *Gharvapsi*programmes to reconvert those who have become Christians.
- Narrow-minded sectarian Vigilantism of extremist elements who oppose Valentine Day, Friendship Day, pub dancing and liquor parties at bars, Western dress of women etc.
- Atrocities against Church personnel and institutions.
- Denial of reservations to *Dalit* Christians which is granted to Hindu, Buddhist *Dalits* and others.
- Imposition of mono-cultural nationalism making inroads into the education system and the framework of the constitution.
- Hindus who believe in Ram as a major deity demand that the temple of Ram be built in the place where stands the Babri Masjid Mosque for the last 400 years in Ayodhya. This has created a lot of tension in the country between the Hindus and the Moslems, particularly since 1991 when this structure was demolished . There have been so many other riots between these two major communities in recent times.

## 4. Church, Culture and Multi-Culturalism

We must humbly admit that at times there have been errors on the part of Christians in relation to various cultures for which Pope John Paul II rendered an apology. However, the Church has recognized the validity of various cultures.

Pius XII holds: “It is necessary to deepen one’s understanding of the civilization and institutions of various peoples and to cultivate their best qualities and gifts.... All in the customs of peoples which are not inextricably bound up with superstitions or errors should be examined with benevolence and if possible, preserved intact." (Pius XII, *Summi Pontificatus.*) Hence, culture has its intrinsic merit and serves as a foundation for the Church's mission of evangelization.

"A culture is strengthened by its openness and its exchange of views with other cultures… we are called to understand and appreciate the values of others, overcoming the temptation of indifference and fear. Never be afraid of interaction, of dialogue, of debate" (Address of His Holiness Pope Francis to "*Roma Tre*" University, 17 February 2017).

In this context, we can assume that The Holy Trinity can be both a source and model for the Church in India to promote unity in diversity everywhere.

Therefore the Church must be in the forefront to promote authentic multi-culturalism within the over- all unity of the nation and of the Church itself. So Vatican II holds: "… the Church, in Christ, is in the nature of sacrament--a sign and instrument, that is, of communion with God and of unity among all men" (LG,1).

Further it says: The universal Church is seen to be "a people brought into unity from the unity of the Father, the Son and the Holy Spirit." (LG, 4).

Yet we must admit that there are caste-based tensions in the Church. Regional, linguistic and sub-cultural diversity within the church does come in the way of the evangelical integration in the Church. Now that the Church's *Dalit* Empowerment Policy has been launched hopefully such narrow rivalries and conflict will decline and promote further unity and integration according to the mind of Jesus who said that all his disciples should live in unity and love. Sustained effort therefor must be made to implement the *Dalit Policy*.

So also the tribal belt also is backward in respects compared to the mainstream communities. Their identity is also threatened and they face displacement, disrespect and marginalization. A lot more needs to be done for them both in the Church and in the country.

There are 22 Rites in the whole Catholic Church. In India we have 3 Rites. The Church is like a rainbow having many colours. All the three rites are so rich in their prayers, spirituality, liturgy, theology, music and their way of living in the Church and society. It is all so precious. Let us preserve it. We need o educate our people to appreciate the different rites and live in fellowship, friendship, trust and understanding with one another., as we were all fortunate to experience here in the Papal Seminary and on the JDV Campus.

While we live by our rite, let us also be always remember that " we are all one, though we are many, because of the one bread that we eat" (1 Cor 10:17).

## 5. Way Forward: Some Concrete Suggestions

Multi-culturalism in India demands that Christians in India live in greater solidarity with people of other religions and the three rites at all levels. There is plenty of scope for such a unity with people.

Along with English language, we should use more and more the local languages, particularly where the Christian communities are perceived to be westernized. Therefore, living together in solidarity will dispel prejudices and misunderstandings and promote trust and good relations.

Developing relationships of friendships and brotherhood with people of other religions and faiths will help improve the climate of hate and distrust.

Therefore, inculturation and inter-religious dialogue should become a way of the Church's pastoral life and mission of evangelization. The 1985 synod of Bishops defined inculturation as "the intimate transformation of authentic cultural values through their integration in Christianity in the various human cultures".

Through such an authentic and sustained inculturation of the Church's life at levels of human life, can the Christians touch the soul of India like Mother Teresa, Fr. Constant Lievans and many other successful missionaries who worked in far-flung areas. The Indian Missionary St. JoesphVazbecame a hüge success in Sri Lanka because he became one with the local people and their culture.

Regular ongoing dialogue in accordance with the directives of *Gaudium et Spes* and *Nostra Aetate* has to be meticulously sustained. The Second Vatican Council clearly laid down the directive principles of inter religious dialogue. Accordingly People Paul VI set up the Pontifical Council for Inter religious Dialogue in 1965.

Announcing the First World Day of the Poor, Pope Francis asks us all to live in effective and life-transforming solidarity and fraternity. "Everyone, independent of religious affiliation, is invited to openness and sharing with the poor through concrete signs of solidarity and fraternity".

As we know well over 30 % of the population in India live in utter poverty. Among the Christians too there is a large number of the poor, living in unhealthy conditions. Elimination of poverty is an immense task of utter urgency. The Church must remove poverty from within the Church as an urgent priority.

Stemming ecological degradation and promoting care of the earth and sustainable development as enthusiastically urged by Pope Francis in *Laudato Si'* is an urgent need. Ecology is an integral part of all people's whatever their cultures. Ecological degradation adversely affects all people, especially the poor and women.

Advocacy at all levels for promotion of moral, human and spiritual values with prophetic critique of anti-human policies is the need of the hour. In the present situation of religious-communal divisiveness and hardships for people across the board, the involvement of the Christian laity in politics for the progress, removal of poverty, peace, integration and unity in variety is an urgent priority. "For the lay faithful, political involvement is a worthy and demanding expression of the Christian commitment of service to others" (Pope Paul VI).

## Conclusion

Christ, yesterday, today and forever is the same. God is ever ancient and ever new. Ecclesia semper reformanda. So in this spirit the Church in India has to minister to the faithful and to the nation. So as the New Evangelization emphasizes we have to do our ministry with new ardour, new method and new expressions and forms. The ultimate aim is eternal salvation enabling people ministered to , to enjoy the fullness of life in Jesus, the Saviour of the world.

3

# Papal Lights for Papalites to be Ministers of Salvation: Pope Leo XIII's Legacy, Pope Francis's Lights

**Francis Gonsalves SJ**

## Introduction: Can India's Sons be Ministers of Its Salvation?

A hundred and twenty-five years ago, when Pope Leo XIII said, "*Filiitui, India, administritibisalutis*", meaning, "Your sons, O India, shall be the ministers of your salvation," he nursed a magnificent vision of beginning a General Seminary for training 'sons of the soil' priests to serve in India. Arguably, one will never know how he envisaged his dream to take root and bear fruit. Nonetheless, after a hundred and twenty-five years of the existence of Papal Seminary – fondly called 'Home of Love' – many of its alumni and professors, past and present, have assembled to look back with gratitude and look forward with hope. Therefore, in this three-part article, I shall briefly look backward in the first part to highlight some innovative ventures that Pope Leo XIII initiated. Then, in the second part, leaping over a century in time, I shall discuss some initiatives that Pope Francis has taken, which accentuate what Leo XIII envisaged. Finally, in the third part, I will provide a few guiding lights for committed Indian Christians – especially for those who felicitously call themselves Papalites – to catalyze so-called 'salvation'.

## 1. Pope Leo XIII's Social, Pastoral and Missiological Innovations

Pope Leo XIII (1810-1903) has the distinction of being the oldest reigning pope in history, governing the church till the age of ninety-three. He is also credited with the third-longest papacy spanning twenty-five years (1878-1903). Being schooled initially at the Jesuit College at Viterbo, Vincenzo GioacchinoPecci (original name of Leo XIII) and his brother, Giuseppe Pecci, later studied at the Jesuit College in Rome. While Vincenzo became a diocesan priest, Giuseppe joined the Jesuits and later became a cardinal. Vincenzo and Giuseppe played a key role in organizing Vatican Council I (1870). During episcopal ministry, Vincenzo had three special interests close to his heart: (a) helping society's poor, (b) renewing the church; and, (c) retrieving the church's intellectual and theological treasures. Success in these three areas would mean victory for the church against two of its enemies: Marxism and Americanism.

Appointed cardinal in 1853, Vincenzo Pecci, founded a number of charities to address social concerns. He began shelters for homeless boys, girls and elderly women. He opened branches of a Bank, *Monte di Pietà*, which provided low-interest loans to the poor. He created soup kitchens and donated much money to victims of earthquakes and floods. Apart from these charitable activities, Leo XIII can be called the 'Father of the Church's Social Doctrine' with his *Rerum Novarum* (1891), the frontrunner of later social encyclicals that, while accepting the rights of individuals for private property, stressed the need for just wages, healthy living conditions for workers, support of workers' family, necessity to work for the common good and equitable distribution of mother earth's God-given resources.

Aware of the need for church renewal and challenged by the intellectualism of those times that promoted Marxism and atheistic materialism, on the one hand, and Americanism's exclusivism, individualism, inhuman industrialization and practical atheism, on the other, Leo XIII revived Thomistic theology, as well as supported the post-Vatican Council I viewpoint that human reason is not an enemy of faith; rather, it can illumine the human will by demonstrating that faith is reasonable. Building upon *Dei Filius* of VC I, in his 1893 encyclical *Providentissimus Deus*, he stressed the importance of Scripture for theological study.

*Providentissimus Deus* was an important encyclical for theology and its relation to the Bible – encouraging the clergy to deepen their study of Catholic Tradition and sacred Scripture, while also cautioning them about the dangers of rationalist interpretations that deny the inspiration of Scripture. His founding of the Catholic University of America in 1889 and the Papal Athenaeum – later renamed Papal Seminary – in 1893 indicate his commitment to renewal among pastors, by fostering intellectual ministry and theological scholarship.

Entrusting this latter venture to Asian Jesuits was probably due to his firsthand experience of being schooled in the Jesuit intellectual tradition.

It will be anachronistic to commend Leo XIII for what we see today as freedom of religion, ecumenical interrelationship and interfaith dialogue, as such. Nonetheless, in his encyclicals like *Immortale Dei* (1885) he exhorted those wielding political power as follows: "All who rule, would hold in honour the holy name of God, and one of their chief duties must be to favour religion, to protect it, to shield it under the credit and sanction of the laws, and neither to organize nor enact any measure that may compromise its safety." He was against coercion in matters of faith. Moreover, he expressed a deep desire for ecumenical unity, echoed in his encyclical letter *PraeclaraGratulationis* (1894). In all this, he extended a hand of friendship to others, ever promoting the common good, collaboration and salvation.

From the above, we can conclude that Pope Leo XIII was a farsighted visionary whose insights in the fields of social development, the education of pastors, as well as ecumenical and missiological outreach laid the foundations for what would be fostered and fine-tuned later. The constraints of space do not permit discussions on the development of Leo XIII's innovations. But, let us move over to our present day, viewing the contribution of Pope Francis in these areas.

## 2. Pope Francis's Social, Pastoral and Missiological Thrusts

In a short span of some five years since his election to the papacy in March 2013, Pope Francis has been receiving both bouquets and brickbats for what some have commended as the 'Francis effect' while others have condemned as Francis's defects towards the end of 2018, with the Church facing its worst crises – now, more internal than external – with scandalous sexual aberrations of clerics, revolt by some members of the hierarchy, accusations of papal digression from 'pure' Catholic orthodoxy and abuse of papal authority in drafting Synod documents.

Pope Francis's critics seem to be condemning him on the basis of being guided by outmoded models of faith, belief, church, society, world and mission. They label him 'liberal' while he is actually '*radical*' – from the Latin *radice*, meaning 'root'. He is rooted and grounded in Christ. Therefrom springs his whole life, vision and mission. Moreover, he seeks renewal, not merely reform. Let us see what this concretely entails in terms of the church's option for the poor, its training of future priests and its pastoral and missiological outreach.

Pope Francis should not be branded a social reformer for his promoting ecclesial poverty, option for the poor, befriending prisoners, helping refugees, reaching out to hierarchs of other churches and religions and care for the earth; for, all these actions are not the outcome of any ideology but rather spring from a profound, personal relationship with Jesus. He tirelessly preaches that this Jesus is the Poor One. This Jesus has a face: mercy! This Jesus had special friends: the poor, sinners, refugees, victims, fishermen, tax-collectors, pagans and Samaritans. This Jesus spoke about Last Judgement and salvation: of only those who love and serve the 'least' of his sisters and brothers (Mt 25:31-44). Finally, this Jesus called some 'chosen ones' to specially serve him – his twelve apostles and disciples like Mary Magdalene, Martha and Mary of Bethany.

Pope Francis believes that Jesus calls you and me for the same mission entrusted to him by *Abba* (Jn 20:19-23) and empowered by the same Spirit promised to all those co-missioned with Him (Jn 14:26; 15:26). This being the case, mission is not simply about *doing* activities, programmes, drawing up policies, and building structures; rather, it is a way of *being*. Francis wrote:

My mission of being in the heart of the people is not just a part of my life or a badge I can take off; it is not an 'extra' or just another moment in life. Instead, it is something I cannot uproot from my being without destroying my very self. I am a mission on this earth; that is the reason why I am here in this world. We have to regard ourselves as sealed, even branded, by this mission of bringing light, blessing, enlivening, raising up, healing and freeing.

'*Being mission*' is so central to Pope Francis's teaching that he repeated this in October 2018 at the World Mission Sunday Mass for Youth:

To live out joyfully our responsibility for the world is a great challenge. … The fact that we are not in this world by our own choice makes us sense that there is an initiative that precedes us and makes us exist. Each one of us is called to reflect on this fact: "I am a mission on this earth; that is the reason why I am here in this world."

By solidly situating mission at the level of *being* (ontology), not simply *doing* or *having* (functionality or operationality), Pope Francis turns the church upside down as Jesus' first apostles did (Acts 17:6). Consequently, mission is not simply some appendix after one pronounces vows, receives ordination, makes pastoral plans and builds institutions; but it defines '*who*' a Christian is and '*Who*' Church is. No mission, no church! Thus, since all of us, Christians, *are* mission, we all have the responsibility of spreading the Good News of joy, mercy and salvation. Salvation is not some afterlife, pie-in-the-sky promise, but an all-embracing venture involving all peoples in all places and at all times. Therefore, one can say that while Pope Leo XIII sowed the seeds for social doctrine, revamping of theology and pastoral updating, Pope Francis 'walks the talk' and brings these dreams and visions to full fruition in order that pastors "with the smell of sheep" might do likewise amidst those of their own flock.

In view of what Pope Francis envisages especially in terms of renewal of church and society, there is urgent need in Jesuit-run institutions like Jnana-Deepa Vidyapeeth, Pune and Vidyajyoti, Delhi, to go back to the roots – listen anew to Jesus' preaching, adopt his praxis and go forth with single-minded devotion, specifically serving those most in need. Such service must neither arise from pity for the poor nor from an obsession to do social work. Rather, our option for the poor and our theological-scriptural-pastoral training must be birthed by radical readings of Scripture, closeness to Jesus, and direct contact with God's people, especially the poor.

Although governing as popes a century apart, we see Pope Leo XIII and Pope Francis as proponents for an indigenous, contextualized and people-oriented approach to pastoral and missiological practice. Aloysius Pieris lauds the distinct 'paradigm shift' of Pope Francis:

Pope Francis is determined to remove the *theological barrier that has distanced the Magisterium from the Masses, the class barrier that separated Shepherds from the Sheep, the language barrier that stood between the Church and the World and the barrier of bias that obstructs both ecumenism and inter-religious collaboration.*

To conclude this section, we can surmise that Pope Francis is not merely suggesting some cosmetic changes in church life, but a real, radical renewal of mindset: a *hridaya-parivartan*, a conversion of heart! Let's see what this concretely entails in the third section.

## 3. Guiding Lights for Papalites to Be Mission and Go Forth as Ministers of Salvation

Building upon Pope Leo XIII's vision and animated by Pope Francis's personalist and 'incarnational' approach to church and mission, let's light a few lamps to direct our footsteps as we – especially Papalites – strive to be 'ministers of salvation'.

"*Be* the change you wish to see in the world" – Gandhi's popular axiom dovetails with "*Be* a mission in the world" of Pope Francis. Although many disagree with Pope Francis's viewpoints, no one dares point an accusing finger at him since he has never lost his moral authority not only in the eyes of Catholics but before citizens worldwide. He was voted TIME's 2013 'PERSON OF THE YEAR' IN HIS FIRST YEAR IN OFFICE, AND HAS BOLDLY VOICED HIS OPINION ON ISSUES RANGING FROM THE REFUGEE-CRISIS TO GLOBAL NETWORKING, AND FROM CHILD ABUSE TO ABUSE OF MOTHER EARTH. IN HIS EXHORTATIONS, HE REGULARLY ACCEPTS PERSONAL RESPONSIBILITY ABOUT THE SORRY STATE OF AFFAIRS, BECAUSE UNLESS CONVERSION BEGINS WITH '*ME-US*', FIRST, I-WE WILL NEVER BE ABLE TO CHANGE OTHERS, AND MUCH LESS, ALTER DIEHARD SOCIETAL STRUCTURES.

Many lay faithful have recently been scandalized by accusations against bishops and priests of the rape of nuns, and minor-girls, pedophilia, accumulating of excessive wealth and profiting from murky land deals. All this militates against priests' claims of being *alter Christus*, visible bodies of Christ, celibates and poor disciples. Hence, we, ordained ministers, must set an example for the laity by first making a *mea culpa* and then leading the laity along a path of personal change and reconciliation. Indeed, the only way we can *be* and build not only a church *for* the poor but also a *poor church*, is by undergoing a spiritual process of self-emptying or '*kenosis*' in imitation of our Lord Jesus (Phil 2:5-11).

Realizing the dire need to have ecclesial intellectuals who would not only serve as apologists by defending Catholic doctrine but also enlighten others about Christ's Good News, Leo XIII chose to revive Thomism. Today, to provide rationale for church renewal, Pope Francis published *Veritatis Gaudium* for ecclesiastical universities and faculties – like our own, Jnana-Deepa Vidyapeeth – exhorting them to re-root theological studies remembering four '*fundamental criteria*': (a) that they are called by the Triune God to build a 'network of relations' which unifies all of creation in a 'global solidarity' that will respond to all peoples – especially heeding the cry of the earth's poor; (b) that 'wide-ranging dialogue' and a 'culture of encounter' is indispensable to effectively engage in ecumenical, intercultural and interfaith initiatives; (c) that inter-disciplinary and cross-disciplinary approaches carried out with wisdom and creativity and are best suited to communicate the richness of Revelation unfolding in our history; and, (d) that there is urgent need for collaboration and 'networking' at all levels – thereby profiting from the rich diversity manifest in our world.

Since four cardinals, some seventy-five bishops and hundreds of diocesan priests have passed through Papal Seminary and are '*Papalites*' of prominence, we can carry the '*Jnana-Deepa*' – the Lamp of Wisdom – to the ends of the earth. Understandably, we now no longer revive Thomism but an indigenous and contextual understanding of the Poor One, Jesus, who struggles in our slums, slogs in our fields, sleeps on our pavements and is crucified on Indian peripheries. With this indigenous and incarnated knowledge Jesus, we go forth to proclaim the 'Joy of the Gospel'. Here, Pope Francis cautions us about two extremes of neo-Gnosticism and neo-Pelagianism, with their disregard for the body and individualism, respectively, that negate the corporate and corporal aspects of Christic salvation. Indic wisdom has the advantage of being *advaitic* at heart, shunning unreal dichotomies that prevent us from living holistic lives.

Let's remember that without a true spiritual awakening, all else will be useless; for we do not seek to be more 'efficient' (which we already sufficiently are!) but more '*effective*' – keeping Christ consciously at the centre of all our missions, remembering that the Spirit always empowers us. Indeed, Pope Francis strikingly states: "Prayer is the first 'missionary work' – the first! – that every Christian can and must do, and it is also the most effective …. In fact, the principal agent of evangelization is the Holy Spirit, and we are called to collaborate with Him."

## Conclusion: Some Takeaways for Papalites to Go Forth

This 125$^{th}$ Jubilee is a *kairos* of grace to look back with gratitude over the pilgrim path which many of our forebears have traversed, often with great difficulty, yet with deep faith. We have spent happy days in prayer, narrating our own stories and celebrating our successes, mindful that all along this yatra, we have been animated by that One whose power made Paul attest: "I can do all things through Him who strengthens me" (Phil 4:13). We sincerely believe that He, Our Guru and Guide, has accompanied us along our journey.

As we return to our ministries, let's recall what Pope Francis says: "time is greater than space;" therefore, we must give priority to time and be concerned about "initiating processes rather than possessing spaces". This demands patience, the rejection of quick fix solutions and the resolve to walk the narrow pathway. It entails having 'less' so as to *be* 'more' and to travel further. Papal Seminary has gifted all those who partook of the Jubilee celebrations three items which are symbolic: (a) badge, (b) cup, (c) cap. Couldn't these three remind us of something significant?

The Papal Seminary badge with our name and seminary symbol on it could remind us of our 'identity' as *Papalites* called to be little lamps dispelling the darkness enveloping India, today. Our patron, St Francis Xavier, challenges us to catalyze the integral salvation of India and Pope Francis reminds us: "I *am* mission" – birthed and branded with the stamp of missionary zeal.

The cup is a symbol of both, joys and sorrows, life and death. Let it be for us a challenge, especially at every Eucharist when we proffer the cup with those words: "Take and drink, this is my blood of the new covenant …" May we be ministers of the new covenant of forgiveness and fellowship, saying "Yes!" to work for God and Jesus' *least* sisters and brothers generously and joyfully.

Finally, let the cap remind us of the need to 'go forth' to shepherd those at the peripheries: the last, the lost and the lonely who need accompaniment and the assurance of God's power and presence in their lives. Many alumni of this 'home of love' have been invested with the zucchetto and mitre for leadership roles in the church. May they wear these with the humility and self-sacrifice of Christ, who bore a crown of thorns, symbolic of his love for us.

As we conclude Jubilee celebrations, let us 'go forth' hand-in-hand with Our Lord Jesus, with all *Papalites* and with all peoples of goodwill, pledging to be diligent sons of Mother India: zealous 'ministers' of her salvation.

## Notes

1. See http://www.papalseminary.in/history for details of the origins and history of the Papal Seminary; accessed on February 7, 2019.
2. See https://en.wikipedia.org/wiki/Pope_Leo_XIII for details on the life and mission of Pope Leo XIII; accessed on February 7, 2019.

3. The two popes who surpassed his papacy in terms of number of years was his predecessor Pope Pius IX who was pope for thirty-two years (1846-78) and Pope John Paul II who was pope for twenty-seven years (1978-2005).
4. https://en.wikipedia.org/wiki/Pope_Leo_XIII for details.
5. See http://w2.vatican.va/content/leo-xiii/en/encyclicals/documents/hf_l-xiii_enc_15051891_rerum-novarum.html for the text of this document.
6. On 4 August 1879, Leo XIII promulgated the encyclical AeterniPatris ('Eternal Father') which, more than any other single document, provided a charter for the revival of Thomism.
7. See J. Neuner and J. Dupius, The Christian Faith in the Doctrinal Documents of the Catholic Church, 6th ed., Theological Publications in India, Bangalore, 1996, nn.220-227.
8. See n.6 of its text; accessible at http://w2.vatican.va/content/leo-xiii/en/encyclicals/documents/hf_l-xiii_enc_01111885_immortale-dei.html
9. See text at the web-site http://www.papalencyclicals.net/leo13/l13praec.htm.
10. 'Liberal' always gives the impression of an attitude of laissez-faire—i.e., naively allowing everyone to do as they please without any regard for established norms or criteria to judge their actions, options and outcomes. However, being radical would imply going back to the roots; here, to the original Christ-event.
11. Reform merely seeks changes from the top to the bottom or from the centre to the periphery of an institution so that the structures of the institution remain unchanged. By contrast, renewal comes in the opposite direction—i.e., from the periphery into the centre or from the base into the top.
12. See his Apostolic Constitution Evangelii Gaudium: The Joy of the Gospel (November 2013), n.273; italics added.
13. http://www.asianews.it/news-en/Message-for-World-Mission-Day:-Together-with-the-young,-let-us-bring-the-Gospel-to-all-43934.html.
14. See Aloysius Pieris, *Helping Francis Renew the Church*, Kelaniya, Tulana Jubilee Publications, 2019, 9.
15. The report of the bishop of Jalandhar repeatedly raping a nun sent shock waves in India and abroad. See https://www.bbc.com/news/world-asia-india-45600402. Accessed on December 5, 2018.
16. https://indianexpress.com/article/india/kerala-priest-sex-scandal-father-robin-kannur-minor-girl-raped-4572713/
17. See https://timesofindia.indiatimes.com/city/mumbai/cops-frame-charges-against-priest-forsodomy/articleshow/.
18. https://indianexpress.com/article/india/controversial-land-deals-in-kerala-archdiocese-hc-directs-criminal-case-against-cardinal-church-group-backs-him-5090055/
19. See: https://press.vatican.va/content/salastampa/en/bollettino/pubblico/2018/01/29/180129c.html for the text of the document. The four 'criteria' are in n.4 a-d. This Apostolic Constitution was published in December 2017.
20. The JDV Faculty had organized an interdisciplinary Symposium on November 3 & 4, 2017, with papers published in a volume under the title: *My Way or God's Way? Neo-Gnosticism and Neo-Pelagianism in Interdisciplinary Perspective*, ed. Francis Gonsalves, Arjen Tete and Dinesh Braganza, Pune: JDV, and Delhi: ISPCK, 2018.
21. See https://millhillmissionaries.co.uk/pope-francis-video-message-to-pontifical-mission-societies/
22. See Evangelii Gaudium, nn.222-225.

PART TWO

# CHALLENGING PROMISES: DIALOGICAL OPENNESS

# 4

# Breaking the Barriers: The Challenge of the Church in India

**Thomas Karimundackal SJ**

## Introduction

Jesus' ministry in Luke's Gospel is very inclusive as he announces the message of the Kingdom to all and brings salvation to all. However, Luke, in a unique way, shows that Jesus goes out to those on the fringe of society to make them partners of the Kingdom. Luke particularly features the reception of Jesus' message by social outcasts, the poor, sinners, tax collectors, women etc. It is in Luke's Gospel that we see more concretely, Jesus breaks down human barriers to cut across his message of the Kingdom of God. The new community that Jesus has envisioned in the Lukan narrative has no boundaries. All the barriers are down; the message is available to all without distinction, especially to those who are exposed in society and those who are thrown into the peripheries of the society. It is a community of justice and righteousness. He shows care and compassion to the poor, the despised, the marginalized, the lost, the broken, the hurt, and the sinful. No one is rejected or ignored by him. Above all, his compassion reaches across racial lines and breaks with convention, and he tenderly cares for each person. Indeed, this inclusive ministry of Jesus in the Lukan narrative serves as a new paradigm for the church in India.

## 1. Jesus Breaks Down Barriers with Gentiles

Luke's account of the gospel appears to be geared towards Gentiles. During his ministry Lukan Jesus shows a special concern towards gentiles whom the orthodox Jew would have considered unclean: Jesus cites the widow of Zarephath and Naaman the Syrian as shining examples (4:25-27); the Roman centurion is praised for the greatness of his faith (7:9). Thus, Luke shows that Jesus' teachings are both versatile and non-discriminatory. Although the salvation of individual Jews remains a possibility for Luke (cf. Acts 2:41, 44; 6:7; 15:5; 21:20; 24:14), the Jews as a nation refused to accept the gospel (cf. Acts 13:45; 14:1-2, 4-5; 17:4-5; 18:6; 19:9; 28: 24-25).

A mission to the Gentiles is previewed in the opening sermon of Jesus before the commencement of his ministry (4:25-27). At the end of the Gospel and beginning of Acts, the resurrected Christ commands his disciples to preach salvation to the nations (24:47; Acts 1:8). Jesus also shows his concern for the "outsider," marginalized members of society, who are included within God's kingdom while "the righteous" find themselves excluded (cf. 2:8-12; 3:8-9; 7:1-10, 36-50; 8:2-3; 10:25-37; 13:22-30; 14:12-14,15-24; 15:1-32;17:11-19).

In 2:32 (cf. Isa 49:6) Luke specifically calls Jesus 'a light to the Gentiles'. In 3:6 (cf. Isa 40:5) Luke quotes Isaiah 40 by stating that 'all flesh will see God's salvation'. Luke, unlike other genealogical accounts of Jesus, traces Jesus to Adam, the father of the entire human race, as opposed to Abraham, the father of the Jewish nation. Thus, Luke announces the universal salvation with the coming of Jesus as savior of the world.

Thus, the Lukan orientation towards a gentile society is in tune with the fulfillment of the Old Testament prophecy (Isa 40:5; 49:6), and it is initiated by the incarnation of the Lord (2:32; 3:6), effected in his ministry (7:1-10; 14:15-24), instructed by him (24:47; Acts 1:8) to be carried out by his disciples (11:1; 15:7,14) as his witnesses (9:15;26:17, 23). In short, Lukan Jesus restores Gentiles to the Kingdom of God.

## 2. Jesus Breaks Down Barriers with the Lost

The Lukan Jesus has a mission to the lost. The entire Gospel of Luke pictures Jesus as reaching out to the lost in forgiveness. We see this demonstrated in the story of the sinful woman (7:36-50), in the parable of the lost sheep (15:1-7), in the parable of the lost coin (15:8-10), in the parable of the lost son (15:11-32), in the story of Zacchaeus (19:1-10). The story of Zacchaeus in 19:1-10 concludes with the statement that the Son of Man "came to seek and to save what was lost" (19:10), which became a primary focus of the Lukan Gospel. The prodigal son was not exactly a model of rectitude and the unrighteous have a way of turning up in the parables in this Gospel (7:41f.; 12:13-21; 16:1-12, 19-31; 18:1-8, 9-14). We see many other instances where Lukan Jesus pays special attention to the lost members of the society, including Gentiles (4:25-27; 7:9), Samaritans (9:51-56; 10:30-37; 17:11-19), women (2:37; 4:25-26; 7:12; 18:3, 5; 20:47; 21:2-3), tax collectors (5:27-32; 7:34; 18:9-14; 19:1-10). He offers forgiveness to a repentant sinner (3:3; 5:20-25; 6:37; 7:41-50; 11:4;

12:10; 17:3-4; 18:13-14; 24:47). In short, Lukan Jesus shows extraordinary commitment to the Lost.

## 3. Jesus Breaks Down Barriers with Samaritans

Luke depicts the Samaritans, a group which is considered as despised, as recipients of the gospel (9:52; 10:33; 17:11, 16; Acts 1:8; 8:1, 5, 9, 14, 15, 9:31; 15:3). Luke refuses to shut the door of the Kingdom of God to any person, and naturally not to the Samaritans (9:51-56). At the outset of Jesus' journey to Jerusalem (9:15-19:27), a Samaritan village refuses to receive him (9:51-56). James and John, his disciples, tell Jesus that they would command fire to come down from heaven and consume them (9:54). However, Jesus "turns and rebukes them" (9:55), pointing to them that they are also part of his community of disciples. Although Jesus was not made welcome in the village (9:53), it is significant that Jesus intended to visit a Samaritan village against the socio-cultural barriers.

Luke alone mentions the parable of the Good Samaritan (10:30-37), and suggests him as a model for his community. Considering the strained relationship between Judeans and Samaritans, a Samaritan taking such dedicated care of an injured Jew poses exemplary challenges to the Lukan community. Lukan Jesus intends to ask his disciples that, if a Samaritan, whom you all despise, already has done what God demands from humans, how much more should you not do to the suffering and needy brethren of your community (10:25)? Jesus argues that, contrary to their prejudiced thinking the Samaritans are devout followers of the Law.

The one grateful leper is also a Samaritan (17:11-19) whom Jesus has reintegrated into the community. This despised Samaritan is the only one who recognized Jesus' power among the healed. Jesus' admiration for this Samaritan's faith in 17:17-18 echoes the word of Jesus in Luke 4:27 which connotes 2Kings 5:1-19a. It is significant that a Samaritan is portrayed as an example of someone open to salvation in contrast to the Jews. In short, Luke depicts the Samaritans as model Law-keepers from the Jewish perspective and model recipients of Jesus from the Christian perspective. Once again Jesus is trying to break down the socio-cultural barriers.

## 4. Jesus Breaks Down Barriers with Outcasts and Untouchables

Luke pays unique attention to the outcasts of the society, namely Gentiles (4:25-27; 7:9-10; 7:11-17), Samaritans (9:51-56; 10:30-37; 17:11-19), tax collectors (5:27-32; 7:34; 18:9-14; 19:1-10), lepers (5:12-16; 17:11-19), shepherds (2:8-20), men with unclean spirits (4:31-37; 8:26-39;9:37-43), the physically challenged (5:17-26; 6:6-11;13:10-17;14:1-6). In 15:1 Luke clearly tells his readers that 'the tax collectors and sinners were all drawing near to hear' Jesus. This is not an isolated incident, for Luke mentions many instances where Jesus goes against the traditional socio-religious barriers and embraces them with a liberative human touch.

In 5:27-32 Jesus purposefully welcomes a group of Israel's outcasts to his community, namely tax collectors, a group which has already been mentioned in 3:12-13 and will be seen again in 7:29, 34; 15:1; 18:10-14; 19:1-10. This episode also mentions Jesus eating with "sinners," an undefined group which Luke mentions some ten times in his Gospel (5:27-32; 7:28, 30, 34, 36-50; 15:1-2; 19:7). Luke tells us of Zacchaeus who was dismissed by the bystanders as 'a sinner' (19:7). To these we may add the people whose diseases rendered them "untouchable and outcasts". Jesus constantly ministers to and even touches these "untouchable and outcasts", whom others avoid at almost all costs, namely lepers (5:13), the dead (7:14), and people with various diseases (8:44-47). In the same way Luke recounts the story of the sinful woman who wept over Jesus' feet and anointed them and of whom Jesus said that her many sins were forgiven (7:37-50).

## 5. Jesus Breaks Down Barriers with Tax-Collectors

Jesus offers hope to the tax collectors, another group of people considered as despised by the orthodox Jewish community, and he shows that they too can enter into God's Kingdom (5:27-32; 7:34; 18:9-14; 19:1-10). One of the disciples whom Jesus called to follow him is Levi, a tax collector (5:27-29), and Jesus eats in his house where the invited guests were mostly tax collectors (5:29). Luke 15:1 informs us the tax collectors and sinners drew near to Jesus to hear him (15:1). On the way to Jerusalem, Jesus stays with the tax collector Zacchaeus, who is a sinner in public eyes (19:7) and Jesus proclaims that salvation has come to his house (19:9).

## 6. Jesus Breaks Down Barriers with Sinners

Luke pictures Jesus as the friend and liberator of sinners (5:27-32; 7:28, 30, 34, 36-50; 15:1-2; 19:7). He alone tells of the woman who anointed Jesus' feet and bathed them with her tears and wiped them with her hair in the house of Simon the Pharisee (7:36-50); of Zachaeus, the tax collector (19:1-10); of the Penitent thief (23:43); of the lost son (15:11-32).

Lukan Jesus offers repentant sinners forgiveness (3:3; 5:20-25; 6:37; 7:41-50; 11:4; 12:10; 17:3-4; 18:13-14; 24:47). Jesus forgives the sins of the paralytic man by healing his physical disability (5:17-26). When the Pharisees complaint against Jesus for eating with tax collectors and sinners, Jesus tells them that, "he has not come to call the righteous, but sinners to repentance" (5:32). In 7:36-50, Luke relates the story of the woman who was a sinner and received forgiveness from Jesus. When the tax collectors and sinners drew near to Jesus (15:1), the Pharisees and scribes complained against him saying that "this fellow welcomes sinners and eats with them" (15:2). Luke is the only

Gospel to affirm that there is more joy in heaven over one repentant sinner, than over ninety-nine who have no need of repentance (15:7). In the Parable of the Pharisee and tax collector (18:9-14), Jesus contrasts the behaviour of the tax collector, who is a sinner with the behaviour of a Pharisee, and again the sinner is found favour before God. In his interaction with Zacchaeus in 19:2-10, Jesus articulates that "the Son of Man came to seek and to save that which was lost" (19:10). In short, Luke shows Jesus' compassionate face towards sinners.

## 7. Jesus Breaks Down Barriers with the Poor

Luke pays special attention to Jesus' dealing with the poor and his teachings about poverty and wealth. The poor or rejected are mentioned in several instances (1:46-55; 4:18; 6:20-23; 7:22; 10:21-22; 14:13, 21-24; 16:19-31; 21:1-4). Although there are also many negative warnings against money and riches (8:14; 12:13-21; 16:1-15, 19-31; 18:18-25), there are also positive examples that illustrate sharing mentality of the rich (8:3; 19:1-10).

In the Magnificat Mary praises God because "he has put down the mighty from their thrones, and exalted those of low degree; he has filled the hungry with good things, and the rich he has sent empty away" (1:52f). The shepherds to whom the angels came to announce the good news (2:8ff.) are from a poor class. Mary offers the offering of the poor for her purification (2:24; cf. Lev 12:8). Jesus' announces at Nazareth that at the center of his ministry is preaching "good news to the poor" (4:18). When he begins teaching, looking at his audience he says "blessed are you poor" (6:20). When he is asked to give his credentials of his identity, he tells the emissaries of John that "the poor have good news preached to them" (7:22). On a few occasions he commands his followers to help the poor (4:18; 12:33; 14:13). He praises the poor widow for her faith in God (21:1-4). On two instances Jesus calls on the would-be disciples to renounce or sell their possessions (12:33; 18:22; cf. 14:33). He exhorts his disciples to give to those in need (12:32-34) and to those who give banquets to invite "the poor, the crippled, the lame, the blind", rather than their rich friends (14:13).

Jesus pointed out the dangers of wealth and the impossibility of serving both God and money (16:13): "woe" to the rich (6:24-25); the parable of the rich fool (12:16-21); the parable of the unjust steward (16:1-13); the parable of the rich man and Lazarus (16:19-31); the rich young man (18:18-30). The rich are strongly warned in the "woes" of 6:24-26. According to Luke, as the rich have already received their comfort, they will be hungry, and they will mourn and weep (6:24-26). The rich fool builds large barns in view of the future, but God calls him to quick judgment (12:16-21). The parable of the unjust steward (16:1-13) leads Jesus to say that "no one can serve both God and wealth" (16:13). Luke alone tells the parable of the poor Lazarus and the rich man

(16:19-31), a story that illustrates Jesus' special concern for those with few possessions. The rich young man refuses to sell what he has in order to follow Jesus, and consequently his attachment to the riches becomes a stumbling block to follow the Lord (18:18-30). The rich young man's attitude towards his possessions leads Jesus to say that "it is easier for a camel to go through the eye of a needle than for a rich man to enter the kingdom of heaven" (18:25). There are also warnings for the rich in the stories of Zacchaeus (19:1-10), and of the widow's mite (21:1-4). The point of all these stories is that there is a proper use of wealth. It is to be used to help the poor.

There is no teaching in the Gospel of Luke which is repeated more often than Jesus' blessings on the poor and his warnings to the rich. Luke is interested in the rich (19:2; 23:50), but he champions the poor because they needed a friend (1:53; 2:7, 8, 24; 4:18; 6:20, 21; 7:22; 14:13, 22; 16:20, 23). In short, Jesus concerns himself with the interests of the poor (1:53; 6:30; 14:11-13, 21; 16:19ff.), and preaching good news to them is characteristic of his ministry (4:18; 7:22).

## 8. Jesus Breaks Down the Barriers of Table Fellowship

The way Jesus restores the people through preaching, healing, and casting out demons in the Gospel is quite significant. Yet unique to Luke is the emphasis on the table fellowship. Meeting around a common table symbolized friendship, intimacy, and unity.Jesus is seen eating with a wide variety of people in Luke, including the crowds (9:10-17), Mary and Martha (10:38-42), his disciples (22:14-38; 24:29-32, 41-43), Pharisees (7:36-50; 11:37-54; 14:1-24), and tax collectors (5:27-32; 19:1-10). In other words, while the Pharisees practiced an extreme exclusivism in sharing meals with others, Jesus practiced a radical inclusiveness in sharing the table with others.

Two aspects of the table fellowship in Luke deserve particular stress:

> The table designates a special relationship between those who sit at the same table. Thus, when Jesus eats with sinners and tax collectors (5:27-32; 7:34; 15:2), it shows his concern and relationship with them. He goes to the house of Zacchaeus and shares a meal with him (19:1-9). He shares meals with the despised, handicapped and disenfranchised (7:22; 14:12-14). Above all, in 15:11-32 a banquet is thrown for the returning prodigal son.
>
> At formal dinners certain table etiquette is demanded in the Palestine, and there should be servants to serve at table. Feet of the guests were washed by servants, the table was served and cleared by servants, etc. In Luke this service is shared by the community and the disciples are fellow-servants, as Jesus himself is a servant at table (22:25-27). The servants are served

at the table of the Lord by Jesus himself in the eschatological banquet (12:35-37).

Only in Luke does Jesus give extended parables of wedding feasts to illustrate future membership and life in the kingdom (14:7-24).The ways of God's kingdom are exemplified through care for the poor and social outcasts, as they are the central recipients of the kingdom (14:12-24). According to the Jewish tradition by associating with the poor, and other unclean social outcasts, the host would become religiously impure and culturally despised. Therefore, in 14:12-24 Jesus calls the host to break the religious boundaries of the Pharisees, and to break the social/economic boundaries between the rich and the poor, the pure and impure. 7:36-50 further reveals Jesus' attitudes toward those who were not extended hospitality by the Pharisees. Because of their lifestyle, they were considered 'sinners' and could not be included in the table fellowship by those considered religiously pure.

In short, Jesus intentionally overcomes all eating traditions of the Jewish society: "he ate with the wrong crowd, ate with unwashed hands, criticized the practice of sitting according to status, encouraged serving instead of being served, and encouraged inviting to one's banquets those who could not repay, such as the poor and disabled. In so doing, Jesus turned every meal into an acted-out parable about the standards of the kingdom of God". He welcomes all to his table, sinner or righteous, poor or rich. He does not fear being compromised by the company he keeps at table. He overturns human expectations by showing his own unique values at table. His meals are indications of the banquet to be shared in the Kingdom of God.

## 9. Jesus Breaks Down Barriers with Children

Luke finds God's plan in events that concern children. This is quite evident in Jesus' approach to the children in the Gospel whether in the healing of a young slave (7:1-10), or raising of a youth at Nain (7:11-17), or raising of a girl in Galilee (8:40-56), or casting of a demon from a boy in Galilee (9:37-45). These narratives taken together - one healing (7:1-10), two resuscitations (7:11-17; 8:40-56), and one exorcism (9:37-45) - represent God's inclusive and restorative grace to the lost, rather than individual testimonies to the presence of children in the Gospel account or the beneficiaries of Jesus' ministry. That is to say, Jesus' care and concern goes to the very deserving members of the society.

Moreover, the inclusion of children among Jesus' followers can be seen most vividly in 9:47-50 and 18:15-17, in which Jesus explicitly exhorts his disciples to welcome little children and infants. 18:15-17 builds on the welcome and inclusion of young children already illustrated in Luke 9:47-50 by explicitly including and welcoming young children and infants into his midst. In these instances Luke not only illustrates the sympathetic character of Jesus towards children, but also clarifies the equal place of children among adult disciples in the Kingdom of God. To receive a child in Jesus' name means to recognize the child's relationship with Jesus as a follower of Jesus and a part of God's Kingdom that Jesus is proclaiming (9:48).

This ethos of welcome and inclusion of children in the Kingdom of God begins in the infancy stories itself (1:2-2:52). The miraculous interventions and angelic announcements in the narrative have made it clear to the reader that God has something special for child John and child Jesus. The angel Gabriel prophesies that Zechariah's son John will "go before [Jesus] to turn the hearts of parents to their children, and the disobedient to the wisdom of the righteous, to make ready a people prepared for the Lord" (1:17). And the same angel Gabriel foretells Mary that her son "will be great and will be called the Son of the Most High, and the Lord will give him the throne of his ancestor David …" (1:32-34). In short, marginalized himself since his birth (Luke 2:1-20), Jesus makes sure that everybody is included in his kingdom.

According to Luke Children are hearers and doers of God's word. Luke puts praise of this unique perspective into the mouth of Jesus himself in Luke 10:21. While thanking the Father, Jesus prays: "I thank you, Father, Lord of heaven and earth, because you have hidden these things from the wise and intelligent and have revealed them to infants; yes, Father, for such was your gracious will" (10:21). At the literal level, children, specifically infants, are thus described as uniquely possessing something that their "wiser" adult counterparts lack. The infantsof 10:21 biologically represent the most vulnerable - and, as a result, the most attentive of all life stages.

In short, children are not simply rhetorical symbol for humility or innocence to the Lukan author. Rather, they are distinct individuals who stand in need of restoration at the word of Jesus to the Society. Luke's concern for children in the Gospel sets a paradigm for a liberative ecclesiology.

## 10. Breaking Down Barriers with Women

Though women are on the fringe of first-century Palestinian society, they are in the middle of Luke's Gospel. Luke takes every opportunity to establish the roles played by women in his story of Jesus and the Kingdom that he has preached (7:36-50; 8:1-3, 48; 10:38-42; 13:10-17; 24:1-12). Lukan Jesus understands and sympathizes with the plight of widows who represent the most vulnerable in society (2:37; 4:25-26; 7:12; 18:3, 5; 20:47; 21:2-3). In these instances we see Jesus as the emancipator of women, particularly of those who are thrown into the peripheries of the society.

Moreover, Luke gives a significant place to women in his narrative. It is in Luke that we read of Elizabeth (1:39-45), of Anna (2:36-38), of the widow at Nain (7:11-17), of the woman who anointed Jesus' feet in the house of

Simon the Pharisee (7:36-50). It is Luke who makes vivid the pictures of the female disciples of Jesus (8:1-3), Martha and Mary (10:38-42), and the women to whom Jesus appeared after his resurrection (24:1-12). Often he refers to women whom he does not name, such as the widow of Nain (7:11-17.), the woman who anointed Jesus' feet (7:36-50), the bent woman (13:11), the poor widow who put all that she had in the treasury (21:1-4) and the 'Daughters of Jerusalem' who lamented for Jesus as he went to the cross (23:27-29.49). Sometimes women turn up also in the parables, as in those of the lost coin (15:8ff) and the widow who bothered the unjust judge (18:1-8).

Often the women characters are paired with men (2:25-28; 4:25-27; 8:40-56; 11:31-32; 13:18-21; 15:4-10; 17:34-35) to show that the Kingdom that Jesus preached is for both genders, and both enjoys equal dignity before God. This can be shown by the paralleling of events involving men and women:

- Annunciation to Zechariah (1:8-23) and Mary (1:26-38).
- Mary's Magnificat (1:46-55) and Zechariah's Benedictus (1:68-79).
- Simeon's praising God for seeing the baby Jesus (2:25-35) and Anna's praising God for seeing the baby Jesus (2:36-38).
- During the sermon in Nazareth, Jesus mentions both widows (4:25-26) and lepers (4:27).
- Healing of the possessed man (4:31-37) follows the healing of Simon's mother-in-law (4:38-39).
- Jesus forgives the sins of the paralytic (5:17-26) followed by the woman who washes his feet 7:36-50).
- The healing of the centurion's slave (7:1-10) is followed by the raising of the widow's son (7:11-17).
- Jesus chooses the twelve apostles from his disciples (6:12-16) but we also see women accompanied him in his itinerary preaching (8:1-3).
- The healing of the Gerasene demoniac is sandwiched with the raising of Jairus' daughter (8:40-42a,49-56) and the healing of the woman with the haemorrhage (8:42b-48).
- Jesus places both Jonah (11:30) and the Queen of the South (11:31) as a sign to his generation.
- The kingdom of God is compared with a mustard seed which a man takes (13:18-19) and with the leaven which a woman takes (13:20-21).
- The parable of the man with the lost sheep (15:3-7) is followed by the parable of the woman with the lost coin (15:8-10).
- Of two men in bed, one will be taken and the other will be left (17:34) and of two women grinding together, one will be taken and the other will be left (17:35).

Luke often shows greater faith and servanthood for the women characters: Mary shows greater faith than Zechariah (1:8-23 vs 1:26-38), Mary sits at Jesus' feet, the position of a disciple (10:38-42), the female disciples who travel with Jesus share their possessions with Jesus and the apostles (8:1-3) etc. In short, "Luke demonstrates God's equal concern for women and men, the equal faith of women and men, and the prominent roles played by women and men."

Allowing women to accompany Jesus (8:1-3) was breaking down barriers on Jesus' part because it would have been scandalous for women to leave home and travel with a rabbi. In Luke 4:38-39 we are told after the cure of Peter's mother-in-law she rose and served Jesus at table. This is against the Palestinian tradition as a woman should not serve men at table. Jesus does the same by allowing Martha to serve him at her house (10:38-42). In 13:10-17 Jesus heals a woman who had a spirit of infirmity for eighteen years and he affirms that she too is a "daughter of Abraham" (13:16), and this is quite significant as nowhere in the Scriptures that a woman is called as "daughter of Abraham". The instances of raising of Jairus' daughter (8:40-42a,49-56) and woman with the haemorrhage for twelve years (8:42b-48) are also sociologically significant. According to Jewish law anyone who touched a corpse would be ritually unclean (cf. Num 19:11-19) but nevertheless Jesus takes the little girl by the hand. Concerning the haemorrhaging woman, Jesus would have been ritually unclean after being touched by her (cf. Lev 12). But Jesus doesn't mind the barriers of the Law but goes against it with a compassionate heart.

## Conclusion

The socio-religious structures of the society of Jesus' time have erected human barriers but Jesus has broken down those barriers. He has not adhered to the social taboos or the restrictions of the society of his time; rather he has tried to liberate people from the clutches of these exploitative and unjust structures. He has shown the love of God to all people and invited them to the Kingdom that he has preached. He showed his concern for the fatigued, the lost, and the broken. He has offered hope to all the socially outcasts, specially to the poor, sinners, tax collectors, Samaritans, children and women. He has healed the sick, diseased, and crippled. He has enjoyed strong friendships with his disciples, followers, and families.The new community that he has tried to form had no boundaries, rather its message of blessing was offered to all, and it embraced all and included everyone. In fact, Lukan Jesus calls everyone to be a neighbour to everyone. Such care and compassion has had no boundaries of race, gender or class. In short, Jesus' ministry in Luke is inclusive, bringing salvation to all by breaking down the social and religious barriers.

Lukan Jesus sets a new paradigm for the Church in India, a church that fosters and witnesses the message of the Kingdom. As Jesus declares himself to be the servant of the Kingdom, sent to serve all, to be the light of the nations and cultures, the Church in India is invited to embrace the message of a 'servant church'. As Jesus has showed that the salvation is available to all- including the gentiles, outcasts and sinners- the Church in India is invited to hug the people who bears the stigma of the lost, broken, unwanted, marginalized and untouchables. As Jesus' ministry in Luke has showed an inclusive character, the Church in India is invited to embrace everyone irrespective of one's cast, creed, culture and biological differences. As Jesus has crossed the socio-cultural barriers of his society to spread the message of the Kingdom, the Church in India is invited to adopt a method of dialogue for spreading the message the Kingdom in its multi religious and multicultural context. As Jesus has brought liberation to all by breaking down the social and religious barriers, the Church in India is called to forego the unjust and exploitative socio-religious structures of the society. As the Kingdom that Jesus has unfolded had a new vision for humanity, its message should be understood in and through the ministry of the Church. Thus, let the Church in India become a place where justice, peace freedom and respect for human rights prevail and a place where Kingdom is present and operative in the world today. Therefore, the primary task of the Church in India is to proclaim the Kingdom of God revealed in the person of Jesus Christ by breaking down all sorts of exploitative and unjust socio-cultural-religious- economic barriers of society.

## Notes

1. D. L. Bock, *Luke Volume 1. 1:1-9:50* (BECNT; Grand Rapids: Baker Books, 1994), 35.
2. For a detailed study on this topic, see J. Dupont, *Salvation of the Gentiles:Essays on the Acts of the Apostles* (Mahwah: Paulist press International, 1979),11-33; J. A. Fitzmyer, *Luke* 1:187-92 (AncB 28; Garden City, 1981); J. Jervell, *Luke and the People of God* (Minneapolis: Augsburg, 1972), 41-74; M. Kiddle, "The Admission of the Gentiles in St. Luke's Gospel and Acts," *JTS* 36 (1935), 160-73; I. H.Marshall, *Luke:Historian and Theologian* (Paternoster Carlisle 1970), 77-144; S. G. Wilson, *Gentiles and Gentile Mission in Luke-Acts* (Cambridge, 1973); D. Ravens, *Luke and the Restoration of Israel* (Sheffield: Sheffield Academic Press, 1995); D. Seccombe, "The New People of God," in: *Witness to the Gospel: The Theology of Acts*, I. H. Marshall and D. Peterson, eds. (Grand Rapids: Eerdmans, 1998) 349-372; R. Wall, "Israel and the Gentile Mission in Acts and Paul: A Canonical Approach," in: *Witness to the Gospel* (Grand Rapids 1998), 437-458; C. W. Stenschke, *Luke's Portrait of Gentiles Prior to Their Coming to Faith* (Tübingen: Mohr Siebeck, 1999).
3. L. Morris, *Luke: An Introduction and Commentary, Vol. 3* (TNTC; Downers Grove, IL: Inter Varsity Press 1988), 49.
4. Their response to the Samaritans' refusal echoes the episode where Elijah threatens fire to fall on the messengers of Samaria's king in 2Kgs 1:1-16. Probably they expect Jesus to act like Elijah, the "Man of God", to make a final break with the Samaritans (cf. Luke 9:5; 10:11; Acts 13:51).

5. For many scholars, this scene is the preview of the Samaritan mission in Acts 8, see O. Tomohiro, *Samaritans in the Context of Multicultural Coexistence Society* (SBL Sessions 2011), 6.
6. It is in stark contrast to Jesus in Mathew who forbade the Twelve to enter any Samaritan village (Matt 10:5).
7. According to Bruners, Luke depicts Jesus as a prophet which is greater than a Elijah-like-prophet by connoting 2 Kings 5, cf. W Bruners, *Die Reingung der zehn Aussätzigen und die Heilung des Samariters Lk 17,11-19: Ein Betrag zur lukanischen Interpretation der Reinigung von Aussätzigen* (Stuttgart: Kothlisches Bibelwerk, 1977), 118.
8. For further studies on this theme, cf. R.T. Anderson -T. Giles, *The Keepers: An Introduction to the History and Culture of the Samaritans* (Peabody: Hendrickson, 2002); C. J. D. Shaye, *The Beginnings of Jewishness: Boundaries, Varieties, Uncertainties* (Berkeley: University of California Press, 1999); C. J. Richard, *Samaritans and Jews; the Origins of Samaritanism Reconsidered* (Atlanta: John Knox Press, 1975); C. J. Richard, "The Samaritans and Acts," *NTS* 28 (1982), 423-434.
9. M. C. Black, *Luke* (NIVC; Joplin, Mo.: College Press Pub. 1996), 15.
10. M. C. Black, *Luke*, 18.
11. L. Morris, *Luke: An Introduction and Commentary, Vol. 3* (TNTC; Downers Grove, IL: Inter Varsity Press 1988), 49.
12. D. L. Bock, *Luke Volume 1: 1:1-9:50*, 35.
13. Sinners would be ostracized from the pure community. Some of the impure occupations are donkey-driver, camel-driver, sailor, shepherd, tax collector, physician, butcher, tanner, weaver, and launderer, cf. J.M. Ford, My Enemy is My Guest: Jesus and Violence in Luke, (Oregon: Wipf & Stock Pub, 2010), 72-73.
14. On Luke's view of wealth cf. L. T. Johnson, *The Literary Function of Possessions in Luke-Acts* (SBLDS 39 (Missoula: Scholars, 1977).
15. The Lukan exhortation in Luke 6:20-26 is very striking when it is compared with its counterpart in the Sermon on the Mount (Matt 5:3-12) where the teaching is much more concerned with spiritual virtues and their reward, cf. J. Dupont, *Les Béatitudes*, Tome II: La bonne nouvelle (Coll. Études bibliques; Paris, Gabalda, 1969); H. J. Degenhardt, *Lukas-Evangelist der Armen*, NovT 1 (1956), 43-53.
16. M. C. Black, *Luke*, 18.
17. M. C. Black, *Luke*, 22.
18. A.T. Robertson, *Luke the Historian in the Light of Research* (Bellingham, WA: Logos Research Systems, Inc. 2009), 28.
19. S. S. Bartchy, "Table Fellowship." in: *DJG*, 796-800.
20. M. C. Black, *Luke*, 28.
21. D. E. Smith, "Table Fellowship as a Literary Motif in the Gospel of Luke," *JBL* 106.4 (1987), 613-38.
22. M. Halvor, *The Economy of the Kingdom: Social Conflict and Economic Relations in Luke's Gospel*, (Philadelphia: Fortress Press, 1988), 130; idem, "Patron-Client Relations and the New Community", in: *The Social World of Luke-Acts*, Jerome H. Neyrey (ed.), (Peabody: Hendrickson, 1991), 249.
23. According to Heil, the conflict between Jesus and the Pharisees regarding the issue of eating with sinners is known to Luke's audience (5:30; 7:34), and in Jesus' ministry, this

woman probably came to him on the basis of the report that he was considered to be a friend of sinners, cf. J. P. Heil, *The Meals Scenes in Luke-Acts: An Audience-Oriented Approach* (SBLMS 52; Atlanta, 1999), 45.

24. M. C. Black, *Luke*, 22.
25. Cf. J. Kodell, *The Eucharist in the New Testament* (Wilmington, 1988), 113.
26. Luke 9:47-50 and 18:15-17 powerfully verbalize what has been implicit throughout Luke's narrative, i.e., children are included as part of the proclaimed Kingdom of God, cf. Green, Gospel of Luke, 651.
27. Luke is the only canonical gospel to give an account of John's birth and Jesus' childhood and the most descriptive in its account of Jesus' birth and infancy.
28. There are many other women who receive brief mention in Luke, See A. Black, "Women in the Gospel of Luke," *Essays on Women in Earliest Christianity*, vol. 1 (Joplin, MO: College Press, 1993), 446-447.
29. D. L. Bock, *Luke Volume 1: 1:1-9:50*, 35.
30. According to Barton, "this fits, of course, with Greek and Roman culture where women were active participants in business, politics, and household management (see, for example, Acts 16:13-15; 17:4, 12). It would have been almost scandalous, however, in Jewish culture where men and women were separated in the synagogue and only men could be taught by the rabbis.", B. B. Barton, D. Veerman, L.C.Taylor, & G. R. Osborne, *Luke* (Life application Bible commentary; Wheaton: Tyndale House Publishers 1997), xxii.
31. W. Barclay, *The Gospel of Luke* (Philadelphia: The Daily Study Bible series, The Westminster Press 2000), 3.
32. D. L. Bock, *Luke Volume 1: 1:1-9:50*, 35.
33. Cf. G. *Lohfink, Jesus and Community: The Social Dimension of Christian Faith*, (Philadelphia 1984), 122-147.

# 5

# Mediation and Spirituality of Reconciliation

**Joaquim Reis**

Mediation and Reconciliation are important topics in the context of what is happening in the Courts of India, as well as in disputes entailing Christian families inter se or with neighbours as well as disputes with the Church Authorities and so on and so forth. In this article I want to talk of the Church in India as an agent of mediation and reconciliation.

## 1. Mediation

We all know the experience of those approaching the Courts of Law in India about the length of time taken for deciding litigation. At times, it is not the one who files the suit that reaps the fruits of the litigation but the next generation. Delay, would be apposite to Justice since unless a man gets speedy justice it would amount to denial of justice. In view of huge arrears in Courts, the Code of Civil Procedure has been amended to provide for mediation and conciliation. Legislature tries to encourage litigants to an Alternative Dispute Resolution either by mediation or by arbitration. Effect of mediation is primarily to solve a dispute between the parties. Basic example would be that A has taken a loan from B and has agreed to repay the same with interest. For reasons beyond the control of B, B is not in a position to repay the amount and A is required to go to Court. In mediation, the mediator will try to either give some instalments to pay the money with interest or to decrease the rate of interest and try to find an amicable settlement between the parties. Arbitration would try to, less legalistically decide who is right and who is wrong.

Mediation is a dynamic, process where a neutral third party assists disputing parties in resolving conflict through the use of specialized communication and negotiation techniques. Mediation is a "party-cantered" process in that it is focused primarily upon the needs, rights, and interests of the parties. The mediator uses a wide variety of techniques to guide the process in a constructive direction and to help the parties find their optimal solution. A mediator is facilitator in that s/he manages the interaction between parties and facilitates open communication

## 2. Reconciliation

Reconciliation is a different ball-game altogether and goes a step further to mediation. For us Christians, Reconciliation is an activity whereby God and the World are brought together through the saving activity of Jesus Christ, and the help of Holy Spirit, relationships are restored and sustained. In Reconciliation, the focus is on the Victim rather on the wrongdoer. Attention is paid to the fact that the victim is hurt and therefore it is required to restore the wholeness of damaged humanity of the victim by giving dignity to the victim which the wrongdoer by his actions took away from the victim. This restoration of dignity to the victim can be found in the Passion, Death and Resurrection of Jesus Christ. Success of this process of reconciliation makes both the victim and the wrongdoer a new creation.

Therefore, in the light of the distinction made by me between mediation and reconciliation, experience shows mediation is a faster process, but for reconciliation, time taken is much more in view of requirement to restore the relationship of victim and wrongdoer.

To buttress my point, I place before the reader, my experience of 1992, where there was a dispute between mother, son and a daughter-n-law. It was referred to the Reconciliation Cell of St. Andrews Church, Bandra. I spoke to the parties individually and jointly and ultimately suggested solutions to the problem. It took some time to get the mother, the son and the daughter-in-law to think alike. Finally, their disputes were solved. That moment when the elderly mother came to thank me for having solved their dispute was a momentous moment for me. Bonds of love and unity in the family were restored and for me it was an experience of an internal joy which no money nor fame could give. Uniting an alienated family restores the relationship of the whole family.

## 3. Transformation of Life

The Conbony Missionary Sisters have beautifully stated that reconciliation allows us to live with the past without being its prisoners. It is the only way enabling us to fend through the darkness of conflict in order to reach out to the open spaces of peace and harmonious togetherness. Before being a collective commitment, reconciliation is a personal journey that cannot be imposed; each one must decide for oneself to forgive the offender. It is a process that starts from the victim, moved by profound motivations marked by gratuity and open to eternity, motivations that reflect the Gospel logic of the "grain of wheat fallen to the ground … that dies and produces abundant fruit" (Jn 12,24) a fruit that many will enjoy.

According to their experience transformation of relationships which comes from acts of reconciliation, brings to life social situations completely different from what seems to be today's mentality. From gestures of reconciliation new styles of life spring up giving credibility to the prophetic strength of the Gospel and make the Kingdom of God present among us.

## Concluding Remarks

Reconciliation is possible to the extent in which conditions of freedom are established that promote truth, justice, compassion and peace:

To compose the truth: demands that the logic of the facts and their meaning be reconstructed in a listening attitude that respects the other in order to find shared solutions.

To give impulse to justice: means to re-establish harmony with sentiments of mercy and compassion while admitting personal responsibility.

The fostering of compassion is an essential element in the achievement of communion; it springs from a humble and benevolent heart always ready to accord beforehand a measure of trust in righteousness that gives life a chance to emerge.

Peace is a fruit to look for by cultivating a heart reconciled with self, with others, with God and with creation in the simplicity of everyday life constantly oriented to the promotion of the good.

All this is finely expressed by Biblical wisdom in Psalm 85:10 'Mercy and Truth have met together: righteousness and peace have embraced'.

I hope that the Church in India becomes both an agent of mediation and reconciliation: between different communities, religious groups, political identities and social strata. In this way the Church can a witness to life with all its frailties, vulnerabilities, complexity as well as joy, hope and goodness!

# 6

# Relationship between Catholic and Protestant Churches: Indigenous People's Perspective

**Jangkholam Haokip**

## Introduction

The worldwide commemorations of the 500th year of Martin Luther's Reformation in 2017 was, at the same time, the mark of 500 years of separation between Roman Catholic and Protestant Church. It was a mixed feeling! On one hand, we are amazed at seeing how God in His love sustains the two divided churches and on the other, how we managed to faithfully maintain and cherish the wounded church, most often unknowingly, for the last Five Hundred Years.

This paper is an attempt to look at the relationship between catholic and protestant churches from an Indigenous perspective. It discusses how, in the process of Christianization, the indigenous people have received their new faith from the Western missionaries and their denominational divides unknowingly. It also explains the fact that before the coming of Christianity, the indigenous people's religion had no room for denominational division because their religious terms and concepts would not limit God into their worldview. The paper then interacts with the views of some theologians on Catholic-Protestant relations and finally puts forward some suggestions for further reflection and practical ministries of the church. It argues for the incorporation of indigenous people's religious insights into Christianity for a more effective faith journey together.

It is our experience that indigenous people, the greatest provider labour service, became the receiving ends of the present-day economic systems. Similar things can be said about them in Christianity.

## 1. Indigenous People's Experience

Here, I would like to share my own story as an indicator of Indigenous people's experience. I was converted to Christianity during my early teen-age. Later, I became committed, sincere and zealous for God. I used to spend time and energy trying to convert others including Catholics. By the way, recently, I happened to join a prayer meeting in the UK where prayer for the conversion of Catholics was still the main concern of the group – the world does not change much!

For me, it was much later on in my Christian life that I realized that at conversion, in ignorance, I was made to separate myself from others including my own relatives because of the Catholic-Protestant divide. Some of you might know Fr Peter Haokip, your own graduate here at Papal Seminary. He is my maternal uncle, but we had no good relationship for a long time because he belongs to the Catholic Church. I realized that I accepted Christianity along with all that came in a package including the conflict histories and 'enemies' of my own missionaries. That is to say, by becoming a Christian, I have adopted some people's form of religion as well as their 'enemies' – that is risky!

We all know that the relationship between Catholics and Protestant churches has not been a good one both here in India and elsewhere. Some might prefer to take the opposite view and say that the relationship has been a good one by referring to several instances of inter-church cooperation in demanding the rights of religion and our rights to propagate our faith but, when it comes to marriage, celebrating Eucharist and other traditions, we find it hard to work together. Praying to Mary, the mother of Jesus, praying for the dead – those are no-go areas for some!

For Indigenous people, this causes us a lot of pain – it pierces into the very heart of Indigenous people's life because, for them, life is shared in a community. In a communitarian life, everybody is related to everybody through different means and a broken relationship is both a sin and shame! Sin, because your existence depends on others, you are a part of a community, but you have separated yourself from the community; and shame, because the goal of life in a community was to establish cordial relationships with everyone, but you, hence your family, do not live up to the expectation. In this case, success was not you trying hard on your own and achieving something by yourself but rather, it was about winning the hearts of others through cordial relationships. The traditional practice of *Chang-Ai* in one example. '*Chang*' means Rice and '*Ai*' means celebration. *Chang-Ai* is a celebration of successful harvest and it is performed by women. In this, success is understood in terms of winning the will and support of nature. The Indigenous Kuki believes that you accumulated plenty of harvest because you are able to establish a cordial relationship with nature (Rice). For them reality is relational and inter-dependent and without relating to others, you cannot survive in the community. It was in such situations that the Indigenous people bore the pain of Catholic-Protestant division.

Another important experience of Indigenous people was that for them religion did not divide people. In other words, people do not divide on the basis of religion. It was true that they have different kinds of worship according to one's own clan culture, but they have a common understanding of God that has no place for superiority of faith claim. They addressed God as 'That which our forebears worshipped.' In other words, they did not want to take the risk of naming God as XYZ bur rather, being aware of the limitation of human knowledge, they safely called God as 'That which our forebears worshipped.' To explain this clearer, the Kuki people have a religious symbol called '*Doibom*', a bunch of articles, hanging in the courtyard of each house. *Doibom* symbolizes the presence of God but it was never perceived that God was confined in the symbol. In other words, the Indigenous people knew the limit of human understanding of God and never uses it to divide themselves. In this situation, the division of Indigenous people through Christianity is too costly for the people. It corrupts their relationships, their culture and their identity. And without an identity, they ceased to be a people. Therefore, this needs to be reflected on seriously and urgently.

## 2. The Need for Relationship

The unity-division-unity dynamic nature of the church is our experiential knowledge from the beginning of the church. In the middle of the 5th century, the Graeco-Roman Church was shut out of the Catholic Church, in the 11th century, the Greek Church got separated from the Catholic Church, in the 16th century the Protestant church was born out of the Roman Catholic and from there came several churches and the trend continues even today. The visible unity of the church was "lost due to historical heresies, schisms, and divisions." Besides doctrinal reasons, some of the reasons for the divisions are social and cultural.

One popular movement for visible unity of the church across all denominations is the Ecumenical Movement which began in the 19th century as the impact of the Evangelical awakening expressed in the Edinburgh World Missionary Conference in 1910. That is to say, the need for church unity was felt by those who were involved in mission. In other words, the call for church unity is a missionary call and hence it is from the heart of God. To strengthen the movement, the World Council of Churches was formed in 1948 and today it has more than 300 members. The Roman Catholic church is working closely with the WCC, but not as a member yet.

In the light of his own experience as a student of the Ecumenical Movement and as a Priest who was in charge of church relations, KuncheriaPathil raises his concerns and writes that the "Roman Catholic Church is in no way ready to change its traditional position that it alone possesses the fullness of 'ecclesial reality'. Hence, they are all defective in varying degrees." His main argument is that despite her close connection with the Ecumenical Movement, the Roman Catholic Church is not yet ready for a visible unity of the church. In fact, he also argues that the stagnancy of the Ecumenical Movement is due to non-cooperation of mainline churches for visible unity of the church including the Roman Catholic Church.

With the same conviction, Cardinal Walter Kasper also calls to repentance and a change of heart on the part of Roman Catholic Church as he writes, "In the ecumenical movement the question is the conversion not only of the others but of all to Jesus Christ. Conversion always begins with ourselves. We Catholics too must be ready for an examination of conscience, self-criticism and repentance."

From the above two views, we can see that part of the problem for church unity is the church itself. The same is also true with the Protestant Church as referred to earlier. The Protestant Church is not ready for unity! We have made the structure so strong that it controls our lives, culture and faith so that we are not able to come together.

## 3. Exploration of the Way Forward

To find avenues for better Catholic-Protestant relations, it is important to consider the following issues. One, our understanding of who God is: We all have some kind of knowledge of God and often have a tendency to hold it as the best and only way of knowing God. This is one area that needs a serious reflection and action. Hans Kung rightly points out that often the feeling of enmity and divide came because of rigidity in our belief and practice of faith. Referring to the hierarchical structure of the church he writes, "Jesus radiated a 'democratic' spirit in the best sense of the word .... This was the original Christian 'liberty, equality and fraternity'. But did not the original church community already clearly have a hierarchical structure with apostles as pillars and Peter as a rock?" The point here is about the structure becoming a hindrance to faith and faith expressions. And the need is to let the truth free. Here, Cardinal Kasper's view is helpful. Kasper encourages the Roman Catholic Church to learn from other churches, saying, "Mainline Churches have to learn some lessons from the success stories of the Pentecostal and Charismatic movements and the amazing growth of the new indigenous Churches in Africa, Asia and South America." The direct implication of this for us is the understanding of God in Indigenous people as referred to earlier. For the Indigenous people, the understanding of God does not divide people because of the absence of any superiority faith claim. This kind of view will pave the way for a better and peaceful relationship between Catholic and Protestant churches.

Two, the understanding of the church: Similar to the understanding of who God is, our understanding of the church is also an important issue. We need to ask some important questions including, what is church? or what is church for? or what is God doing through the church? A creative missionary theologian and thinker LesslieNewbigin suggests that we understand church not in terms of a finished product but rather in a futuristic sense. He writes, "The nature of the church is never to be finally defined in static terms, but only in terms of that to which it is going. It cannot be understood rightly except in a perspective which is both missionary and eschatological." In a similar way, Yves Congar talks about the importance of looking forward and backward. Looking forward includes looking into the past and appreciating the tradition where we stand and that would also help the church accept the legitimacy of other expressions in other circumstances. This is a useful insight that helps us focus more on what can be achieved through collaboration than pointing out the past wounds.

In the same line of thought, Ephraim Radner in his *Hope among the Fragments* suggests that we look at the church not in terms of 'what is the church?' but rather in terms of 'how is God using the church?' and in doing this, according to him, we will be able to understand 'what is God's calling to the church'. For him, God's call for the church is to accept all including the Jews and the Gentiles. He calls this 'one new man' that is the inclusive community of all people. Radner's view of the church is also helpful because it directs our focus on God and God's purpose in and through the church.

Emphasizing the place and role of ecumenical relationships for unity, Kasper argues, saying, "In mission, the Church makes rooms in itself for the richness of peoples and cultures in a creative way; likewise, in ecumenism, it is enriched by the gifts of the other churches and enriches them with its own." In this case, the paradigm of unity in diversity is realized in the Holy Trinity wherein the three individual identities are not abolished for the sake of unity. Envisioning the future of the church, Kung asks an important question, 'Which church has a future in the third millennium?' and suggests four conditions as the answer. They are all relevant for us:

The church must not turn back and fall in love with the Middle Ages or the time of the Reformation or the Enlightenment, but be a church rooted in its Christian origin and concentrated on its present tasks.

It must not be patriarchal, fixated on stereotyped images of women, exclusive male language and predetermined gender roles, but be a church of partnership, which combines office and charisma and accepts women in all church ministries.

It must not be narrowly confessional and succumb to confessional exclusiveness, the presumption of officialdom and the refusal of communion, but be an ecumenically open church, which practices ecumenism inwardly and finally follows up many ecumenical statements with ecumenical actions like the recognition of ministries, the abolition of all excommunications and complete Eucharistic fellowship.

It must not be Eurocentric and put forward any exclusivist Christian claims and show a Roman imperialism, but be a tolerant, universal church which has a respect for the truth that is always greater, it must therefore attempt to learn from the other religions and grant an appropriate autonomy to the national regional and local churches.

Kung is a man ahead of his time. He predicted the coming of what is now known as 'World Christianity', where there is more respect and acceptance for those in the margins including women, Indigenous people and others, and ecology. In other words, he prepares the ground for the participation of Indigenous people in re-imagining and reclaiming the unity of the Church of Christ.

## Conclusion: An Indigenous Way

By way of concluding, I would like to come back to Indigenous people's experience and offer two proposals. For Indigenous people, reality is relational, hence, life is shared in community which includes nature. Breaking up of a relationship in this context is not only a sin but also shame. For these reasons, first, faith must be expressed responsibly in order to bridge gaps between denominations. This is about creating or leaving space for God to judge our belief and action. This is about holding uncompromising faith in Christ and expressing it with humility. It is not about leaving faith but expressing it without condemning others. The reason for this is the fact that we only experienced God and do not own God. Here, we are talking about putting faith in its rightful place. For this reason, in some sense, faith and social identity can be put together at the same level. Identity is a social construct and it is a gradual process. It is based on history, but history is vague. When the past is recent and memories are clear, they cannot be called history but when they become old and blur, we look back and construct a history by collecting data. For this reason, it is difficult to say 100 per cent of history is right but at the same time, we cannot live without history. In a similar way, faith is faith - we cannot leave it nor be too fanatic about it. It is the way we perceive and respond to the reality which is beyond our comprehension. Moreover, for Indigenous people, the understanding of God was imported and the division of the church was our accidental adopted wounded history. Therefore, an Indigenous resource is necessary to reconstruct the understanding of God and the church for unity. The Indigenous people's voices have been silenced for the last five hundred years and it is the right time to claim and use Indigenous resources for the realization of their place in the future Kingdom that God is creating because, heaven will not be complete without them (Rev. 7:9).

Secondly, besides preparing a theological foundation for unity, we also need to start working together in our own capacity. One way to mend relationships is to re-start following the cultural web of relationship in a community, or, to invite each other to important events in life. In my own experience, on my wedding day, I invited a few Catholic fathers and it was the first time when Catholic fathers entered my church wearing their cassocks. I broke the record but thankfully there was no strong opposition. Further, I am initiating a new project for the study of Indigenous resources and World Christianity in North East India. I am delighted to say that here, both Catholics and different denominations of Protestant churches are involved. Fr Peter Haokip whom I referred to earlier is one of the active members in the Advisory Board. In fact, in recognition of his contribution, the Library of the centre is being named as 'Fr. Peter's Library'. This is both mending relationships and anticipatory participation in the future Kingdom God is creating.

I conclude this small reflection in the words of Kasper, "As we move nearer to Jesus Christ, in him we move nearer to one another."

## Notes

1. Kuncheria Pathil, *Future of the Ecumenical Movement* (Delhi: ISPCK, 2017), p. 25.
2. Pathil, *Future*, p. xix.
3. Pathil, *Future*, p. 34.
4. Walter Kasper, *That They May All Be One: The Call to Unity Today* (London: Burns & Oates, 2004), p. 17.
5. Hans Kung, *The Catholic Church* [Translated by John Bowden] (London: Phoenix Press, 2001), p. 16.
6. Pathil, *Future*, p. 35.
7. Lesslie Newbegin, *The Household of God* (London: Wipf & Stock, 1953), p. 25.
8. Yves Congar, *Diversity and Communion* (London: SCM Press, 1984), p. 166.
9. Ephraim Radner, *Hope among the Fragments: The Broken Church and Its Engagement of Scripture* (Grand Rapids, Michigan: Brazos Press, 2004), p. 217.
10. Radner, *Hope*, p. 221.
11. Kasper, *That They May All Be One*, p. 4.
12. George Karakunnel, 'The Identity and Role of Individual Churches' in Jacob Kavunkal et al., *Church in the Service of Asia's People* (Pune: Jnana-Deepa Vidyapeeth, 2003), pp. 275-290, (p. 287).
13. Kung, *The Catholic Church*, p. 213.
14. Kasper, *That They May All Be One*, 17.

7

# Carefronting Saffronisation

**Vishal G. Jadhav**

## Introduction

Since the present political coalition has come to power, it has systematically subordinated democratic institutions in the country. This leadership has also been a cause of political tensions based on identity politics in recent times. Swachh Bharat or 'clean India' has been one of the major clichés on which the Modi government has overtime gained legitimacy and popularity amongst the masses. Pictures of Narendra Modi and other Bharatiya Janata Party (BJP) members sweeping the streets and roads abound in the media. These pictures and media tactics seek to win over the support of the common man, who begin to relate to the metanarrative i.e. 'Janata ki Sarkar' (People's government). Further Narendra Modi's strategies of reaching out to the masses through Chai pe charcha and Mann kibaat are intertwined with this metanarrative of Swachh Bharati and Shining India.

However, one needs to critically dissect this narrative of the BJP as it has more implications than meets the eye. The discourse on cleanliness is not new in India as there have been many social reformers, political leaders and religious gurus who have advanced this notion. For instance, Sant Gadge Maharaj of Maharashtra selflessly worked towards cleanliness. Mahatma Gandhi also espoused the cause of cleanliness by associating it with godliness. Dr. B.R Ambedkar exhorted dalit communities to adopt a path to dignity by maintaining good health and cleanliness. He urged dalits to cease animal sacrifice as part of religious rituals and campaigned against vices such as alcoholism.

Various social scientists have argued that since the BJP is a right wing party and has the support of the Rashtriya Swayamsevak Sangh (RSS) and its affiliates such as the Bajrang Dal, Patit Pawan Sanghatna, Vishwa Hindu Parishad (VHP) etc., the Swachh Bharat Abhiyan needs to be examined through a critical lens. This paper attempts to deconstruct the Swachh Bharat Abhiyan narrative by examining it through the various facets of the term and the agenda of the BJP and its alliances.

## 1. The Pure and the Impure

In sociology the idea of purity and pollution or the sacred and profane is generally linked to the idea of inclusion and exclusion. For instance, as Louis Dumont in his epic work *Homo Hierarchicus* demonstrates that caste is linked to the purity- pollution binary. The savarnajatis are involved in non-polluting occupations and they practice vegetarianism. The lower castes on the other hand are meat eaters and also consume alcohol. This generalization leads to further universalisation of these binaries. The 'shudras' therefore are deemed to be inferior in terms of their capacity. In the works of M.N Srinivas, it becomes clear how the process of sanskritisation entails the movement of individuals from the realm of the 'polluting' to one of 'purity'. The individuals gradually over a period of time, sometimes over generations adopt practices of commensality, clothing/dressing and other cultural codes of the upper caste. This over a course of time provides potential for 'passing off' as savarna.

It is important to note that caste as a social marker reveals one's social and cultural practices and preferences in great detail. Food and culinary practices are definitely embedded in caste and kinship practices. For instance, Marriott (1968) has examined in great detail about the transactional "matrices" of the numerous local inter-caste food exchanges that occur in North India. He had documented the food ritual based on the principle of purity and pollution- these are five food types – the"raw", "water boiled" *(kacha)* or "ghee fried" *(pakka)* foods, alongside the "food remnants" (particularly the eaten "leftovers" or *jutha),* garbage *(kuda),* and faeces*(gu).* The village which he was observing (Kishangarhi) had thirty-six different caste groups and therefore he adopted multitransactional ranking matrices, rather than the usual binary food exchange scorings (Marriott 1968: 142.-146, 156-158). Dumont (1960) similarly observed that Indian foods and food ways revealed distinct-and indispensable-cultural, linguistic, moral, and material grammars of action patterns, purposes, and meanings (see Khare 1976b: 1-27, 47-80; Khare 1992).

In such a case where food habits are deemed to be an integral part of one's status and position in the caste hierarchy, how does one explain the ban on cow slaughter and ban on consumption of its meat in India? The answer to this could be in the Hindutva rhetoric of creating a nation of Hindus. In this sense then, anyone who is a beef consumer, is polluted. Only those practicing vegetarianism, supposedly the Brahmins represent the other end of the spectrum i.e. purity. If one were to stretch one's imagination, the idea of cleansing the nation of 'polluted beings' may even suggest conversion of members of other religions into Hinduism also termed as *GharWapasi.* This term is quite similar to the one that the Arya Samajists use called the 'shuddhi movement'.

The examples of *GharWapasi* from various parts of the country suggest that the right wing in India may be wishing to purge the individuals of their pollution and accommodate them into the 'Hindu' nation. It has also been suggested by scholars that the ban on cow slaughter has economically affected two communities most in India. One being the Muslim community and the other the dalit communities. The Muslims and the dalits are involved in activities related to cow slaughter. Due to this ban, they have had to shut down their abattoirs, leather tanning business, and leather related occupations. Further both these communities because of their economic marginality depend on beef for their staple food that provides the requisite proteins.

It has also been suggested by scholars that the Gujarat carnage affected businesses of the Muslims the most. The reports suggest that members of this community were targeted and eliminated so as to create an atmosphere of fear and uncertainty. The rhetoric of creating one Hindu nation then is itself anchored in this metanarrative of cleansing the impure. It is also therefore not surprising that the metaphorical cleaning of the Ganga, itself is related to the idea of cleansing it of its impurities. In such a case the overuse and misuse of the Aadhar card and biometrics can only lead to surveillance and targeting. Just as in the Anti-Sikh riots, where the census and other government registers were used to pin point addresses of the Sikhs, so too, the Aadhar card can be misused to locate and eliminate individuals from the impure category.

In the case of the Muslims in India, the GOI's Sachar Commission (2006) has suggested that nearly 40-60% of Muslims in India are artisans. Often they are settled in urban areas and have poor access to formal employment, literacy, and modern skills. In addition they face discrimination based upon communal, /religious, and /sectarian ideologies, which that legitimate these practices discrimination.

Studies have argued that the scheduled castes have continuously faced discrimination in the labour market in spite of having access to education. Though formally freed from traditional bondage systems and (extra legal social relationship,) they continue to face both wage and occupational discrimination in both rural and urban areas (The World Bank, 2011).

When one takes this argument to another level, the idea of ending corruption and retrieving black money is also part of cleansing the economy and polity of impurities. The demonstration drive set off by the government was to ensure that there would be a complete end to black money and this would ensure better tax compliance. However, as the reports by various scholars suggest, demonetization drive was a complete failure as it did not deliver the desired results. Some scholars suggest it was only a populist ideology that the government adopted to dupe the common man. Scholars also suggest that the demonetization drive hit the unorganised sector the most which constitutes 93 percent of the total economy of India. The aftereffects of the drive suggest that the government never intended to end black money; instead it sought to use certain information from this drive to threaten political leaders and political parties.

## 2. Rhetoric of the Glorious Past

In the interest of creating a 'samaj' the BJP and its affiliates seem to create this rhetoric of a glorious past for India. They blame the colonial era for the decimation of the Indian economy and society. They argue that the immoral British rule in India led to gradually deteriorating educational system. They now suggest that the society must go back to 'vedic' forms of learning. Some of the members of the BJP even suggested a complete revamp of the educational system. In this new system the college teachers will have a new responsibility which is conducting societal level interaction. They will have to work with the community programmes organised by their respective departments. They no longer have to work towards research and other related activities. It seems that the state wishes to use the labour of the college teachers to propagate their ideology.

Most importantly, this ideology has had the maximum impact on the women of the country especially those who are in the age group of 18 to 50. This age group is the most important section especially as this group is termed 'youth' by the government and this is the section of women who are generally employed in the large market. Generally, women are thought of as unclean as every month they have to undergo the menstrual cycle. The orthodox, right wing party deters women from entering temples or attend any 'auspicious' celebration and cultural event in the name of pollution.

It is also not surprising that this brand of right wing ideology exhorts girls and young women to dress in a 'traditional' manner such that they do not attract undue importance. Moreover, the parents and other elders in the family have an additional responsibility i.e. constant surveillance such that the women does not loose her virginity, which then defiles the women and her family. In contrast women from various other communities can be 'defiled' as they deserve it.

There is the violence with which women are reinserted into official kinship relations of which the khap panchayat is the most visible reminder. As student bodies are changing, with higher proportions of hitherto underprivileged castes and groups, including women, seeking higher education, the hyper-visibility of women from all backgrounds taking control their destiny is becoming too much for some sections to bear. Class differences combine in important ways with differences based on region, language and caste.

Our contemporary visual culture is saturated with messages that teach us that sexualised violence and violent male sexuality is normal. Love is unidirectional, declared by men, and succumbed to or accepted by women. They are often loved to death by men who, once spurned, wield the axe, knife or acid bottle. Indian cinema has carefully nurtured this version of loving, a unidirectional flow of feeling from man to woman, whose outcomes are always predictable. Many new entrants to the university system, who come from a very wide variety of socio-economic backgrounds, envy and fear the economic and social independence of women, themselves often from Dalit and OBC communities.

A strict vigilantism is initiated by the state on the reproductive facilities of the women and also on her sexuality. The state hesitates in arresting any one from the vigilante groups if any thing goes wrong. An Indian women (*nari*) has to ensure that she protects her chastity from the various prying individuals. To ensure that she is protected, the right wing parties suggest that the brother is an important element. It is during 'Rakshabhandan' that the sister acknowledges the brother/s as her saviour. Such an ideology is informed by patriarchy as an idea and practice.

Another agenda of the BJP is to ensure rapid economic growth but only of those who are rich and powerful. The rhetoric 'Make in India' is another fulcrum on which this whole meta-narrative is build upon. The indigenization of knowledge and culture is one of the major agenda of the present government.

The recent announcement of levying the GST is also not new. The new move is supposedly going to usher in a phase of easy payment of taxes. However in this whole effort of digitalization, it is argued by scholars that it is the marginal and middle class that bear the brunt of the developmental rage.

## Conclusion

This paper sets out to map the various meaning that the word 'Swachh' connotes. The etymology of the term is found in Sanskrit is (*swa* = self and *achh* = goodness). This meaning of Swachh encompasses several meanings. It could mean cleanliness from the body to the soul/mind. It could mean end of corrupt practice. It could also have a meaning for the environment. Thus cleaning of 'Ganga Maiyya' is a metaphoric expression of cleansing one's motherland of unwanted and polluted individuals. Following this mode of thought, then it becomes necessary to cleanse oneself of all the impurities. In this narrative then the impure are represented by the lower caste individuals,

Muslims and other minorities and also women who are thought to be the guardians and carriers of the family's dignity.

The attempt to invisibilise Mughal history for instance is one way of cleansing the memory of the nation. The ban on cow slaughter is to inform the minorities that this is a Hindu nation-state and therefore they have to respect their practices and culture, but this is not reciprocated but instead, the government wishes to pass a uniform civil code so as to take away any concessions provided to the minorities. Similarly, the talk of ceasing the protective discrimination policy is to ensure that the dependency of the scheduled caste increases and thus it may get easier for them to internalize the hegemonic ideology. The Dadri incident is not lost out on the memory of the nation and the government has yet to provide an answer. So it is with the patriarchal nature of the agenda and also the anti-dalit stance that we are concerned of.

Thus we are called to carefront the saffronising forces with gentleness and firmness. In the spirit of care and compassion. With love and trust. We can make our own the prayer of Tagore:

This is my prayer to thee, my lord---strike, strike at the root of penury in my heart.

Give me the strength lightly to bear my joys and sorrows.

Give me the strength to make my love fruitful in service.

Give me the strength never to disown the poor or *bend my knees before insolent might.*

Give me the strength to raise my mind high above daily trifles.

And give me the strength to surrender my strength to thy will with love."

8

# Women and the Challenge to the Indian Church

D. J. Margaret FMA

## Introduction

India is truly incredible in terms of its diversity and progress in many fields. However, women belonging to the marginalized sections of society are subjected to multiple exploitations. Women have become victim of the patriarchal culture, social ethos, economic domination, political power, oppressive religious rituals and customs. Moreover, the Church also plays its own role in discrimination against women. Within this context, can women today bring necessary transformation within themselves, in Indian society, in the Church and world? Can the Church respond adequately to the challenging situation of women in India? How effectively can women carry out the ministries of the Church today?

My paper first briefly mentions the context of women in India, and in the Church. Then, it highlights the prospects of women being agents of transformation with a theological perspective – focusing on the First and Second Testaments, the Church's teachings, and Popes' views on women's empowerment. Finally, it focuses on the role of women in the challenging ministries of the Church and proposes a few suggestions for ministry today.

## 1. An Overview of the Context of Women in India

An array of factors has affected the current status of women in India: political autonomy, social reform, economic emancipation, religio-cultural awakening, information and technological development, etc. Indian women fare very well in every sphere – education, social work, economics, politics, religion, sports, science and technology – though the following realities of their lives call for a creative response of the Church in India.

## Socio-Economic Context

In spite of the enormous progress made in all aspects of human life, gender inequality continues to be a part of the fabric of our society today. No matter what their circumstances, female children, young girls and women nationwide face a wall of resistance in their struggle for gender equality and justice. We cannot deny the harsh reality of our society, which has more obsessive and morbid preoccupation with male progeny and blatant discrimination against females throughout their lives from the time of their birth. A woman has to struggle to define her space from womb to tomb,[1] on account of sexual assault, trafficking and prostitution, honour killing, domestic violence, single motherhood, widowhood, migrant and refugee women, peasant women, etc.

## Political Context

Though political equality has been guaranteed in the Indian Constitution (art. 15), this has not helped women to play their role as partners. Women have built an illusion of equality and power, which is frequently used as an argument to resist special protective and acceleratory measures to enable women to achieve their just and equal position in society. Most women are kept out of the political power structures that govern our society. The much-debated 33% reservation issue is still a sign of resistance.

## Religio-Cultural Context

Women are confronted with the reality of a multi-religious context. The institutional religions have generated discriminatory laws and legitimized the subordinating position and roles of women in society.[2] Each religion has a treasure of myths and legends, which through description of events and activities emphasize certain values.3 In a tradition-ridden Indian society, the women are submerged in the "culture of silence and submission", and "a culture of dominance and dependence."

## The Context of Women in the Indian Church

The above mentioned context of women in society is part of women's life in the Church too. We know that women are regular Church goers, faithful supporters, active collaborators and propagators of the faith. In spite of the odds stacked high against women, many women give remarkable contributions, regionally, nationally and internationally as foundresses, social workers, leaders, lawyers, journalists, scientists, missionaries, administrators, theologians... But often women are not treated as equal in the life and mission of the Church in India.

In the Churches where the ordination of women as deacons and even as ordained ministers is permitted, women are still to attain complete equality of status within the Church's power structure. There is no place for women in the hierarchy of the Church. In the matter of rendering justice and equal opportunity to women and promoting their integral well-being and growth, there has been and is a persistent contradiction between the church's preaching and practice. The discipleship of equals, which marked the early Christian Church, which is outlined in the gender policy for the Catholic Church in India (2009), is yet to become a reality.

Thus, despite constitutional guarantees of justice, socio-economic and political assurance of a life of freedom, equality, equity and dignity, many challenges are ravaging the lives of women in India. The situation of women in the Indian Church too is not satisfactory. The above context of women both in the society and the Church call for an adequate and radical response from both men and women so that each one can give their best for the transformation of society and Church.

## 2. Women Agents of Transformation: A Theological Perspective

The Creator God draws people out of their own captivity and invites them to be co-creators with him in his ongoing process of creating a new heaven and earth. Having placed their trust in this God of justice and equality, women find ample examples in the Bible of those who were God's agents of integral transformation.

### First Testament

God chose women and prepared them to carry out His plan of salvation. In seasons of oppression and bondage, women like Jochebed and Miriam thwarted the cruel edict of a tyrant King and saved the life of baby Moses by their united efforts of courage and faith (Ex 2: 1-10).

In the wilderness, in the entry into Canaan, in sieges, in battles, in captivities, women wielded immense influence and power. Rahab the harlot risked her own life to save the life of Joshua's spies (Josh 2:1-24). Shiphrah and Puah (Ex 1:8-22) protected the lives of innocent babies. Mahal and her sisters demanded and obtained the family property inheritance (Num 27:1-11; 36:1-3; Joshua 17: 3-6). Rizpah (II Samuel 21) acquired justice with a long fight against injustice.

Among the many prophets that God sent, we find Deborah who was both judge and prophetess accompanying Barak in the battle (Judg 5:6-8). Within this story we find Jael who played a vital role in bringing victory to the people of Israel. Huldah the prophetess (II Kings 22: 8-20; II Chr 34: 14-28) authenticated a 'Book of the Law' discovered in the Jerusalem temple and initiated a nationwide reform and spiritual renewal.

Judith provided political and spiritual leadership (Jdt 13:18). Esther used her influence to save her people from the Persians (Esther 9). Abigail (I Sam 25) accomplished a peace-making treaty with King David through her swift judgment and apt diplomacy. Thus these women stand out powerfully as models in nation building and peace building.

## Second Testament

The society in which Jesus was born, grew up and carried on His ministry was one in which the superiority of the male was taken for granted. But Jesus and His ministry emerge clearly as transcending patriarchal limitations.

## Jesus: A Paradigm Par Excellence

The attitude of Jesus towards women constituted a challenge to the society of his day. Every encounter of Jesus with women illustrates his concern for them and his attempt to take them beyond the confines of Jewish male-dominated patriarchal society: Jesus accepted the sinful woman (Lk 7:36-50); had compassion on the widow of Nain (Lk 7:1-17); and healed the woman with the flow of blood (Lk 8:42b-48). Many women were included among the disciples of Jesus (Lk 8:1-3). He not only taught them but, as in the well-known incident of Martha and Mary (Lk 10:38-42), made it clear that there was no question of their right to be instructed for discipleship.

Jesus contextualized gender relations, sometimes transcended centuries of patriarchal distortions. Jesus liberates the woman of Samaria (Jn 4:1-42) and she becomes a part of the liberating thrust of his discipleship.[4] Seeking healing for her daughter, the Syrophenician woman (Mk 7:24-30; Mt 15:21-28) frees Jesus to heal, to transcend the racist and gender boundaries of his society. In the story of Martha and Mary (Lk 10:38-42) Jesus challenges the conventional opinion and praises Mary's option to listening to Him (Lk 10:41-42). Another reference to Mary and Martha is in John 11:1-44 where Martha does not fit in the society's stereotype. Martha confesses a faith that recognized God as the source of Jesus' power.5 In the incident of a woman caught in adultery (Jn 7:53-8:11) Jesus indicates what needs to be changed, the system, so that men and women can live new lives, with a new vision.6 The episode of a woman anointing the head/feet of Jesus (Mk 14:3-9; Jn 12:1-8), though going far beyond culture restriction is a sign of female discipleship.7 Discipleship is defined by acts of love and one's response to Jesus.8 It is a great challenge to patriarchy.

The women who travelled with Jesus during his public ministry (Lk 8: 1-3), passion and death (Mt 27:55-56, 61; Mk 15:40, 47; Lk 23:49, 55) are now to become the first witnesses of Jesus' resurrection (Lk 23:49, 55; 24:1-8, 10-11; Acts 1:14). Women's presence at Jesus' resurrection confirms their faithfulness to His person and His work (Mk 15: 40, 16:9-10, 20; Mt 27:55-56;

28:10; Lk 8:1-3; 24:1-12; Jn 19:25; 20:18). All the gospels indicate that women were the first ones to see Jesus alive and hear his voice. Mary Magdalene is the first one to have seen the risen Christ (Jn 20:1-18) and is commanded by him to "go and tell" the Good News to others. Thus she becomes 'the apostle of apostles'.[9]

## Mary: A Role Model for Women

Mary's role in the whole event of the Incarnation (Lk 1:26-38), the Redemption (Jn 19:25-26) and the birth of the Church (Acts 1:14) summarizes the quality of her response to the life and the mission of God. Mary's life manifests concrete instances where she puts her faith into concrete deeds of service: Service to her cousin Elizabeth (Lk 1:39-45, 56); Intervention at the wedding feast at Cana (Jn 2:1-11). Mary's song, the *Magnificat (Lk 1:46-55), envisions a new era of justice and equality.*

Mary's entire life is a constant proclamation and epiphany of Jesus to a variety of people: to the shepherds (Lk 2:8-20), to the Magi (Mt 2:1-12), to Simeon (Lk 2:22-35), to the prophetess Anna (Lk 2:36-38), to the wedding guests at Cana (Jn 19:25-27), to the Church in prayer at Pentecost (Acts 1:14-2:13). Thus the exemplary life of Mary can help women to become authentic agents of social transformation.

## The Church's Teachings on Women

The issue of women's rights and participation in social and political life came to the forc in the 1890's. It was Pope Leo XIII who first responded to the needs of women in the world in his social teaching.[10] The successive popes have developed emphasizing women's status, their feminine nature and their appropriate roles as homemaker, wife and mothers. Pius XII encouraged laywomen to get involved in Catholic action and in social movements.[11]

Pope John XXIII in the encyclical *Pacem in Terris* affirmed women's equality and encouraged them to reach their full potential for the benefit of all society.[12] To mark the "year of woman" in 1975, Pope Paul VI said: "We desire to scc progress for the role of women in professions and society; the dignity and the mission for women must continue to be preserved. God has made them to be sensitive daughters, strong and pure virgins, loving wives, and especially holy and worthy mother, and finally devout, hardworking widows."[13] This is in conformity with the traditional roles of women.

The Vatican Council II offers two different reflections on women. The first, implicitly, is in terms of wife and mother, in the image of Mary and the church, and the second is the paradigm of human liberation in the light of the gospel. In its closing remarks the Council stated, "the hour has come when the vocation of woman is being achieved in its fullness, the hour in which woman acquires in the world an influence, an effect and a power never hither achieved. Thus it endorsed and promoted a new era of thinking about woman's role and status in the church and the world."[14]

Pope Paul VI in his apostolic letter *Octogesimaadveniens* reaffirms women's equality, and states that this equality gives them an equal right to participation in all facets of social, cultural, economic and political life. He says that in spite of the constant appeal of the church to the people, the gender discrimination still persists.[15]

We find the new directions with regard to women's role in society and the Church in the recent papal teachings. For example in *Familiarisconsortio* John Paul II stresses on the following points in relation to Christian anthropology and women: Women have equal dignity with men and consequently they have 'inalienable rights proper to a human person'; God manifests the dignity of women in the highest form possible by assuming human flesh from the Virgin Mary… and presenting her as the model of redeemed woman; the works and actions of Jesus towards women confirm their dignity and equality.[16]

In his Apostolic Letter *Mulieris Dignitatem*, Pope John Paul II renders thanks to the Most Holy Trinity for the 'mystery of woman' and for every woman-for all that constitutes her feminine dignity, for the 'great works of God', which throughout human history have been accomplished in and through her.[17] The same Pope interestingly argues that women are essentially equal to men in dignity yet, by their vocation as virgins and mothers, they are called to higher things. As a consequence, women are not eligible for priesthood.

Pope Francis states that by creating male and female bodies differently, God shows us that what God's intends for men and women is to have separate roles and purposes in the church and in the family.[18] Feminine genius is needed in all expression in the life of the society and the Church.[19] He further, explains that "masculinity and femininity are not rigid categories."[20] Women have the capacity for leadership, and men have to take on tasks in the family in order to accommodate the wife's work schedule. To the nuns in New York the Pontiff said, "Women of strength, fighters, with that spirit of courage which puts you on the front lines in the proclamation of the Gospel. I wish to say 'thank you,' a big thank you... and to tell you that I love you very much."[21] It is stated that after long days of intense prayer and reflection, Pope Francis had appointed a Commission for the Study of the Diaconate of Women.[22]

The final document of the synod on youth, "The Faith and Vocational Discernment" on the role of women in the life and mission of the church endorses the need for greater decision-making roles for women in the church. It states, "Young people have asked for a greater recognition and appreciation of women in society and in the Church." It acknowledges that many women play an irreplaceable role in Christian communities, but in many places it is a struggle to give them a place in decision-making processes even when these processes do not require specific ministerial responsibilities.[23]

The document states that a Church that seeks to live a synodal style must reflect on the condition and role of women within it, and also in society. It demands for change through courageous cultural conversion and in daily pastoral practice. It affirms that an area of particular importance in this regard is the presence of women in ecclesial bodies at all levels, including in leadership functions, and ecclesial decision-making processes…This is a duty of justice, inspired as much by the way in which Jesus related to the men and women of his time, as well as by the important role some women have played in the bible, in the history of salvation and in the life of the Church.

In *Ecclesia in Asia*, the Synod raised special concern for women who face discrimination and violence at home, in the work place and within the legal system. To fight against all forms of injustices and discrimination, women need to find collaborators in the Christian community and therefore the Synod recommended the local churches to promote human right activities on behalf of women. Its aim should be the attitudinal change on the role of men and women in the family, the society and the church.[24]

In India, the 'Gender Policy for the Catholic Church'[25] addresses the concerns of women, who are doubly marginalized and oppressed. It promotes the egalitarian message of Jesus, with the vision of a collaborative church with gender justice. It desires to make a favourable situation for women that will create co-partnership in the family, society and the world. It aims to bring about the required change of mindset and attitude through a proper understanding of the specific roles of both men and women in our homes and workplaces, in our human interactions and social relationships, in the church and society at large. The church in India needs to uphold the dignity and the freedom of women by encouraging their role in its life and mission in the world.

## 3. Women's Role in the Challenging Ministries of the Indian Church Today

If the status of women in society has to improve, then there has to be a radical change within the family.[26] If the society has to change its attitudes, then women and men must play their respective roles as authentic partners; and women's contribution and commitment are needed in the following areas.

### A Holistic Family Care

The family is not only the nucleus of society but, more importantly, the powerhouse of society. Peter Sharkey rightly said that a contented family increases the likelihood of a contented person.[27] Hence women together with the members of the family, need to build a contented and happy family. In the parish, (group of families) women can embody the prophetic spirit of Jesus in social protest, in solidarity with the poor and the marginalized to uphold human rights and life, justice and harmony.

## An Integral Environmental Care

The encyclical of Pope Francis '*Laudato Si': Care for Our Common Home*'[28] awakens women to an integral ecology of cosmic wholeness and interconnection with earth. Pope Francis states that earth is our common home and we are called to be instruments of God our Father, so that our planet might be what he desired when he created it and correspond with his plan for peace, beauty and fullness. Women could make this, our cosmic home into a loving habitat for all children's children.

## An Embodied Spiritual Care

Women today are developing a more woman-defined and woman-oriented spirituality which draws on female experiences and feminine metaphors, and is more inclusive in its language and thought.[29] Women's spirituality stresses concrete embodiment and advocates an embodied rather than an idealized, abstract spirituality divorced from everyday experience. It helps them to claim not only their rightful place in the social and religious sphere; it deepens their faith or sustains them through the prolonged, dreadful reality of domestic abuses and social discriminations.

## Partnership in Ministry

"Man and woman are both equally created in the image and likeness of God (Gen 1:27), together they are called to form one unit (Gen 5:2). The partnership of men and women in the ministries of the church is rooted in the life story of Jesus Christ. They must work together for just distribution of their roles and responsibilities in the ministry of the Church. By their joint contributions, they can become capable of redefining their roles and ministries in the Church today.[30] Their partnership in ministry can make an effective impact on the integral well being of the society.

## Possible Suggestions for the Church's Ministry to Women

The following suggestions are proposed for an effective ministry of the church to women in India.

## Individual and Collective Empowerment of Women

The journey of individual and collective empowerment has to lead to the recognition that, women are valuable and significant, able and powerful. Women need authentic role models and increased visibility and stability in public and private spaces of power and influence. The Church needs to engage in female empowerment and gender equality for the definition and enhancement of the society.

## Safe and Secure Environment to Live and to Work

Employment has enabled many women to enter the labour market and benefit from economic autonomy. The Church can provide women a safe and secure environment to live and to work in free from prejudices, abuses and harassments. For better working environment and efficiency and productivity of female employees, a fundamental change is required in the attitudes of the employers, policy makers, family members, church leaders, and the public at large.

## Care for Single Mothers

A single mother has to face continuous newer challenges every day. Aside from the financial and familial aspect, single mothers have to deal with the emotional, physical and psychosocial components of being single in a complex society. Strong steps should be taken to protect single mothers and children from abusive social context. It is the collective responsibility of every church to ensure the single mothers safety, security, and surety of life and love.

## Support for Widows

Widows should be made aware of their legal and constitutional rights. They must be provided financial support, psychological help, social and religious acceptance. The church can bring about an attitudinal change in society to end social disparity, stop religious and cultural discrimination and ensure social justice to the widows. It can help women face life's challenges bravely and to move forward in life confidently.

## Emancipation of Peasant Women

A comprehensive and gender responsive approach will improve peasant women's productivity and shared household responsibilities, change societal beliefs that unpaid care work is primarily the responsibility of women. The emancipation of peasant women doesn't just mean an end to patriarchal practices or prejudices in their society but also liberation from all problems faced by them. Women's liberation is pointless if millions of peasant women are not liberated and emancipated.

## Need for Church's Special Response

Apart from the above mentioned groups of women needing church's ministry, the following groups of women need church's special and specific responses of care and support: abused women, war affected women, refugee women, trafficked women, women forced into prostitution, women in prison, women who suffer from terminal illnesses, tribal women and dalit women.

## Conclusion

The life experiences of women in the family, Church, and society show that they are being empowered with strength to cope in the challenging circumstances of life, by utilizing personal, familial, Church and societal resources. These resources direct the whole of their lives. To make the ministry of women in Church and society more effective, women need to be emancipated and empowered. This calls for equal space in familial, church and social decision-making forums and reciprocal relationships. Women need to evolve a new understanding of themselves as persons, their dignity and rights and also attitudes that will guide their involvement in the creative ministries of the Church.

In a multi-religious society like ours, women need to join hands with all the people of goodwill in the promotion of integral human development and the care of the environment. This calls for a new inclusive systems and structures in the society and the Church that will respond in a variety of ways and at various levels in the struggles of people. On the part of the Church, women have to be reinstated into the life and the mission of the church with freedom, equality and dignity. The Church must create an atmosphere where women can responsibly contribute for the betterment of the church and the society. Finally, everyone has to realize that the wholeness and integrity of the human community is assured only when men and women work together for the realization of God's kingdom. This demands from both women and men a profound relationship, an active co-operation and collaboration for the transformation of the society and the church.

## Notes

1. Rehana Ghadially, ed., *Women in Indian Society* (New Delhi: Sage, 1988), 181.
2. Kritika Bhardwaj and Ashok K. Sharma, *Nobel Peace Prize Winner Malala: The Crusader of Fearless Freedom* (New Delhi: Diamond Pocket Books (P) Ltd, 2015), 60-74.
3. Anita Ghai and Rachana Johri, "Religion, Feminist Politics and Muslim Women's Rights in India", in *Women and Law Critical Feminist Perspectives*, ed. Kalpana Kannabiran (New Delhi: SAGE Publication, 2014), 264-273.
4. Anna Vareed Alexander. *Biblical Women Our Foremothers. Women's Perspective* (Indore: Satprakashan Sanchar Kendra, 1997), 51.
5. Pheme Perkins, "The Gospel According to John", in the *New Jerome Biblical Commentary* (New Jersey:Prentice Hall, 1990), 970.
6. Gail R. O'Day, "The Gospel of John, Introduction, Commentary, and Reflections", in *the NewInterpreter's Bible Commentary*, vol. IX Luke and John, (Nashville: Abingdon Press, 1995), 630.
7. Antoine E. Nachef, *Women in the Eyes of Jesus. Yesterday, Today & Forever* (New York: St. Pauls, 2003), 94.

8. Alan Culpepper, "The Gospel of Luke", Introduction, Commentary, and Reflection", in *The New Interpreter's Bible Commentary*, vol. IX Luke and John (Nashville: Abingdon Press, 1995), 703.
9. Ross Saunders, *Outrageous Women. Outrageous God. Women in the First Two Generations of Christianity* (Australia: E.J Dwyer Pvt. Ltd, 1996), 65.
10. Cf. Leo XIII.*Rerum Novarum*.Encyclical on Capital and Labor (1981), 26. ttp://W2.Vatican.Va/Content/Leo-Xiii/En/Encyclicals/Documents/Hf_L-Xiii_Enc_15051891_Rerum-Novarum.Html (accessed 28 September, 2016).
11. Richard Leonard. *Beloved Daughters.100 Years of Papal Teaching on Women* (Melbourne Australia: David Lovell Publishing, 1995), 15.
12. John XXIII, *Pacem in Terries* (1963) Nos. 35-37, 44-45.
13. MargaBühring, *Women Invisible. A Christian Odyssey in Christian Feminism* (Great Britain: Burns & Oates, 1993), 112.
14. Leonard, *Beloved Daughters*, 23.
15. Paul VI's *Octogesimaadveniens* (1971), No. 13.
16. John Paul,*Familiarisconsortio*No.22-24.
17. Pope John Paul II, *Mulieris Dignitatem* (Boston: Daughters of St. Paul, 1988), No.31
18. Jamie Manson, "It's Time to Be Honest about Pope Francis and Women" National *Catholic Reporter*(May. 19, (2016), https://www.ncronline.org/blogs/grace-margins/its-time-be-honest-about-pope-francis-and-women (accessed 29 October, 2016).
19. Pope Francis, *Evangeli Gaudium* (EL), Apostolic Exhortation (Kerala: Carmel International Publishing House, 2013): 103.
20. Francis, AL, 286.
21. Lauren Barbato, "Pope Francis Says Women are The Future of The Church, So Where are They?" posted on Sep 27, 2015, https://www.bustle.com/articles/113294-pope-francis-says-women-are-the-future-of-the-church-so-where-are-they (accessed 29 October, 2016).
22. Daniel Burke and Holly Yan, "Pope Francis Creates Commission to Study History of Female Deacons", CNN, posted on August 2, 2016, http://edition.cnn.com/2016/08/02/world/pope-francis-female-deacons/ (accessed 29 October, 2016).
23. Gerard O'Connell, "Youth synod final document urges 'accompaniment,' endorses women in church leadership", posted on October 27, 2018,https://www.americamagazine.org/faith/2018/10/27/youth-synod-final-document-urges-accompaniment-endorses-women-church-leadership (accessed 11 Nov. 18, 2018).
24. Mary John Mananzan, ed., *Women and Religion* (Manila: Women's Studies Series, 1988), 1.
25. "Empowerment of Women in the Church and Society", *The Gender Policy for the Catholic Church in India 2009*, (New Delhi: CBCI Commission For Women Catholic Bishops' Conference of India, 2010).
26. Eka Kapoor et al., *Women of Vision* (New Delhi: Roli Publication, 2013), 87-98.
27. Peter Sharkey, *The Essentials of Community Care* (New York: Palgrave Macmillan, 2007), 34.
28. Francis, *Laudato Sí'* (LS), Encyclical Letter (2015).
29. N Nason-Clark, "When Terror Strikes at Home: The Interface between Religion and Domestic Violence," *Journal for the Scientific Study of Religion*, 42/3 (2004): 303-310.

30. John Gray, *Men are from Mars, Women are from Venus* (London: HarperCollins Publishers, 2012), 9-15. See also Padmini Saminathan, "Revisiting the Theme of Women's Empowerment: How Leadership Matters", in *Interrogating Women's Leadership and Empowerment*, ed. Omita Goyal (New Delhi: Sage Publication, 2015), 13-29. Meeta Deka, *Women's Agency and Social Change: Assam and Beyond* (New Delhi: Sage Publication, 2013), 77-122.

# 9

# Mental Health Crisis: Service of Contemporary Indian Church

**Rony George**

## Introduction

We live in a broken world, beset with overwhelming problems: disease, pain, death, sorrow, sin and mental illness – clinical depression, bipolar disorder, borderline personality disorder, schizophrenia, and panic attacks. Our culture assumes people diagnosed with mental illness are stuck, doomed to struggle for the rest of their lives against a problem without ever experiencing real and lasting change. As Christians we know better. The world is broken, but God has invaded that world with the power, light, and hope of his Son Jesus Christ. Whether you're tormented with panic attacks or thinking of committing suicide, Jesus can help.

Many people over the years have studied the Bible from a medical point of view offering diagnoses for the symptoms and signs that appear to have afflicted numerous individuals in the Bible. The Holy Bible, accepted by Christians all over the world as the Word of God, has always remained relevant with its eternal message of love, peace, and hope. Various interpretations of the exact text of the Bible have been arrived by scholars and laypeople alike. The Bible is not just a religious text. It is also a historical account of the Israelites in the Old Testament, to the birth of Christianity in the New Testament

The official Church has made remarkable statements on the need to take care of the mentally sick people.

**Pope John Paul II** at a conference for health care workers in New York on November 1996 said "Whoever suffers from mental illness 'always' bears God's image and likeness in himself, as does every human being. In addition, he 'always' has the inalienable right not only to be considered as an image of God and therefore as a person, but also to be treated as such."

**Pope Benedict XVI** for the 14th World Day of the Sick on 11 February 2006 urged all of us: "I therefore encourage the efforts of those who strive to ensure that all mentally ill people are given access to necessary forms of care and treatment. Unfortunately, in many parts of the world, services for these sick people are lacking, inadequate or in a state of decay. The social context does not always accept the mentally ill with their limitations, and this is another reason difficulties are encountered in securing the human and financial resources that are needed. One perceives the need to better integrate the two approaches: appropriate therapy and new sensitivity towards disturbance, so as to enable workers in the sector to deal more effectively with these sick people and their families, who would be unable on their own to care adequately for their relatives in difficulty."

After exploring the theological framework of mental illness, this articles proposes some guidelines that the Church can follow to improve the living conditions mental patients, whom the Church hold dearly.

## 1. Theological Framework on Mental Illness

The National Catholic Partnership on Disability (NCPD) sets forth the following framework as a guide to the Church's ministry for and with people with mental illness:[1]

### Human life is Sacred. Every Person is Created in God's Image

"One of the fundamental truths of Christian belief is that each human being is created in the image and likeness of God (Genesis 1:26-27). The Catholic Church unconditionally embraces and faithfully proclaims this truth. It is the foundation for human dignity. Our commitment to this truth is measured through actions on behalf of the vulnerable and alienated in society, especially the poor and suffering."(*Affirming the Dignity of the Mentally Ill,* Nebraska Bishop's Conference, January 2005.)

Since all people are created in the image of God, their dignity and worth cannot be diminished by any condition including mental illness:

"Whoever suffers from mental illness 'always' bears God's image and likeness in themselves, as does every human being. In addition, they 'always' have the inalienable right not only to be considered as an image of God and therefore as a person, but also to be treated as such." (Pope John Paul II, *International Conference for Health Care Workers, on Illnesses of the Human Mind, November 30,1996.)*

## Suffering is Redemptive When United to Christ

"Those who share in the sufferings of Christ are also called, through their own sufferings, to share in (eschatological) glory." (*Salvifices Doloris, Apostolic Letter from John Paul II,* July 15, 1999, p.22).

## We are the Body of Christ

"The great strength of community is the uniqueness and giftedness of each member. The more each person uses their gifts, the stronger the community and the richer the relationships in that community. People are liberated if and when they use their gifts. People are imprisoned when they are prohibited or not enabled to use their gifts. Parishes are communities with great potential to receive and nurture the giftedness of people with disability. The Christian community is one in which all people can claim an equal place and contribute

Knowledge and attitudes toward mental illness among Christian leaders and members of the Christian community:

Despite the widespread prevalence of mental illness and the increasingly high need for mental health care, patients with mental illness continually fail to receive adequate or timely treatment. Among other reasons, stigma against and misunderstandings of mental illness prevent millions of people from promptly seeking appropriate medical attention, thereby distressing not only those affected, but also their families and communities. In particular, recent research on attitudes toward mental illness among Christian leaders and members of the Christian community has demonstrated that knowledge regarding causation remains limited among Christians, as well as that negative views toward mental illness are widespread in that community. In response, this paper highlights the considerable amount of stigma and misinformation, if not outright lack of knowledge, regarding mental illness, its causation, and approaches to treatment among Christians, all of which are factors that can contribute to the under-recognition and undertreatment of people with mental health disorders. Its aims are both to improve the understanding of attitudes and views toward mental illness among Christian leaders and the Christian community and to illuminate how those perceptions can prompt the under-recognition and under-treatment of individuals with mental illness. To those ends, a systematic search of international literature was conducted from September 2015-April 2016 to analyze current literature on Christianity and mental health, Christians' attitudes toward mental health, and their impact on treatment-seeking behavior in the Christian community. The paper's contribution is part of an important effort to de-stigmatize mental illness and increase awareness among clergy to promote the use of mental health services among Christians given the services' role as a source of care for members of the community.2

In 2007, Matthew S. Stanford studied 293 self-identified Christians who completed an online survey addressing a range of psychiatric disorders, including mood disorders (39.9%), schizophrenia and other psychotic disorders (30.4%), anxiety disorders (15.7%), substance use disorders (6.8%), eating disorders (4.1%), and other forms of mental illness (3.1%). Stanford's results showed that churches were significantly more likely to dismiss women's mental illnesses than men's or to tell women more often than men to avoid taking psychiatric medication, if not both. Although most mentally ill survey respondents were accepted by their churches, approximately 30% of them reported negative interactions with their congregations, including abandonment, the church's equating mental illness with the work of demons, and the suggestion that the mental disorder had resulted from personal sin. In a 2012 study published by Baylor University that examined 5,899 members of 24 Christian churches representing four Protestant denominations, only 27% of people with mental illness and their families reported attending church. A major reason expressed by respondents who reported nonattendance was that they did not feel welcome at their churches. By extension, the study highlighted that although most families with mentally ill members wanted their churches to assist them in dealing with mental illness, most of their churches neglected to address such illness in their congregations. In 2013, LifeWay Research interviewed 1,001 Americans in a telephone survey that posed four questions about mental illness. The results indicated that nearly half of all pastors interviewed rarely (39%) or never (10%) spoke about mental illness. In fact, only one in six pastors (16%) spoke about mental illness in sermons at least once per year, while roughly a quarter of them (22%) were reluctant to help people who suffer from acute mental illness, chiefly because it takes too much time. Interestingly, a third of US citizens and nearly half of evangelical, fundamentalist, and born-again Christians believed that only prayer and Bible study could dispel serious mental illness. By comparison, most respondents (68%) thought that they would feel welcome in church if they were mentally ill, although approximately 54% of respondents said that churches should do more to prevent suicide. Among evangelical, fundamentalist, and born-again Christians, however, that number jumped to 64%. In 2008 Stanford and McAlister investigated one church and found that it had dismissed the mental health diagnoses of 41.2% of members of the congregation who participated in the study. Participants who were told that they did not have a mental illness were more likely to attend church more than once per week and to describe their church as conservative and charismatic.

## 2. Mental illness and the Church's Mission

In general, the church tends to handle mental illness in one of three ways: ignore it, treat it exclusively as a spiritual problem, or refer people to professionals and wash our hands of their trouble.

When we ignore it, we acquiesce our responsibility to be the church, who "must clothe yourselves with tenderhearted mercy, kindness, humility, gentleness, and patience" (Colossians 3:12). We send the message that our faith isn't big enough to handle problems we don't understand. Mental illness does raise challenging questions, but such questions do not threaten God. And they are not inconsistent with Christian theology—all creation is groaning under the weight of our sin. Our minds are no less cursed than the rest of us.

When we treat mental illness as a spiritual problem, prescribing more faith or prayer, we suggest suffering people aren't eligible for God's grace. We behave like the Pharisees, whom Jesus said "don't practice what they teach. They crush people with unbearable religious demands and never lift a finger to ease the burden" (Matthew 23:3-4).

Our bodies, minds, and spirits are interconnected in ways too mysterious for us to unravel. And technically, all sicknesses are ultimately spiritual in origin—they entered our world as a result of humanity's rebellion against God. But to assume that disorders and diseases which attack the brain have direct spiritual causes and solutions is to misunderstand the way we are made. Mental illnesses are real, treatable, and manageable conditions caused by genetic, biological, or environmental factors, or some combination of the three.[3] To withhold or discourage medical and psychological intervention is as cruel as to deny treatment for a broken arm or a case of diabetes. I find it baffling that people who believe other physical ailments should be treated only with faith and prayer are considered cultists or heretics—but such a perspective on mental illness is accepted within mainstream Christianity.

Yes, mental illness can be fostered, or exacerbated, by people's choices. But such people are no less deserving of compassion and help than those with other lifestyle-related diseases like HIV, diabetes, and heart disease. And just as most pastors do not claim they can heal broken bones and cancer through their seminary training, church leaders should know when they're in over their heads with psychological issues—and they usually are.

At the same time, when we refer people to professionals without walking alongside them with love and acceptance, we abandon them to a system that doesn't give people what we might hope it will. Churches must refer people to professional help—but they must also confer with those professionals and provide friendship and love to suffering people.

## 3. Some Concrete Suggestions

Churches can help in many ways. Some of them are:

**Talk about it.** Every year, more than 25percent of the U.S. adult population suffers from a diagnosable mental illness—mostly quietly and in shame.

**Assemble a network**. Before a crisis, find professionals with a variety of specialties. Build relationships with them, ask for advice, and be ready to partner when someone needs care.

**Foster friendships**. People affected by mental illness need friends who will not abandon them when they're symptomatic.

**Walk through treatment.** Visit the hospital. Bring casseroles. Help with the cost of medications. Ask how treatments are going. Minister to people with mental illness in the ways you minister to people recovering from surgery or enduring cancer treatments.

## 4. Mental Health Awareness

Mental health is a major concern worldwide and India is not far behind in sharing this. If we evaluate developments in the field of mental health, the pace appears to be slow. Dr. Brock Chisholm, the first Director-General of the World Health Organization (WHO), in 1954, had presciently declared that "without mental health there can be no true physical health." More than 60 years later, the scenario has not altered substantially. About 14% of the global burden of disease is attributed to neuropsychiatric disorders. The burden of mental disorders is likely to have been underestimated because of inadequate appreciation of the inter-play between mental illness and other health disorders. There remain considerable issues of priority-setting based on the burden of health problems and of addressing inequalities in relation to determinants and solutions for health problems.[4]

Progress in mental health service delivery has been slow in most low- and middle-income countries. Barriers include the existing public-health priorities and its influence on funding; challenges to delivery of mental health care in primary-care settings; the low numbers of those trained in mental health care; and the lack of mental health perspective in public-health leadership. There have been numerous calls for invoking political will, for enhancing advocacy and for galvanizing community participation; all with scant improvement in outcomes.

Thus, it becomes now opportune to explore the paradigm of mental health awareness as a means of combating stigma, enhancing prevention, ensuring early recognition, and also stimulating simple and practical interventions within the community. Today there are opportunities in terms of growing acknowledgement of mental disorders as key targets of global health action, as well as of leveraging new technologies particularly internet, big data and cell phones in amplifying simple field interventions found successful in primary care and other echelons.

## Mental Health Awareness

Mental health awareness campaigns have yielded positive outcomes. Some of the strategies undertaken to target awareness and address stigma around mental illness include participation by family members, sensitization to treatment and social inclusion. Lack of knowledge about the mental illnesses poses a challenge to the mental health care delivery system. Research has highlighted the role of community-based systems in low-income countries and has also yielded positive results in creating awareness, thereby impacting participation

Awareness and health literacy are two sides of the same coin. Stigma and discrimination are negative consequences of ignorance and misinformation. There are a few studies which have measured mental health literacy in the Indian context. One study found mental health literacy among adolescents to be very low, i.e. depression was identified by 29.04% and schizophrenia/ psychosis was recognized only by 1.31%. Stigma was noted to be present in help-seeking.

These findings reinforce the need to increase awareness of mental health. Mental health literacy is a related concept which is increasingly seen as an important measure of the awareness and knowledge of mental health disorders. Health literacy has been described as "ability to access, understand, and use the information to promote and maintain good health. Mental health literacy encompasses recognition, causes, self-help, facilitation of professional intervention, and navigating the information highway.

## 5. Components of Mental Health Literacy

The following components are very significant in fostering mental health literacy.

Knowledge of how to seek mental health informatin.
Attitudes that facilitate recognition and help-seeking.
Knowledge and beliefs about professional help.
Knowledge and beliefs about self-help.
Knowledge and beliefs about causes.
Ability to recognisepyschological distress.

The impact of stigma has led to the institution of various programs worldwide to challenge the stereotypes and discrimination that generate social disability. Mental health awareness programs have had favorable impact and can produce positive change in people's views of mental illnesses.

However, more robust evaluations are needed to assess the long-term impact of approaches to increasing mental health literacy worldwide.

## Road Map for Mental Health Awareness

For the large Indian population to be involved in its own mental health, the only way forward is through enhancing mental health awareness which will generate its own demand. With rising awareness, it can be expected that early recognition and access to treatment will follow, as will the adoption of preventive measures. It can also be expected that with enlarging awareness in a democratic society, advocacy, leveraging of political will, funding, and cross-synergies shall follow. It is envisaged that bulk of the awareness contributions shall flow from the following six platforms.

## Conventional Media

Media has been the cornerstone of the previous action in the field of mental health awareness. Celebrity endorsements, like the recent one by actress Deepika Padukone who shared her experience of depression, together with succinct tag-lines of advertisements and content-rich narrations and documentaries; have been the mainstay of media drives so far.

Making evidence-based mental health information easily available to journalists and other content providers like internet portals from trusted and reliable sources like Indian Psychiatry Society, research organizations, medical colleges, etc., through their websites is a relatively simple step. Accessibility of simply translated jargon-free content in various regional languages in written and spoken forms will go a long way. It also behoves professionals in the mental health domain to take the lead in engaging and partnering with the media. Encouraging recovered patients to make their success stories accessible to all shall make good the paucity of authentic narratives.

## Government Programs

Despite some complains regarding the amount of money spent, the government remains the biggest single spender in the mental health sector. While most new interventions remain isolated and confined to urban areas, it is only the public health system through large programs which can reach the rural masses. Apart from the National and District Mental Health Programs, the National Rural Health Mission is on its way to becoming the vehicle for delivering mental health as a part of integrated primary care at the cutting edge of the public healthcare system. Seeing that it partners with existing private and alternative care providers in a nonthreatening manner, shall help such large interventions synergize and succeed.

## Educational System

Most chronic and debilitating mental illnesses have their onset before 24 years of age when most are a part of the educational system. From including mental health narratives in curricula toward, de-stigmatization, removing discrimination and early detection, to empowering stakeholders for early detection and simple interventions; the educational system yields myriad opportunities for enhancing mental health awareness.

## Industry

The organized sector suffers significant loss of effective workforce through mental ill-health. Not only as a part of corporate social responsibility but also to maintain productivity, it becomes important to engage with mental health awareness in a concerted fashion.

## Internet, Social media and cellphones

Hand-held devices and the social media can truly be game-changers in the propagation of effective mental health interventions through focussed amplification, and not just in increasing information. With the greater utilization of big data, the understanding of subtle and distributed patterns over large volumes shall inform decision making.

## Crowd Sourcing

The ultimate convergence of information and technology in a free society results in crowd-sourcing which breaks down barriers of geography, historical incquitics, and economies of scale. It is the true involvement of communities real and virtual, harnessed to make a change. Thus, dynamic ideas of individuals can synergize with the success stories of nongovernmental organizations to amplify them across geographies and time. Crowd-funding is a successful model in testing radical ideas which flounder outside the mainstream.

## 6. How the Church Can Help Someone Facing Mental Illness

Facing mental illness is not an easy process. Regardless of how informed we are, this process is not easy. Trying to walk this difficult journey by yourself only makes it harder. Often, in the arena of mental illness, what the church has to offer are not superior answers—if the problem is biological or environmental, the church should provide very similar advice as our secular friends in the mental health field.5

While the initial guidance the church provides would, in many cases, be the same, the church should always provide a superior context of living out those answers—a sphere of relationships where everyone acknowledges we are broken people in need of redemption, thereby, negating the stigma that makes overcoming these struggles so painfully isolating. Counseling is never merely principles and suggestions; it is also a context that facilitates a journey.

That is the ideal; a stigma-free, redemptive community. But the question remains, "How do we produce more of that reality in our churches?" Unfortunately, as Amy Simpson says in her book *Troubled Minds*, mental illness is often the "no-casserole illness" in Christian circles; a form of suffering from which the church, uncharacteristically, moves away from suffering people instead of towards them.[6]

One of the reasons we move away instead of towards people is confusion and uncertainty about what we should do. When we don't have good answers, it is often easier to just avoid the people who generate the questions. It is unlikely the church will offer the unique care of a redemptive community if its people are uninformed about and intimidated by mental illness.

A particular individual or church does not have to be able to do everything in order to do some very significant things powerfully well. Consider the example of someone in need of knee surgery. There is a surgeon who repairs the ligament; a physical therapist who helps the individual regain a full range of motion; family and friends who care for day-to-day needs and provide encouragement; and a physician who oversees the pain medicine management. A similar set of roles can exist in the struggle with mental illness.

This metaphor is not meant to imply that the church only plays the "friends and family" role. A given church, pastor or friend may be well-equipped to provide various levels of intensive soul care. But it is their responsibility to know the limits of their ability to help and be willing to invite other members on the care team with needed, supplemental expertise.

With that in mind, let's consider many things that the church—as a corporate entity or through its personal relationships—is uniquely equipped to do. Many of these functions have little-to-no secular alternative; ongoing gatherings of adults for mutual encouragement and instruction are rare in our culture.

As individuals or groups the Church can help as follows:

**Teach a balanced view of mental illness as a part of an ongoing education process.** A church has many venues through which this education can occur. Mental health does not need to be the "focal point of the church" in order for the church to effectively disciple people in the care of their interconnected mind, soul, and body.

**Sermon Illustrations**: Speaking of depression, anxiety, trauma, addiction, and other struggles in an informed, unstigmatized way will go a long way toward giving people the emotional freedom to talk about their struggle with friends and seek the help they need.

**Testimonies:** Someone sharing their story has a powerful influence on any group's culture. As someone tells their story of wrestling with mental illness they should (a) speak of how personal faith, a community of care, wise care of their body, and counseling played a role in their recovery; and (b) clarify that this is their personal story and not necessarily the map of how God guides every person with a similar struggle in their pursuit of hope and wholeness.

**Follow Up Blogs**: A blog that follows up on a sermon or testimony can be a great way to connect people who still prefer to remain anonymous with helpful resources. The ultimate goal is to create an open community of care, but the process may involve facilitating many smaller steps in that direction.

**Adult Education Classes or Conferences**: There are a growing number of excellent Christian books on various types of mental illness. These classes or events can simultaneously comfort and equip. Having classes like this communicates that your church is a "safe place" for these conversations and that these topics are a relevant part of living a God-honoring life.

**Support Groups**: While a class or event is educational (over-viewing a subject), a support group is therapeutic (taking someone on a journey). While support groups can create cliques within a church, they can also provide a context for a greater transparency as a next step toward more general authenticity. When starting these groups, a church would want to think through how to prevent a support group from becoming someone's long-term community and, thereby, inadvertently reinforcing their struggle as their identity.

As you can see in the examples above, a church is a unique context for allowing people to become progressively known, instructed, and loved. Where else in our culture could each of these levels of education and connection be provided within a context of ongoing community.

**Befriend those who are struggling with mental illness with multiple people so no one person carries the full weight of responsibility.** We often fail to realize that no professional qualifications are required to be a friend. As Amy Simpson in Trouble Minds wrote, "When churches have antibiotic-like expectations for mental health treatment, they communicate, 'go get treated, then you can come back and you can be a growing Christian with us.'"

**Have a relationship that includes but transcends the struggle with mental illness.** In a purely professional setting, a struggle with mental illness is why an individual is known and cared for. This adds to the stigma and results in a mindset that says I have to be "all better" to be known authentically. With a professional counselor or recovery group if you get better, you "graduate" from having people who know and care for you.

**Help people sort their struggles into categories of sin, suffering, and identity which can be caused by biology, environment, or choice.** Emotional unrest and embarrassment make it difficult to sort out how to best categorize struggles. One of the main goals for this presentation is to equip people for these conversations. The more these conversations can be hadeffectively in natural relationships the earlier people will receive care, the longer they will stick with their care, and less ashamed they will be to embrace the care God wants for them.

**Attend a counseling session with your friend, take notes, gain an understanding of their struggle, and serve as an echo of key truths or practices recommended by the counselor.** This would require the permission of your friend and the cooperation of the counselor. But many counselors are willing to cooperate with this kind of counseling-advocate model, and it can greatly enhance both the short-term and long-term effectiveness of counseling.

This list is not exhaustive. Instead, it is meant to be the beginning of a brainstorming exercise. But there is a danger in thinking through what the church could do: our personal initiative gets lost in the corporate possibilities. For instance, we think "the church ought to mentor underprivileged students," but we don't take the step of volunteering at the nearest school.

Undoubtedly, mental illness is a difficult subject to address because of its complexity and highly personal nature. Everyone is affected by mental illness; either personally or someone they love. As a result, it is a subject that must be discussed and addressed in the church. Let's not let our silence hurt people by leaving them to struggle in isolation.

## Conclusion

The church is equipped to advocate for and walk alongside people with mental illness. Our shame and abandonment are the last things people affected by such illness need. Like it or not, the church is the first place many turn in crisis. And fair or not, the church's silence or rejection feels like rejection from God. We cannot keep turning away from the most vulnerable among us. *It's time to be part of the solution.*

## Notes

1. "Theological Framework on Mental Illness | NCPD - National Catholic Partnership on Disability." Accessed February 11, 2019. http://www.ncpd.org/ministries-programs/specific/mentalillness/framework.
2. Santiago Almanzar, Clarion Psychiatric Center, Universal Health Services, USA. Citation: Santiago Almanzar. "Christianity and Mental Illness: Evil or Sickness?". EC *Psychology and Psychiatry* 4.5 (2017): 181-188.
3. Health (US), National Institutes of, and Biological Sciences Curriculum Study. Information about Mental Illness and the Brain. National Institutes of Health (US), 2007. https://www.ncbi.nlm.nih.gov/books/NBK20369/.
4. Srivastava, Kalpana, Kaushik Chatterjee, and Pookala Shivaram Bhat. "Mental Health Awareness: The Indian Scenario." Accessed February 11, 2019. https://www.ncbi.nlm.nih.gov/pmc/articles/PMC5479084/.

5. For this section, I am indebted to Hambrick, Brad. "5 Ways the Church Can Help Someone Facing Mental Illness." ERLC, June 8, 2015. http://erlc.com/resource-library/articles/5-ways-the-church-can-help-someone-facing-mental-illness.
6. Simpson, Amy. *Troubled Minds: Mental Illness and the Church's Mission*. New York: READHOWYOUWANT COM LTD, 2013.

# 10

# Church of the Poor and for the Poor

**Jose Thayil SJ**

Pope Francis said, "When the cardinals were counting the votes of the secret election to elect the pope, I was sitting next to Cardinal Claudio Hummes, Archbishop Emeritus of Sao Paolo, Brazil. When the votes in my favour reached 77 votes – the two-thirds majority of the 115 cardinals required to attain the papacy – Hummes embraced me and kissed me and said: 'Don't forget the poor.' Then I thought of the poor and all the wars, as the votes were still being counted."[1] Jorge Mario Bergoglio had been pope for only three days when he first uttered the phrase 'How I would like a church that is poor and for the poor', that has since become a catchphrase for his papacy. It's a fitting sentiment for a pope who took his name from Francis of Assisi, a saint renowned for his love affair with Lady Poverty.[2]

Speaking to a large gathering of 5000 journalists gathered for an audience, the newly elected Pope explained how he came to choose the name Francis: "And those words of Cardinal Claudio Hummes came to me: the poor, the poor. Then, right away, thinking of the poor, I thought of Francis of Assisi.... He is the man who gives us this spirit of peace, the poor man"[3]St. Francis of Assisi, who died in 1226, renounced his family's fortune for a life of charity and poverty and is also revered by environmentalists because he loved nature and preached to animals.[4]

## 1. Church that is Poor

Though Jesus is God, he humbled himself to become one like us in everything but sin: "Let the same mind be in you that was in Christ Jesus, who, though he was in the form of God did not regard equality with God as something to be exploited, but emptied himself, taking the form of a slave, being born in human likeness. And being found in human form, he humbled himself and became obedient to the point of death - even death on a cross." (Phil 2:5-8)[5] God became poor to enrich us by his poverty. "For you know the gracious act of our Lord Jesus Christ, that for your sake he became poor although he was rich, so that by his poverty you might become rich" (2 Cor 8:9). Though Jesus belonged to ordinary middle class, He declassed Himself, by becoming a wandering charismatic, in the company of socially and economically poor. His dignity and worth did not come from His possessions, or the position he held in society. He was a man with great authority, as people often remarked (Mk 1:22, Mt 7:29). His authority came from his simple and poor life. He practiced what he preached. Authenticity comes from leading a simple life. Jesus instructed the seventy whom he sent out on mission to go as simple and poor missionaries. "Carry no purse, no bag, no sandals…….Remain in the same house, eating and drinking whatever they provide, for the labourer deserves to be paid." (Lk 10:4-7) In this world of competition and consumerism, having more and more is considered the ideal. But Jesus tells his disciples to be poor and experience the internal freedom. The option to be poor comes from the very heart of the mission of the church. When we, as poor people, approach the poor and suffering, we discover a privileged place of encounter with Christ, who is already there amongst his beloved poor who know and experience his suffering in a special way.

According to the encyclical, "The Joy of the Gospel", by Pope Francis, the poor have much to teach us. Because of their suffering, they know Jesus and the Gospel better than us. We are called to find Christ in them, to lend our voice to their causes, but also to be their friends, to listen to them, to speak for them and to embrace the mysterious wisdom which God wishes to share with us through them. We need to let ourselves be evangelized by them. We are called to find Christ in them. We need to be aware that ignorance of the poor is ignorance of Christ.[6]

A holy man (sadhu) was passing through a forest and he found a large precious stone. When he came to a village, one of the villagers saw this precious stone and asked the holy man whether he can part with that precious stone. The holy man willingly gave the precious stone to the villager. After that the villager was so much worried that the precious stone may be stolen by someone and he couldn't sleep the whole night. The next day morning he told the holy man to take the precious stone back and tell him the secret that makes it possible for the Sadhu to give the precious stone away so easily. The holy man told the villager that he was happy and peaceful with or without the precious stone. Unless one discovers this inner wealth, this kind of detachment, one cannot live poverty meaningfully. One may be forced to live in poverty by the economic system, but that can only lead to misery. We come across many who go on grumbling about their lack of facilities, amenities, comforts, etc. and are in search of money to improve their situation. Jesus said, "Blessed are the poor". He did not say "Blessed is the poverty".

Pope Francis wants the worldwide Church to take on a simple life-style. Pope Francis certainly wants to practice this in his own life and attempts to inspire the Roman Catholic Church and the people at large to think and act from the perspective of the poor. He shows an example for this. On the night he was elected he shunned the papal limousine and travelled on a bus with other cardinals. He went to the Church-run hotel where he had been staying before the conclave and insisted on paying his bill. Pope Francis, the former Cardinal Jorge Bergoglio, has also urged Argentines not to make costly trips to Rome to see him or for his installation, but to give that money to the poor instead.[7]

It is a hopeful sign that the church is slowly becoming a poor church mainly because the church is going to be predominantly a Third World Church. The Church is growing in Africa, Asia and Latin America and dying in Europe and USA.[8]

## 2. Church for the Poor

Church becomes a Church for the poor by being at the service of the materially and spiritually poor. We typically associate this way of being for the poor with works of mercy. The 25th chapter of Matthew's Gospel sets forth our obligations to the "least of our brothers and sisters": feed the hungry, give drink to the thirsty, welcome the stranger, clothe the naked, care for the sick and visit the imprisoned. The church traditionally adds a seventh: bury the dead. There are also the spiritual works of mercy: instruct the ignorant, counsel the doubtful, admonish sinners, suffer wrongs with patience, forgive willingly, comfort the afflicted and pray for the living and dead. These are concrete ways in which the church can be for the poor, providing material and spiritual goods that are otherwise lacking.[9]

According to the Gospel, we will be judged by our care for the "least of our brothers and sisters." So to be a "church for the poor" we need to involve ourselves with the works of mercy, which points ultimately to God's mercy, by way of his chosen poverty. This way the church can fulfill the dream of Pope Francis to become a church for the poor.[10]

Christ identifies himself with the poor in a special way: "Whatever you did for one of these least brothers of mine, you did for me." Therefore, if we want to be close to Jesus, we must be close to the poor and be at their service. Unless the church itself becomes poor, it will not be able to serve the poor. Only through identification will the church be able to perceive reality from the perspective of the poor.[11]

Like the poor, we need to receive everything with gratitude and accept with joy a certain austerity of life. We also need to be grateful to the simple gifts people give. Our real wants are very few while our imaginary wants are very many. We are not rich by what we own, but more by what we are able to do without.

The preferential option for the poor is something we undertake not out of a sense of duty, but out of a sense of gratitude for the extraordinary gift of God's love. The way we receive that gift is precisely through the way we share it with those who are very dear to Jesus. Pope Francis emphasizes the great tradition of Catholic social teaching, which begins with the assertion that we are all God's children and that all of us have a dignity that derives from being created in the image and likeness of God. According to Catholic social teaching, any society or any system that attaches value to human persons solely by what they produce or by what they consume is a fundamentally materialistic and atheist system. And the causes of poverty therefore are not only simply selfishness of persons but also bad systems or structures that promote, encourage, and reward certain forms of behaviors over others. The fundamental insight of liberation theology is the preferential option for the poor, and that's an insight that has now become part and parcel of Catholic social teaching and is cited over and over again in official Catholic documents. I don't think there is any doubt that this pope affirms and believes in the preferential option for the poor.[12]

What does that preferential option for the poor look like in practice?

The preferential option for the poor is simply the attempt to read the gospel and to understand God from the perspective of the poor. A poor individual need not be any better than a rich individual. But the poor class is definitely seen as better than the rich class. The rich oppress the poor by making use of their wealth and influence. The poor in a very special way is identified with Jesus Christ. That is why we will be able to find God in the poor, the hungry, the naked and the outcast. By our identification with such people, we will be identifying with the crucified Christ.

## How can parishes help Indian Catholics live out such a preferential option for the poor?

One of the ways we can show our preferential option for the poor is to work for the rights and dignity of poor people. It also means being with the people and developing friendship with the poor and the marginalized. There is a need to shift from 'doing for' the poor to 'being with' the poor. For example, by using a faster mode of transport, we may be able to reach out to more people much faster than using public transport or walking. If we want to be more effective, we need to identify ourselves with the normal mode of transport of the people we want to serve. Absolute poverty is when people don't have money to meet their most basic needs, such as food, shelter and clothing. Practicing relative poverty means to be in solidarity with the people we are serving. According to George Eliot, one way of getting an idea of our fellow countrymen's miseries is to go and look at their pleasures. For example, when the poor villagers hire an LCD projector for one day, they try to use it to the maximum, even at the cost of losing their sleep. This is because they cannot afford to hire it again the next day.

Until we can be with and accompany the victims of society, we cannot work for justice. Otherwise, we impose our own needs on them. The Peruvian liberation theologian Gustavo Gutierrez is fond of saying that the option for the poor demands friendship with the poor. The poor people have to become the subjects of development rather than the objects of development. That means that they should be part of the decision making process. We need to work for justice by fighting against injustice.

In many of the mission stations in North Indian dioceses, the priest in charge along with catechist and parish sisters often visit the far away villages on a regular basis. The mission stations also make arrangements for the education of the Catholic children and run hostels to accommodate them.

Many dioceses and religious congregations in India are concerned about immigrants from other countries as well as from other parts of India. Many of them are exploited by the local people in various ways. The Church has started NGOs and offices to help them to get their rights as immigrants and labourers. The Church is beginning to see the immigrant as a messenger of Christ, who himself was a refugee in Egypt. The main reason for not being open to accept refugees in our midst is our obsession with security and privacy.

In our obsession with creating lives that are fully controlled, invulnerable, and completely secure, we isolate ourselves from those in our society who are vulnerable, powerless, and poor. Not because we hate them, but because the poor remind us that, ultimately, we're all going to die and our lives are not in our control. Jesus was crucified because he associated himself with the "wrong" people—with sinners, with prostitutes, and with tax collectors. Although not explicitly a political act, it is nevertheless in some ways the most radical political act because it completely overturns people's expectations and assumptions about who we are as a society and who God is.[13]

In following Jesus, then, we are challenged in our own society to break down the barriers that we have set up between ourselves and the sinners, prostitutes, and tax collectors. We need to reach out to them, not only for their good but for our own, to be liberated from our obsession with security, control, and power, to yield ourselves to the God in whose hands we exist and live and can thrive. It's liberation for all of us. We're all in this together. As Martin Luther King Jr. used to say, "As long as one black person is enslaved, we're all enslaved." We need to understand that intrinsic connection between our own wellbeing and the wellbeing of all people.[14]

## Practical ways to serve the poor in the present context

Firstly, the Church can take a special interest in educating the poor children with a view to getting them employed in future job market. Other than the formal schooling, the Church can start vocational training programmes to prepare them for self-employment, if needed. Our colleges and vocational training centres can organize campus recruitments so that jobs are assured after they finish their studies.

Secondly, the church can also be sensitive to the poor by making our facilities accessible to them. In most cases, the biggest asset a church has is its facilities, and often they are underutilized. Therefore, it is important to consider using our buildings and grounds to meet the needs of the poor we serve. They may need computer with internet facility to access to apply for jobs. Students may need a place to complete their homework assignments or just to play computer games.

Thirdly, the church can collaborate with other NGOs to get financial support for the smart students to continue their further studies. They can also offer short courses to equip the poor in language facility, public speaking, computer education, etc.

Fourthly, although the Church doesn't encourage dolling out money and other items to the poor on a regular basis, in times of emergency, the Church could think of helping the poor financially. The Church can serve the poor in times of financial crisis by becoming their temporary employer. In this way work gives a sense of dignity to the poor. The Church should be mainly concerned about providing development opportunities rather than relief activities.

The above mentioned ways are not exhaustive. There are many more different ways of helping the poor and the needy depending upon the context and the situation of the people.

## Conclusion: Challenge for Pope Francis

Financial Transparency

If Pope Francis is serious about preaching a "poor church" to the world, he'll be challenged to make sure the Vatican keeps its financial matters transparent. This was an area Vatican had lost its credibility many a times.

In Vatican leaks there were letters written by a former senior official in the government of the Vatican City State, today the pope's ambassador to Washington, D.C., describing widespread corruption in Vatican finances. Although the amount of money is small by the standards of large organizations, the charges nevertheless gave the Vatican a big blow. The Vatican bank has also faced persistent charges of shady dealings. Both the president and the director, Italian layman Paolo Cipriani, were placed under investigation by Italian authorities in 2010, and at the same time $30 million in assets were seized for allegedly failing to follow European anti-money-laundering protocols. The money was released in May 2011, and no criminal charges have been filed against the two officials.[15]

Pope Benedict XVI may be seen as a reformer in Vatican financial matters. He created a new "Financial Information Authority" in the Vatican, empowering it to inspect the books of other departments. That was a minor cultural revolution, since the various Vatican offices are accustomed to being semi-autonomous entities accountable only to God and the pope. Benedict also brought in a renowned anti-money-laundering expert to run the agency, a Swiss lawyer named René Brülhart. The appointment clearly shows the efforts of Vatican to rectify the financial mismanagements.[16]

Pope Benedict had initiated a first-ever evaluation of the Vatican's financial operations by Moneyval, the Council of Europe's anti-money-laundering agency. Never before has the Vatican opened its financial and legal systems to external, independent review, with the results made public. Pope Francis will be forced to continue these reforms if he has to be credible. After cleaning up the Vatican, the Pope has to make efforts to change the perceptions of people through communication experts regarding Vatican management of finances.[17]

## Simplicity vs. Security

Pope Francis shows his concern for the poor, sick, children and the marginalized by going out to meet them and being available to them. The pope insisted on travelling in an open jeep in the Vatican rather than in the bulletproof pope-mobile. This expresses his desire to mingle with the ordinary people rather than being cut away from them. Though he cannot do such things every time, such expressions have a great symbolic value.

Vatican security personnel are greatly worried that the Pope is exposing himself too much, though such expressions have great apostolic significance. We can recall how John Paul II was shot on 13 May 1981 while he was travelling in an open jeep. This had nearly cost him his life and the pope-mobile was designed as a compromise between accessibility and safety.

Pope Francis' charming ways with the ordinary people gives a terrible time to his security personnel. The pope is aware that he cannot preach love, compassion and concern if he is cut off from the ordinary suffering humanity. At the same time, the pope also has a responsibility not to place unreasonable burdens on his security personnel. So he as the "Pope of the Poor" has to strike a balance between availability and security.

## Notes

1. https://www.ncronline.org/blogs/ncr-today/challenges-vision-poor-church-poor accessed on 9.2.2019.
2. https://www.ncronline.org/blogs/ncr-today/challenges-vision-poor-church-poor accessed on 9.2.2019
3. https://www.americamagazine.org/issue/213/they-know-suffering-christ accessed on 7.2.2019.
4. https://www.ncronline.org/blogs/ncr-today/challenges-vision-poor-church-poor accessed on 9.2.2019
5. https://www.americamagazine.org/issue/213/they-know-suffering-christ accessed on 7.2.2019
6. https://www.americamagazine.org/issue/213/they-know-suffering-christ accessed on 7.2.2019
7. https://www.reuters.com/article/us-pope-poor/pope-francis-wants-church-to-be-poor-and-for-the-poor-idUSBRE92F05P20130316 accessed on 9.2.2019
8. https://www.uscatholic.org/articles/201307/how-can-we-be-church-poor-27539 accessed on 9.2.2019
9. https://www.americamagazine.org/issue/213/they-know-suffering-christ accessed on 7.2.2019
10. https://www.americamagazine.org/issue/213/they-know-suffering-christ accessed on 7.2.2019
11. https://www.americamagazine.org/issue/213/they-know-suffering-christ accessed on 7.2.2019
12. https://www.uscatholic.org/articles/201307/how-can-we-be-church-poor-27539 accessed on 9.2.2019
13. https://www.uscatholic.org/articles/201307/how-can-we-be-church-poor-27539 accessed on 9.2.2019
14. https://www.uscatholic.org/articles/201307/how-can-we-be-church-poor-27539 accessed on 9.2.2019
15. https://www.ncronline.org/blogs/ncr-today/challenges-vision-poor-church-poor accessed on 13.02.2019
16. https://www.ncronline.org/blogs/ncr-today/challenges-vision-poor-church-poor accessed on 13.02.2019
17. https://www.ncronline.org/blogs/ncr-today/challenges-vision-poor-church-poor accessed on 13.02.2019

11

# Reimagining the Study and Teaching of Philosophy for Our Time

**Joseph Kaipayil MCBS**

## Introduction

The importance and relevance of philosophy has come to be recognized more today than ever before in recent history. In many colleges and universities philosophy is now an essential component of interdisciplinary studies. The public interest in philosophy is increasing. UNESCO's initiatives to promote philosophy are laudable. All these call for reimagining the study and teaching of philosophy for our contemporary time – a task worthwhile for philosophy studies in ecclesiastical institutes as well.

## 1. Philosophy and Its Ageless Exigency to Remain Relevant

Humans are cognitive beings by nature. As cognitive beings we seek to know the world we experience – the world which we ourselves are a part of. It is this capacity for intellectual activity that distinguishes us as *Homo sapiens.*[1] Aristotle said it aptly: "All men by nature desire to know."2 This epistemic quest is the basis of all knowledge domains, not to mention philosophy.

Philosophy, with its insistent noetic and methodological commitment to critical thinking and its reasoned positions on our life and the world we experience, has been with humanity for the last two and a half millennia.[3] And it will remain with us as long as human beings are able to think. The usefulness of philosophy, both as an answer to our epistemic quest to know and as a guide to an examined life, is a proven fact by its long history and universal presence.

In the wake of positivism and technological innovations, philosophy was kind of dethroned from its high pedestal during the major part of the last century. Of late, however, philosophy made its comeback. Philosophy is now an essential interdisciplinary component in arts and science departments of many colleges and universities.[4] Interest in philosophy is also growing outside academic circles. The most remarkable impetus for philosophy's revival came from UNESCO's initiative though.

In Catholic higher education, philosophy was always considered a respected academic subject. In ecclesiastical institutes of clerical training, philosophy is a prerequisite for theological studies. That said, it does not mean philosophy is always pursued with enthusiasm at these places. As often as not, philosophy study and teaching is faced with disinterest. There could be various reasons for it.[5] Nonetheless, we cannot afford to ignore the importance and significance of philosophy at a time when the international community recognizes philosophy as a reasoned necessity, when secular academia is convinced of philosophy's bearing on academics and careers, and when the public readership and interest in philosophy is on the increase. This calls for reimagining the study and teaching of philosophy for our time – a challenging job that is worth the effort.[6]

## 2. UNESCO's Clarion Call to Reinvent Philosophy

UNESCO has been actively promoting philosophy as a catalyst for social transformation since late 1990s.[7] The UN agency is strongly of the opinion that people should be trained in the art of philosophical thinking, so they may sustain and promote democracy, world peace, and tolerance. For UNESCO, philosophy is not so much about philosophers and philosophical systems as about method of rational independent thinking. And UNESCO sees philosophy as a school of freedom. Akin to a school, philosophy educates human beings to achieve enlightened intellectual and ethical freedom, by helping them to develop their capacities for critical thinking, independent judgment, and sound reasoning. The UNESCO handbook, *Philosophy: A School of Freedom, calls people of all ages to engage in philosophical reflection for the sake of democratic peaceful society and an examined (reasoned) meaningful life for individuals.*[8]

The UNESCO handbook charts out four levels at which philosophy learning and practice can be done, namely philosophy at preschool and primary school levels, philosophy in secondary education, philosophy in colleges and universities, and philosophy outside academia. Paying heed to UNESCO's suggestions to involve people of all ages and of all walks of life in philosophy is surely one way to reimagine philosophy for our time:

Children, with their sense of wonder and intellectual curiosity to know, are very philosophical. They continually question the world around them and ask existential questions about life. The role of the teacher is to support children in their thinking about their questions. This will help them develop their thinking skills and ability to understand and relate with themselves, other people, and the world.

Philosophy in secondary school is more challenging, because adolescents are argumentative and questioning. They seek to clarify to themselves their self-identity and their relationship with others; they seek to affirm and reassure themselves as individuals with freedom of thought. Hence the essential function of philosophy at secondary level lies less in learning to reason, but more in learning to have a critical approach to knowledge and value systems.

Coming to philosophy at college/university level, teaching is secondary to research and personal learning. Even as keeping traditional course structures, more practical and seminar-style courses with increased student participation should be introduced. It may be noted that sufficient academic freedom is a necessary precondition for any genuine philosophical research in colleges and universities, [including ecclesiastical institutes].

The place and role of philosophy outside academia is being increasingly recognized these days. In the context of the wider civil society, the need to philosophize – to think critically and creatively – arises from people's need to formulate for themselves or for their communities the values and existential purposes that give meaning to their personal and social lives. In the face of personal and societal problems and difficulties, people still have faith in the ability of reason to stand back a little and find a reasoned solution.

## 3. Philosophy in Ecclesiastical Institutes: Certain Concerns

Now I will briefly consider certain questions which I think are important, in regard to the study and teaching of philosophy in Catholic ecclesiastical institutions in general and in India specifically. To address them, or to at least acknowledge them, is another way of reimagining philosophy for our time, I suppose.

### (1) Methodological Independence

Regardless of where it is practiced, whether it is in church circles or otherwise, philosophy is a non-theological (secular) subject and it should be treated as such. The validity and rationality of any philosophy is to be determined by appeal to human reason and our empirical experience. If we take a faith-based yardstick to philosophy, we would be reducing/elevating philosophy to theology and harming the good of both disciplines. Even as theology can draw from philosophy concepts and arguments to understand and articulate faith and philosophy can make use of insights from theology, both disciplines should maintain their reciprocal autonomy.

There was a time when philosophy was misjudged as "ancilla theologiae" (servant of theology). Though the expression, "philosophia ancilla theologiae," can be interpreted to mean philosophy's usefulness for theology, the original intent was to censure philosophy's independence.[9] But the Church's official position is that philosophy should be given autonomy of thought to investigate philosophical problems according to the methodology proper to it.[10] Furthermore, the Church puts confidence in the ability of natural reason to demonstrate the rationality of the Christian view of the world, the human person, and God, placing in a proper light the relationship between philosophy and theology.[11] To be sure, treating philosophy as mere handmaid of theology can still be seen in some places.

## (2) Identification of Christian Philosophy with Thomism

Thomas Aquinas is surely one of the very fine thinkers the Church has ever seen, and he has inspired a host of philosophers and theologians to this day. But oftentimes his philosophy, or the philosophy shaped by his thought, and "Christian philosophy" get identified with each other en bloc. Thomism's ascendency was thanks to Leo XIII's encyclical, *AeterniPatris, in 1879 and subsequent establishment of the Pontifical Academy of St. Thomas Aquinas the very same year.*[12] Thomism soon became the dominant philosophical system of the Catholic Church and was to be normative in the training of priests at church seminaries until Vatican II. In the neo-scholastic circles, Thomism was considered the "philosophia perennis" (perennial philosophy).[13]

But as John Paul II made clear in his encyclical, *Fides et Ratio*, in 1998, there is no official philosophy of the Church, since the faith as such is not a philosophy.[14] At the same time, there is a Christian way of philosophizing – a philosophical speculation conceived in dynamic union with faith.[15] And the Church acclaims Aquinas and his thought as an authentic model for such a philosophizing.[16] Thus the Church accords to Aquinas a special place in the perennially (enduringly) valid philosophical tradition, without, however, taking any position on properly philosophical questions or demanding adherence to particular theses.[17]

## (3) Natural Theology and Classical Theism

Natural theology's focal point has always been the God of classical theism. The classical notion of God as articulated by Aristotelian-Thomism put overly emphasis on God's transcendence and simplicity. This created a deep-seated divide between God and the world, which both philosophy and theology found hard to explain.

The classical God which is unqualifiedly transcendent, absolutely simple, and characteristically disjointed from the world is almost incompatible with the biblical God who is thoroughly personal, relational, and involved in the world.[18] Besides, in place of classical mechanistic world view, modern science presents a more inclusive, holistic, and organic view of the world. In recent times, neo-classical theism, also called panentheism, revisited the God-question form an inclusive point of view. I think the neo-classical solution is not adequate either.[19] Instead, what I would propose is a relationalist model.[20] The relationalist view of God, which I may propose for natural theology, not only suits the Trinitarian concept of God but also derives insights from it. The Incarnational and Eucharistic model also goes well with relationalism.

## (4) Political Philosophy

Ever since the publication of John Rawls's *A Theory of Justice* in 1971, political philosophy is prominent in contemporary philosophical and political discourse. Political philosophy is indispensable for the survival of a genuine democracy. When religious, ethical, and social ideologies divide people in a democracy, the only way forward is an informed political discourse and political consensus. This is very true of India, which is not only the largest democracy in the world but also a very unique democracy with its vast cultural, linguistic, and religious pluralism. India is in great need of a political philosophy tailored for its needs – secularism, respect for human rights, inclusive economic growth, and check on populist nationalism.[21] A political philosophy for India should incorporate the Constitutional values such as liberal democracy, federalism, and social inclusiveness.

The importance of political philosophy is now recognized by the Church in the revised philosophy curriculum for ecclesiastical institutes.[22] Since political philosophy is relatively a new entrant to Catholic academics, the discipline is still in the making as regards its content and method. However, one should keep in mind two things. First, political philosophy is to be exercised in wider context of defending human rights and basic freedoms that are essential for the common good of constitutional democracy.[23] Second, political philosophy must incorporate the cherished values of Catholic social doctrine: grounding of basic freedoms in human dignity, promotion of the common good, principle of subsidiarity, preferential option for the poor, and stewardship of creation.

## (5) Indian and Chinese Philosophies

Certainly, Indian philosophy is very much present in our philosophy departments, both secular and ecclesiastical. Thanks to the cultural openness of Vatican II, Indian philosophy was received with grater warmth in Catholic institutes of India. The need for the study of Indian philosophy is acknowledged by the official teaching authority of the Church too.[24] In most places, Indian philosophy is taught as part of history of philosophy. This is not enough, I suppose. Ideas and concepts from Indian philosophy need to be assimilated into systematic courses as well. But my great concern is whether we are approaching Indian philosophy critically and with sufficient philosophical rigor or we are still in the traditionalist framework of interpretation, namely Indian philosophy is spiritual in contrast to Western philosophy which is rational. Another vestige from the past is the faith-based division of classical schools into orthodox (astika) and heterodox (nastika). What is required is to approach and critique Indian philosophy as philosophy as such and not as religious thought.[25] Another concern we need to address, I believe, is the overly emphasis on Shankara'sAdvaita and the consequent neglect of other classical systems.[26]

The Indian, the Chinese, and the Western philosophies are the world's three major traditions of philosophy, because of their long history, rich literature, and wide range of ideas. But there is only a very meager presence of Chinese philosophy in India. This lacuna needs to be filled. Owing to their common Indo-European heritage, the classical Indian and Western philosophies have a shared worldview that tends to spirit-matter (mind-body) dualism of a sort. On the other hand, the classical Chinese worldview is more holistic and integrated. Heaven, earth, and the human being form a triad. This cosmic, ecologically sensitive outlook is remedial to any one-sidedly anthropocentric and theocentric thinking.

## (6) Refocusing the Objective of Philosophy Study and Teaching

Philosophy is not basically about thinkers, systems, and doctrines. Philosophy is more about method and perspective; philosophy is more like a way of thinking and a way of life. If our only insistence is on learning and teaching some ideas, a good many of our young graduates are likely to pass out of our philosophy institutes disenchanted with philosophy and not seeing any use for what they have studied. At the end of the day, what matters is the way of philosophizing the students learn. The study of philosophy should increase in them a capability for critical thinking and independent judgment and an ability to articulate and communicate ideas. So the focus of philosophy study and teaching needs to be on forming a philosophical mind in the student. Philosophy is not a way of thinking alone, but it is a way of life as well. The study of philosophy should be a transformative and enlightening experience for students. Philosophy should make one more humane and compassionate, socially and ecologically more relational, and less dogmatic and more tolerant toward differences.

For all these to happen, the style of teaching also needs to change. The beaten path of lecturing and passing exams has to give way to a more participatory model. A philosophy student is not a learner alone; in the first place, she is a teacher to herself. Hence what is conducive for philosophy is a dialogical model. Philosophy in all three major traditions – Indian, Western, and Chinese – started as dialogues. A student who has learned to philosophize through a dialogical way will be able to help others to find for themselves reasoned solutions to their problems.[27]

## Conclusion

To conclude, reimagining philosophy for our time, or for any time, is transforming philosophy into philosophizing and philosopher from being a sheer seeker to a reasoned guide (to themselves and others).

## Notes

1. The species name *Homo sapiens* (Latin: wise man) was applied to modern humans by the Swedish biologist Carl Linnaeus in 1758.
2. *Metaphysics*, 980a21.
3. The three major philosophical traditions of the world – the Indian, the Chinese, and the Western – emerged and took distinctive characteristics during what is commonly called "axial age" (roughly 800 BCE to 200 BCE).
4. In certain western universities there is even an increase in the number of students majoring in philosophy, before they fan out into careers ranging from law and business to medicine, technology, and education. For example, the number of philosophy majors at the University of California, Berkeley, grew 74 percent in the last decade (Berkeley News, May 10, 2011).
5. I think the main reasons why philosophy is looked upon with disfavor are the following: (1) in many, if not most, instances philosophy is not a student's choice but something they are asked to do; (2) philosophy is a conceptual discipline that requires a certain amount of intellectual inclination for it, which some students may lack; (3) sometimes philosophy is taught in a manner which makes the subject look like something that is over one's head and without any reference to and relevance for life; (4) in some faith circles there may also be a misconception that philosophy is antithetical to faith.
6. By reimagining philosophy I do not mean to propose any new philosophy or even reinterpreting what philosophy is for our time. After all there is not much of an old and new distinction in philosophy. Unlike in natural and social sciences and even theology, there is no linear development of ideas in philosophy. There is only a recycling and reinterpretation of ideas and concepts. The history of philosophy mostly means how different ideas and concepts came to be focused (highlighted and emphasized) at different periods. So the task at hand is to make philosophy relevant and meaningful for us – to relate philosophy to contemporary needs.
7. In 1995, UNESCO adopted the "Paris Declaration for Philosophy," which stated that philosophy contributes to the training of citizens by exercising their capacity for judgment, which is fundamental in any democracy. In 2002/05, UNESCO instituted World Philosophy Day, with the objective of promoting an international culture of philosophical debate that respects human dignity and diversity, democracy, and world peace. In 2007, UNESCO published a groundbreaking book on the status and prospects of teaching and learning philosophy, called *Philosophy: A School of Freedom.*
8. UNESCO, *Philosophy: A School of Freedom* (Paris: UNESCO, 2007).

   (1) The expression "philosophia ancilla theologiae" (philosophy is the handmaid of theology) is attributed to the eleventh-century churchman Peter Damian who had a negative view of philosophy. (2) Cf. John Paul II, *Fides et Ratio* (1998), 77.

9. See *Fides et Ratio* (1998), 75, 106; Congregation for Catholic Education, *Decree on the Reform of Ecclesiastical Studies of Philosophy* (2011), 7, 15.b; Pope Francis, *Veritatis Gaudium* (2017), 81.1.
10. *Veritatis Gaudium*, 81.1; *Fides et Ratio*, 77. As Karl Rahner sees it, theology's need for philosophy cannot be undervalued, because theology of its very nature presupposes philosophy as a condition of its own possibility. See Karl Rahner, *Theological Investigations*, vol. 6 (London: Darton, Longman and Todd, 1969), 71-72.
11. Leo XIII had been introduced to the writings of Thomas Aquinas by his older brother and Jesuit theologian Giuseppe Pecci.
12. The term "philosophia perennis" was originally used by AugustinusSteuchus in 1540 to show that there is a long and continuous philosophical tradition since classical antiquity that is in essential harmony with Christian faith.
13. *Fides et Ratio*, 76. Incidentally, John Paul II's own philosophical and theological thinking was influenced not only by Thomism but personalist-phenomenological tradition as well. See for his philosophical personalism, Avery Dulles, "John Paul II and the Mystery of the Human Person," *America Magazine*, February 02, 2004; Fergus Kerr, *Twentieth-Century Catholic Theologians* (Oxford: Blackwell Publishing, 2007), 165-70, cf. 187.
14. *Fides et Ratio*, 76.
15. *Fides et Ratio*, 78.
16. *Fides et Ratio*, 43, 60, 78, 106; *Veritatis Gaudium*, norms 64.1.
17. A biblically based theology might look less like defending dogmas and more like paying attention to how God was already at work in the world, particularly in the lives of his people.
18. While classical theism's was an extrinsicist understanding of the relationship between the natural and supernatural orders, neo-classical theism's is an intrinsicist one. The neo-classical proposal of radical reciprocity between God and nature leads to their mutual enrichment and consequently compromises the former's autonomy.
19. The limited scope of this paper does not permit me to go into any details of relationalism, let alone the version of philosophical relationalism I pursue, namely ontological relationalism.
20. What *The Washington Post* columnist E. J. Dionne Jr. said is applicable to any democracy, but all the more true for India: "If liberal democracy does not survive and thrive, every other problem we face becomes much more difficult." See E.J. Dionne Jr., "The most consequential question facing the world," *The Washington Post*, August 23, 2017.
21. *Veritatis Gaudium*, norms 55.1.a, 66.1.a.
22. One's primary attention should not be on the defense of religious freedom, and here we may heed to what the Jesuit theologian John Courtney Murray said long ago: the freedom of religion stands or falls with the freedom of the people. See John Courtney Murray, "The Schema on Religious Freedom: Critical Comments," (1964), Murray Archives, Georgetown University.
23. Cf. *Fides et Ratio*, 72; *Veritatis Gaudium*, norms 66.1.a.
24. Long ago, the great Indologist Max Mueller had warned the native scholars of the danger of mixing up the philosophical with the religious in the Indian culture. See F. Max Mueller, *The Six Systems of Indian Philosophy* (London: Longmans, Green and Co., 1928), xix.
25. The ascendency of the Shankara Vedanta was more due to historical factors than philosophical reasons. During the British period, German idealism was the prominent European philosophy in India. Both European and Indian thinkers found in Shankara'sAdvaita a

philosophical counterpart to Western idealism, especially the Hegelian idealism. Moreover, the early orientalists like Paul Deussen and Max Mueller considered Vedanta, particularly the Shankara's version of Vedanta, as the culmination of Indian thought. Following the lead of the orientalists, Swami Vivekananda and other Neo-Vedantins propagated Shankara's philosophy at home and abroad. Cf. Richard King, *Orientalism and Religion: Postcolonial Theory, India and 'the Mystic East'* (London: Routledge, 1999), 93, 128.

26. One recent and successful example of using philosophy to help others is philosophical counseling. The German philosopher Gerd B. Achenbach initiated philosophy counseling in the early 1980s, and from Germany it spread to other parts the world, especially North America. Philosophical counseling consists in helping individuals or groups critically examine the ideas and perceptions associated with their specific problems and come to terms with more realistic and meaningful beliefs and perspectives.

PART THREE

# SPIRITUAL OPENNESS: MYSTICAL DEPTH

12

# Spirituality for the Diocesan Priests of Today

**Joseph Ponnore**

## Introduction

The situation of the Indian Church today is extremely complex. On the one hand, there are a lot of committed pastors who are actively engaged in the shepherding ministry entrusted to them. There are very good number of clergy who goes on with great pastoral and missionary enthusiasm in their own given pastoral context. On the other hand, despite such a great pastoral ministry being done very enthusiastically, there are also darker shades that call our attention. There is an ever growing number of sex abuse cases by the clergy. The missionary zeal and spirit seem to be stagnated in many parts of the country except for some pockets and corners. The general climate that we are actively involved in the mission work is not there anymore! Where is the spirit of *Ad Gentes?* Gone are the days when mission used to be the central focus of the Church. We are faced with large number of clergy and religious who are grossly lethargic if not totally indifferent. In many situations, the pastoral ministry has come down to the bare minimum of just administering the sacraments. This is not to deny the spontaneous and enthusiastic pastoral ministry being done by some priests and religious.

This article looks into the diocesan priests of India and proposes the outlines of a spirituality. It looks into the special task of the diocesan clergy, their call to holiness and on their pastoral charity.

## 1. The Task of Diocesan Clergy

The situation in the families is also equally disheartening as family values are very much on the decline. Just as the Synod of Bishops discussed on the challenges facing the family today, we have become all the more aware of struggles, anguish, and pain of the families of today. Challenges faced by the family today are in fact, show-casing the challenges faced by the Church today! The *Humane Vitae* by St Pope Paul VI, nearly four decades ago, has proved to be prophetic in spelling out the devastation now being experienced in the families, and consequently in the Church. Systematic destruction of "family" has subsequently also inaugurated the decadence within the Church. By and large we have a secularised clergy[1] that is leading a Church that is more and more secularised. Is this secularised clergy an outcome of a secularised theology? The secularisation process within the Church has received faster momentum with the advent of the latest communication gadgets and applications, which have effectively left the clergy 'time-starved' for any creative and enthusiastic pastoral ministry. This process has also led the Church into dangerous fragmentation; leaving it into 'isms', 'ideologies', ethnic and linguistic groupings.

It is in this volatile situation that the diocesan priest is called upon to the primary task of leading and guiding the people of God into union with the Triune God. It is this situation of the clergy themselves, families, societies and the Church at large that calls us to "return to the mystery of Christ". Without *knowing Christ*, no priest can effectively minister to the People of God today. This is why theology needs spirituality and vice versa.[2] We cannot afford to have a theology without God. Without ***knowing*** and ***loving*** **Jesus**, the Saviour, the Word that became flesh, no genuine theological formation is possible.3

The Church, especially the Church in India, stands in need of reform and renewal. An external *aggiornamento* is just insufficient. The Church needs to breathe positive and renewed synergy. The Church needs to stand up, take clear position without ambiguity. But if this has to happen, the frontline soldiers have to be renewed, reformed, re-energised, and revitalised with clarity of spiritual focus and a sense of mission. According to available data, the number of the diocesan clergy in India is higher than the religious priests and total parishes numbered were 8583.4 Out of these many parishes, vast majority of the parishes are manned by the diocesan priests across the country. As such, they are the foot-soldiers at the ground zero because substantial number of the religious priests is at the moment held up in the institutions. Hence if any serious renewal is to take place in the Church, it has to begin with the diocesan priest. It is an urgent need to revitalise and renew our clergy so as to be able to ensure that the Church effectively faces the challenges before her.

## 2. Holiness: The Biblical Vocation

The call to be holy is the most basic and fundamental vocation in the Bible. Every baptised Christian has received this call to holiness. The message of the Bible to those who wish to follow the Master Jesus has always been *to be holy.* A Christian's journey is in fact a pilgrimage of constant striving to be holy. There are several Biblical references that vouch for the most basic call of man to sanctity. Some of them are: "Blessed are those with a pure heart, for they shall see God" (Mt 5:8); "For those who keep the holy laws in a holy way will be acknowledged holy, and those who accept the teaching will find in it their defense" (Wisdom 6:10); "I beg you, dearly beloved, by the mercy of God, to give yourselves as a living and holy sacrifice pleasing to God: such is the worship of a rational being" (Rom 12:1); "For your part you shall be righteous and perfect in the way your heavenly Father is righteous and perfect" (Mt 5:48); "The will of God for you is to become holy and not to have unlawful sex" (1 Thess 4:3); "Strive for peace with all and strive to be holy, for without holiness no one will see the Lord" (Heb 12:14); "God has called us to live, not in impurity but in holiness" (1 Thess 4:7); "All of you, the elected of Christ, are part of them, you, the beloved of God in Rome, called to be holy" (Rom 1:6); "to God's Church which is in Corinth; to you whom God has sanctified in Christ Jesus and called to be holy" (1 Cor 1:2); and "to the Church of God in Corinth, and to all the saints in the whole of Achaia" (2 Cor 1:1). As St. Teresa of Calcutta said, "holiness is not a luxury for a few, but it is a simple duty for you and me". There is no "elite Christian" syndrome that distinguishes the Christians with the call to be holy and those without it. All baptized are to be holy.

## 3. Holiness: The Second Vatican Council's Renewed Call

The Second Vatican Council taught of holiness very emphatically in its dogmatic constitution on the Church, *Lumen Gentium.* The fifth chapter of Lumen Gentium on the universal call to holiness (Lumen Gentium 39 - 42) clearly spelled out the above said biblical teaching in sharp focus:[5]

> The Church, whose mystery is set forth by this sacred Council, is held, as a matter of faith, to be unfailingly holy. This is because Christ, the Son of God, who with the Father and the Spirit is hailed as «alone holy», loved the Church as his Bride, giving himself up for her so as to sanctify her (cf. Eph 5:25-26); he joined her to himself as his body and endowed her with the gift of the Holy Spirit for the glory of God. *Therefore all in the Church, whether they belong to the hierarchy or are cared for by it, are called to holiness,* according to the apostle's saying: 'For this is the will of God, your sanctification' (1Th 4:3; cf. Eph 1:4)

This renewed call by the Council has been taken up with great enthusiasm and seriousness by the lay faithful. The present times witness a great blossoming of holiness among many lay faithful. Many of them have even accepted their vocation to be lay evangelizers, actively involving themselves in the preaching of the Word, and in the spreading of the Gospel to non-Christians even at the cost of a lot of personal sacrifices.

It is in this pastoral context that the diocesan priests are called to live their priesthood. The diocesan priest entrusted with the shepherding ministry of leading the flock to be holy has no option, but to become an authentic witness of holiness to all those who are under his care. He is to be a signboard as to how one can strive for holiness in the midst of very normal daily chores of life with its own ordinary struggles, pains, sorrows and joys.

The Council has taught through *Lumen Gentium* how anyone can strive for holiness in the simplest way. It has taught in unequivocal terms that the only way to holiness is the way of love.[6]

> God is love, and he who abides in love abides in God, and God abides in him" (1 Jn 4:16). God has poured out his love in our hearts through the Holy Spirit who has been given to us (cf. Rom 5:5); therefore the first and most necessary gift is charity, by which we love God above all things and our neighbour because of him.

Thus anyone who wants to be holy, regardless of one's state of life, can begin to walk this way of love. All those who begin to walk this path of love – love that is poured out on the cross of Jesus – can eventually hope to become saints as St. Francis de Sales would state in his book: *Introduction to Devout Life*.[7]

## 4. Spirituality for the Diocesan Priests of Today

One of the difficulties faced by the diocesan priests until recently has been that, the spirituality of the diocesan priest was almost never considered in the theological and formation centers. It was very often a neglected and ignored subject in most of the seminaries in India.[8] As a result, there was hardly any clear cut focused understanding of the spirituality of the diocesan priests. Most often, those involved in the formation (largely religious men) tried their best to give whatever spirituality they knew from their own specific religious / spiritual contexts and experiences. Due to this lack of clarity regarding the pastoral context and the spiritual focus required for the diocesan clergy, many of them adopted whatever they thought to be useful for their meaningful priestly life and existence, which in many cases were only mediocre.

St. John Paul II's post-Synodal Apostolic Exhortation *Pastores Dabo Vobis*, states:[9]

> The internal principle, the force which animates and guides the spiritual life of the priest in as much as he is configured to Christ the head and shepherd, is pastoral charity, as participation in ***Jesus Christ's own pastoral charity,*** a gift freely bestowed by the Holy Spirit and likewise a task and a call which demand a free and committed response on the part of the priest.

Pastoral charity of Christ is the essence of the spirituality of the diocesan priest. What is this pastoral charity of Christ? Christ had a profound experience of his Father's love and he was impelled to share that same love of his Abba with his own brothers and sisters. Therefore, Christ's pastoral charity has both a vertical as well as horizontal dimension; both a gift freely experienced as well as a task to be accomplished. Christ gave himself totally as a self-gift to his brothers and sisters, as he was in intimate communion with his Father. John the Evangelist has presented to us this pastoral charity as self-gift in a beautiful figurative language "I am the good shepherd. The good shepherd gives his life for the sheep. Not so the hired hand or any other person who is not the shepherd and to whom the sheep do not belong. They abandon the sheep as soon as they see the wolf coming; then the wolf snatches and scatters the sheep. This is because the hired hand works for pay and cares nothing for the sheep. I am the good shepherd. I know my own and my own know me, as the Father knows me and I know the Father. Because of this I give my life for my sheep". (Jn 10:11-15). Jesus has further stated in the Johannine gospel: "There is no greater love than this, to give one's life for one's friends" (Jn 15:13). St. Paul also alludes to the same concept when he writes to the Ephesians: "as Christ loved the Church and gave himself up for her." (Eph 5:25). This is the love that Christ has experienced from his Father; and this is the love that he pours out from his cross on Calvary. Jesus hanging on the cross is an icon of his pastoral charity.

It is this pastoral charity of Christ, which is the essential core of the spirituality of the diocesan priest. Accordingly, "The physiognomy of the spirituality of the diocesan priest is then a close following of Christ's pastoral charity. It means, like Christ, the diocesan priest is to experience the Father's love in Christ as a gift and to horizontally share that gift with his brothers and sisters as a total self-gift. All the other means to holiness for the diocesan priest issue forth from the pastoral charity."[10] All his pastoral ministry of breaking the Word, administering the sacraments, guiding and building up the Christian community, and proclaiming Jesus Christ and his gospel well up from this pastoral charity which is imitation of Christ's own pastoral charity. In this sense, to borrow a technical term from the religious parlance, the "charism of the diocesan priest" is *to live thepastoral charity of Christ*.

Eucharist is the heartbeat of the pastoral charity of Christ. If pastoral charity of Christ is his self-gift to the Church, so is also true with the Eucharist. The pastoral charity of Christ is in fact his own self-gift to His Father and to

His brothers and sisters. Pastoral Charity understood as the self-gift of Christ to His Father and to the humanity at large is very intimately linked to the understanding of the Holy Eucharist. Pope Francis on 16th August, 2015, said Eucharist is Jesus himself, where he offers himself totally. Eucharist is the Self-Gift of Christ himself to his people. Eucharist is then Christ giving himself to us. Therefore, Eucharist is the expression and manifestation of the pastoral charity of Christ. Jesus Christ celebrated his last supper with his own disciples to reveal his self-gift to the sinful world and then he walked up to Calvary and ultimately to the cross to give himself totally as a gift to the world. Both his pastoral charity and his Eucharist have same content and meaning: his self-gift to others. Hence devout and meaningful celebration of the Eucharist nourishes the pastoral charity of the diocesan priest because the Eucharist strengthens him to live out his pastoral charity. In this sense, we can state that the spirituality of the diocesan priest is *Eucharistic spirituality***.**

## 5. Pastoral Charity

Pastoral charity of the diocesan priest has four dimensions, namely, Christological, Ecclesial, Pastoral and Missionary. These four dimensions are four different aspects of the same pastoral charity.

Firstly, imitating the pastoral charity of Christ makes the spirituality of the diocesan priest fundamentally ***Christo-centric spirituality.*** The Christological dimension of his spirituality invites him to be configured to Christ, as Good Shepherd, as Head and Spouse of the Church.[11] The three-dimensional configuration of the diocesan priest to the figure of Christ involves a process of becoming more and more like Christ the good shepherd, the head and spouse of the Church. The diocesan priest is to be poured out into the mould of Christ as the good shepherd who readily lays down his life for taking care of the sheep. Christ became the head of the Church not by bossing over it; but by serving the Church "to the point of death, even death on a cross" (Phil 2: 8). Therefore, configuration of the diocesan priest to Christ as the head of the Church does not mean to 'rule' over the Church, instead, it means to serve the Church to the point of laying down one's life. Con-figuration of the diocesan priest to Christ as the spouse of the Church demands a spousal commitment to the Church just "as Christ loved the Church and gave himself for her" (Eph 5: 25). The qualification of this spousal commitment of the diocesan priest indicates the depth and intimacy of his love for the particular Church to which he is incardinated. Therefore, this three-dimensional configuration to Christ can effectively be called as the Christological dimension of the pastoral charity of the diocesan priest.

Secondly, following the pastoral charity of Christ means for the diocesan priest to give himself as a self-gift to the particular Church to which he has been incardinated and belong to. Incardination of a diocesan priest to his diocese is not just a juridical or organisational matter; but it is a profoundly "theological point of belonging and dedicating oneself to a particular Church in which the universal Church truly exists and is present. In that sense, the diocesan priest is juridically, and more importantly, theologically bound to the particular Church in which he is ordained."12 This makes his spirituality essentially an *ecclesial spirituality.* His love for the Church to which he belongs is a spousal love. Hence one of the criteria for discernment in his life is his whole hearted love for the Church. The diocesan priest, as a consequence of his incardination to his diocese, is the permanent collaborator of his diocesan bishop, the head of the particular Church. Just as, "the joy and hope, the grief and anguish of the men of our time, especially of those who are poor or afflicted in any way,"[13] are those of the Church, so too, the diocesan priest considers the joy and hope, the grief and anguish of the particular Church as his own. This requires him to be in ecclesial communion with his diocese at all levels, namely, to be in communion with his bishop, with brother priests (diocesan *presbyterium*), with the religious working in the diocese and with the lay faithful. For this reason, the diocesan priest needs to cultivate basic qualities required to be a builder and animator of community. Apart from the ecclesial communion, his ministry has to be oriented to build up the Church; both by proclaiming the Word effectively as well as by the devout celebration of the Sacraments. *Lumen Gentium* taught that Mary is the archetype of the Church. Therefore devotion to Mary would help the diocesan priest in fulfilling the ecclesial dimension of his pastoral charity.

Thirdly, pastoral dimension of the pastoral charity manifests all pastoral ministry that the priest does voluntarily while con-figuring himself with Christ. The pastoral ministry of each diocesan priest will be conditioned by the geo-political, socio-economic and religious context in which he finds himself. Depending on the different needs of a particular situation, pastoral dimension of the pastoral charity will be determined. This is why the diocesan priest has to be a man for all seasons and all people. This demands great generosity, flexibility and availability on the part of the priest. Hence he puts on various roles: the role of an understanding father to children and the young, caring and concerned elder, affectionate son to elderly and lonely, barefoot counselor to those confused, spiritual guide to the sinners, healer of the injured, teacher of faith to the ignorant and wavering ones and above all a faithful, reliable and committed priest. While ministering to the poor and the needy in this way, he is gifting himself to Christ his master and to his body, the Church. Thus in and through his effective pastoral ministry, he is being sanctified. This is clear from *Pastores Dabo Vobis* 24: "The priest's mission is not extraneous to his consecration or juxtaposed to it, but represents its intrinsic and vital purpose: Consecration is for mission. In this sense, not only consecration but mission as well is under the seal of the Spirit and the influence of his sanctifying power."

Finally, we look at the missionary dimension of his pastoral charity. Ever since, the Second Vatican Council entrusted the responsibility for the mission to the Bishops, Vatican has discontinued the practice of entrusting territories to religious congregations for the mission work. Accordingly, the diocesan bishop is directly made responsible for the mission of the Church. The diocesan priest being a permanent collaborator of the Bishop participates in this responsibility of the Bishop for mission.[14] As Vatican II teaches, the Church is missionary by her very nature. For this reason too, the diocesan priest, who has a spousal relationship with the Church shares in the missionary responsibility of the Bishop because it is also equally the responsibility of the diocesan priest to love the Church totally, by actively involving himself in the missionary tasks before him. In this sense, the spirituality of the diocesan priest is intrinsically a **missionary spirituality**.

## Conclusion

"*Filiitui India, administritibisalutis", "Your own sons, O India, will be the heralds of your salvation",* these words of Pope Leo XIII, reverberate in our hearts his great vision for the Church in India as we celebrate the 125th year of the establishment of the Papal Seminary. These words of Pope Leo XIII have a special resonance for the diocesan priests. They are called upon to be heralds of salvation wherever they are. They can truly be heralds of salvation only if their hearts are inflamed by the love of the Good Shepherd and his Church for the care of souls.

These words of the Pope can truly be realized only when the clergy passing through the portals of this 'home of love' or any other seminary of this country have a clear spiritual focus and goal, with a heart burning with love of Christ. India, a holy land of spiritual heritage, is urgently looking for genuine spiritual men. Hence, the need for the diocesan priests of India to be immersed into the pastoral charity of Christ and to live the same wholeheartedly with all its Christological, Ecclesial, Pastoral and Missionary dimensions.

Hence I conclude this paper with some concrete suggestions so as to transform the challenges to opportunities for the Church in India:

The Church in India needs to introduce a year of spiritual formation for the diocesan priests.[15] Some Regional Bishops' Councils have already begun this and the result in those regions is showing positive impact. It is high time that the spiritual formation of the diocesan clergy is taken more seriously with the due priority it deserves.

On-going formation of the diocesan clergy needs to be taken more seriously and more systematically as often many of them do not get opportunity for this as many of them are bound by their pastoral commitments.

The diocesan clergy needs to be encouraged to join one or other spiritual movements or fraternities for their spiritual upkeep and welfare. For instance, Apostolic Union of Clergy, Priests of St. Francis de Sales, etc.

All three *sui iuris* Churches to have their own fraternities of the diocesan clergy, helping them to come together from time to time to share their pastoral experiences and discuss issues that are affecting the life of the Church.

Dioceses need to have regular priests gathering at the deanery / forane / vicariate and diocesan level for their regular spiritual recollections and for the experience of fraternity.

Seminaries in India need to prioritize spiritual, pastoral, and missionary formation along with the academic formation. For this reason, seminaries should also include sufficient pro-pastoral programmes in their academic curriculum. The Church in India needs pastors more than ever with the "smell of the sheep", with a profound love for the Church in order to become the true "heralds of salvation" for India.

The Church in India needs to have a national level pastoral institute for the updating of pastoral endeavors and sharing of creative pastoral and missionary initiatives.

## Notes

1. This is not to refer to the diocesan priest. Ever since Second Vatican Council, diocesan clergy is not called as secular clergy in the original Latin text of the Conciliar documents of Vatican, because of the inherent negative connotation of the word "secular". If at all one finds in the English translations the word "secular clergy", it is due to the fact that the translator has not taken notice of the subtle changes the Council has initiated.
2. See S.M. Schneiders, "Theology and Spirituality: Strangers, Rivals or Partners?", *Horizons* 13/2 (1986), 253-274. See also Annice Callahan, "The Relationship between Spirituality and Theology". *Horizons* 16/2 (1989): 266-274.
3. The Church fathers theologized because they were deeply in love with the Lord Jesus. Their profound love is visible in all their writings.
4. Cf. www.catholic-hierarchy.org/country/sc1.html as on 13th July 2015. This figure need not be exact. For instance, the www.CBCI.in shows a total of 174 dioceses and not 149. Yet this figure gives a general understanding of the grass-root reality.

| Catholic | Population | Catholic % | Dioceses | Diocesan Priests | Religious Priests | Total Priests | Parishes |
|---|---|---|---|---|---|---|---|
| 17,005,000 | 1,098,096,000 | 1.55% | 149 | 11,437 | 8,509 | 19,946 | 8,583 |

5. *Lumen Gentium* 39. Emphasis is mine.

6. *LG* 42.
7. See Francis de Sales, *Introduction to the Devout Life*, tr. & ed. John K. Ryan, (New York: Image Books, 1972, 1989).
8. This is not to deny the fact that the seminarians were given general understanding of Christian spirituality and the demands and responsibilities of ministerial priesthood in their seminaries. But this was clearly insufficient because it did not give them a clear spiritual focus, emphasis and goal for their pastoral ministry.
9. John Paul II. *PastoresDabo Vobis*. Boston: St. Paul Books & Media, 1992, n. 23. Emphasis is mine.
10. John Ponnore, *Spirituality of the Diocesan Priest*, (Raipur: 2016[2]), 177· See also Juan Esquerda Bifet, *Priestly Spirituality and Mission: Signs of the Good Shepherd*, (Bangalore: National Office of the Pontifical Mission Organization, 1995), 102-103.
11. See John Paul II. *Pastores Dabo Vobis* 21-23.
12. John Ponnore, *Spirituality of the Diocesan Priest*, (Raipur: 20162), 120. See also *PastoresDabo Vobis*, n. 31-32.
13. *Gaudium et Spes* 1.
14. See *Lumen Gentium*, n. 17, 48; *Christus Dominus*, n. 6: *Ad Gentes* n. 2. All citations from the Second Vatican Council are taken from: Vatican Council II, The Conciliar and Post Conciliar Documents, ed. Austin Flannery, O.P., (Mumbai: St. Pauls, 2016).
15. See for details on the subject: John Ponnore, "Spiritual Formation of the Diocesan Priest" in *Vidyajyoti, Journal of Theological Reflection*, Vol. 68, No. 8 (August 2004), 595-605.

13

# Prophetic Mysticism in the Consecrated Life of India

**Fabian Jose UMI**

To transform the world, the Lord has chosen men and women who are capable of transmitting his love to the people through the radical path of consecrated life. The consecrated life is a gift which the Father has given to the church by means of the Spirit so that, in faithfulness to the Gospel, the most characteristic traits of the life of his Son Jesus, the chaste, poor and obedient one (Mt 8:20; Phil 2:8), and the unfathomable riches of his mystery (Eph 3:8), might be present in the world to draw everyone toward the kingdom of God. The life which is consecrated is an integral part of the ecclesial reality which looks towards the emerging new horizon with a desire to fulfill its role in a relevant manner in this world. The consecrated men and women committed to Christ have a mission in the 21st century as mystics and prophets to heal the wounded church which is bruised by the technical and secular cultures of India. Jesus rooted in His *Abba* is an example for the consecrated men and women to live a credible life amidst the challenges of India.

## 1. Consecrated to Follow Jesus the Mystic and Prophet

The integration of mysticism and prophecy is fully reflected in Jesus. From the *Abba* experience and its living memory, the heart of Jesus looked to the world and saw in nature and the simple realities of human life, the face of God, the finger of the Father, the presence of his love, the exuberance of his creative fantasy, and the signs of his mystery. As a mystic he found the loving face of

*Abba* in anyything and everything. The Biblical scholar John Dominic Crossan, makes this insightful observation about Jesus' inner peace: "The serenity and security passed by Jesus to his followers, derives not from knowing hidden mysteries from the past or the present, but from watching nature's rhythms of here and now."[1]

The mystical experience of Jesus included an experience of oneness with nature and the universe. He experienced God as an *Abba* or caring Creator to the birds of the air and the lilies of the field. His love for God's creation was expressed in these words, "Look at the birds, think of the flowers, take the fig tree for a parable, look around on fields ripe for harvest, or let the children come to me (Mt 6: 26-28; Mk 13: 28; Lk 18: 16; Jn 4: 35). Jesus called people to conversion, to a radical obedience to God, not out of fear, but as the result of the experience of His love leading to the fellow human beings. Jesus lived in perfect harmony with God, nature, self, and others.

As a prophet, Jesus challenged everyone to live by love that cuts across frontiers and prays for persecutors and killers. Service shall no more be self-regarding or reward-counting but shall be abundant, outgoing and free. His power-filled words and deeds were far more reminiscent of the great prophets of ancient Israel than of the hair-splitting 'canon-lawyers' of the scribal schools of his day.[2] Jesus' love was not calculative but went beyond all the measures. It was so royal and free that it could not be blocked or fettered, detoured or conditioned by human caprice. On good people and bad people, on those who love and those who hate or care not, God continues to cause His sun to shine and His rain to fall (Jn 3: 16; Mt 6: 25-34; Mt 10: 29-31; Mt 5: 43-48). Jesus encountered God amidst the challenges of the daily realities.

Following the path of Jesus, the consecrated men and women are called to be rooted and grounded in Jesus Christ and to become emissaries. Jesus being rooted in his *Abba,* broke the fetters of all boundaries. He was filled with passion for God and compassion for the humanity. As disciples of Jesus, the consecrated are invited to rekindle divine fire in them.

Give me the love that leads the way,
The faith that nothing can dismay;
The hope no disappointments tire;
The passion that will burn like fire
Let me not sink to be a clod
Make me thy fuel, flame of God.[3]

Filled with the fire of Christ's Spirit within, the consecrated persons are invited to launch into the prophetic dimension of their call. As Pope John Paul II rightly puts it, "There is a prophetic dimension which belongs to the consecrated life as such, resulting from the radical nature of the following of Christ and of subsequent dedication to the mission characteristics of the

relates to motor skills, a similar methodology is used by psychology schools like NLP to develop personality traits. A psycho-spiritual parallel could be used to adapt the structures of the Spiritual Exercises to produce the same functions.

## Conclusion

Karl Rahner's 'future' is today and his Christian of the future is the Christian of today. This 'today' is a time when the old absolutes no longer hold. There have been major paradigm shifts in almost all spheres of human activity: Darwin in anthropology; The Theory of Relativity and Quantum Mechanics in Physics; DNA in biology and numerous pioneers in Psychology, all have shattered old institutions and while opening vast new frontiers for human endeavour they have also demolished old certainties. It is futile to imagine that Religion as a human institution can escape this inexorable trend. For a Christian, only one thing is certain and is that Jesus Christ is the same, "yesterday, and today, and forever" (Heb 13: 8). In practice what this means for us is that the revelation of Jesus is the same yesterday, today and forever and this revelation is that God is Love. This is the Ultimate Reality and to experience this, the only way is to become one with Jesus and the task before all Christians is to find a way to do this.

## Notes

1. Theological Investigations XX, 149.
2. Experience of the Holy Spirit, *Theological Investigations Vol XVIII*, p. 193.
3. Ibid.
4. Austin, James H. *Zen and the Brain: Toward an Understand of Meditation and Consciousness*. Cambridge: MIT Press, 2015.
5. Loyola, St. Ignatius of. *The Spiritual Exercises of St. Ignatius of Loyola*. San Franciso: Ignatius Press, 2018.
6. Schäfer, Lothar. 2006. "Quantum Reality, The Emergence of Complex Order from Virtual States, and the Importance of Consciousness in the Universe". *Zygon*®. 41, no. 3: 505-532.
7. Pandikattu, Kuruvilla. *Ever Approachable, Never Attainable: Science-Religion Dialogue in India*. Pune: CreatiVentures, 2015.

## 15

# *Hetser Panim*: In Search of Answers to Personal and Systemic Problems in the Life of Pastoral Clergy

**Nishant A. Irudayadason**

The Hebrew phrase *hetserpanim* (הֶסְתֵּר־פָּנִים) means "hiding of face," and is often used when discussing the hidden-yet-revealed role of God in the Book of Esther. The sages note that there are two types of divine "hiding." The first is such that the person is unaware even that God is hiding, whereas the second type understands that God is hiding, openly, if you will, and that the partial disclosure constitutes an invitation to seek Him. To find God, we must seek His face, but this means coming out of hiding ourselves - moving beyond our shame - to believe that God's love and Presence is "for us," even in the darkness. "We find what we are seeking only by understanding that we are being sought."

What we intend to do is to bring out the sage within us to be open before God and to address some of the challenges that we face in pastoral ministry. Of course, while we are aware of many contemporary problems we face including religious fundamentalism and inhuman globalization, our response has been scanty if any. One of the reasons, I think, is that we are not perceived to be credible and may be rightly so. Rather than discussing those well-known problems, I would like to focus on some innate concerns in our life as priests that prevent us from adequately responding to the global challenges. My emphasis would be on the "in search of answers" than the challenges themselves. But we need to first specify what those challenges are.

So, my paper has two parts. The first part will spell out some of the challenges that I personally consider important and the second part will propose some meaningful and practical ways to deal with them.

## 1. The Challenges

The challenges are two-fold: personal and systemic or psychological and social. I will deal with only one issue in each aspect and leave the other aspects for the readers to address. When we speak about personal challenges what comes to my mind immediately is the need for recognition. In my interaction with my friend priests, I often notice that they feel they are not recognized enough either for their talents or for their hard work. Contemporary political philosophers like Charles Taylor, Nancy Fraser and Axel Honneth have extensively dealt with the idea of recognition.

For Taylor, recognition is related to the question of identity which he defines as "a person's understanding of who they are, of their fundamental characteristics as a human being". (Taylor, 1994: 25) He goes to say that non-recognition or misrecognition can harm the person, "can be a form of oppression, imprisoning someone in a false, distorted, and reduced mode of being". (Taylor, 1994: 25) Thus Taylor argues that recognition is a vital need. Honneth thinks that it is through recognition "that individual learns to see himself from the perspective of his [or her] partner in interaction as a bearer of equal rights" (Honneth, 1992: 194). Lack of recognition sometimes can be a source of motivation but through negative emotional experiences. According to Fraser, recognition guarantees equal participation of all members of the society in the social life (Fraser and Honneth 2003: 36) While there are minor variants in their approach to the idea of recognition, that recognition is an important social need is incontestable for all of them

However, our need for recognition may not always stem from our accomplishments. Sometimes it may be the result of our sense of insecurity, which in turn is the effect of our lack of self-acceptance. We want to be someone else – what we are not –, forgetting that each one of us is precious, uniquely gifted and beyond comparison with anyone. We also need to be realistic that we are not indispensable. When we are not aware of our sense of insecurity that cripples us, we tend to cripple others. Instead of having spiritual and moral power, we end up becoming arrogant and authoritarian.

Fr. Gabriel Ringlet from Belgium holds that the sexual abuse that we unfortunately witness in the Church is the result of spiritual abuse. Through the numerous sessions he had with the victims of sexual abuse, he arrived at the conclusion that spiritual abuse often precedes sexual abuse. Some priests find a kind of enjoyment in the fact that other people are spiritually dependent on them. Sometimes this spiritual abuse gradually leads to sexual abuse. There is a kind of terrible convergence between spiritual abuse and sexual abuse because when these two converge the victims do not perceive violence in being abused but feel accompanied by a certain emotionless sweetness.

Any streak of authoritarianism is a pointer that we may begin to abuse people. Legalism and hypocrisy are products of the authoritarian streak. We impose on others in the name of Church Law what we ourselves fail to practice forgetting that realistically speaking we need to enforce what is enforceable. This makes us lose sight of the original vision and the call of Jesus to be at the service of others. We hear critical voices that say that we wash the feet of some people on Maundy Thursday as a mere tokenism and expect people to wash our feet rest of the days.

Another fall out of the sense of insecurity is our false pride. False pride when coupled with the culture of market leads us to narcissism. We fall in love with ourselves in a lopsided manner that we think that the whole world is centred on us. This is manifested in our desperate need to occupy the centre stage everywhere and always. We seek for opportunities to make huge posters for ourselves in parish functions and preach without any message and that too with a powerful audio system only to admire our own voice. What saddens me is the extravaganza displayed during ordinations including photos in the invitation card and in banners when we claim that we commence our journey of pastoral service.

Let us now turn our attention to the systemic problem. In an empirical study conducted by Paul Parathazham on the perception of people about priests, a clear majority of them said that they want their priests to be persons of integrity and they said that priests are hardly honest. While integrity and honesty have many dimensions, we can infer that they want us to be transparent about financial details and accountable to the parishioners for the expenses incurred in the parish. People are not financially illiterate, and they know that our life style does not reflect our supposed spirit of simplicity. People do not see us credible when it comes to financial management.

It is important that our material needs are taken care of, but it should not be seen as misused. This problem is systemic because in many dioceses priests' financial needs are not properly addressed. We all know this problem but continue to ignore it under some pretext of pseudo spirituality. When the basic material needs of priests are not met with, dishonesty is an inevitable outcome. We tend to appropriate money from parish funds for our own needs and unfortunately it leads to further greed. Financial stability is an important concern which unless addressed systemically will lead to many problems.

The major problem it leads to is the division among priests. All priests want to have a "better parish." By better parish we do not mean parish that are spiritually nourishing and pastorally fulfilling but financially beneficial. This creates a class consciousness among priests of the "haves" and the "have-nots." Sadly, many priests work their way to get a parish or an institution that can make their life easy and comfortable. Whichever way we can achieve this, we strive to do even if it means promoting polarization in terms of caste, language or ethnicity. No doubt that casteism is a pervading evil in our society, but what is worse is that we begin to play the caste card not because we want to work for the welfare of any caste group but because we have certain self-vested interest of our own. No matter how many seminars or lectures we may attend to eradicate caste discrimination, we do not meet with even a minimum success because caste becomes an easy façade to cover up for financial malpractices. In our self-justification, we find fault with our bishops and other priests rather than making a genuine introspection. In my little experience no priest who has a strong caste affiliation has done anything substantial for his caste group but makes use of his caste group to ensure his upward mobility.

## 2. Concrete Suggestions

Now that we have identified two major challenges – one personal and another systemic, let us now search for answers which we can to implement in our little ways in our respective parishes. Since I have been in formation for more than a decade now, I will suggest some concrete ways in which we all can strive to work together towards our common goal of letting God be seen in our lives rather than letting him be eclipsed by personal and systemic problems.

The question of the formation of future priests and religious is crucial. Based on the findings of professionals responsible for ensuring the selection and training of seminarians in Switzerland, the report published in 2017 says that the resistance to psychological training and a denial of emotional problems among seminarians can grow into strong hostility to any psychological work on oneself. According to Isabelle Mäder, psychologist-psychotherapist consultant at the Seminary in Givisiez, Switzerland from 2004 to 2016, many candidates for the priesthood have weak emotional and psychosocial maturity. It does not matter in itself: we all have our flaws and weaknesses. This becomes problematic when the person does not dare to confront it. Normally, a person seeks therapy freely. But in the seminary, this accompaniment is imposed. The context creates a climate of hesitation. Added to this is the habit of confiding in a spiritual father, often not well-equipped to guide the seminarians surmounted by modern-day problems rather than a psychiatrist, which makes the process more complex.

The psychological dimension of formation to priesthood is necessary. It is not enough that the seminarians are offered a few courses on Psychology and occasional talks on emotional maturity, but a fraternal life that hints at the talents and flaws of each candidate to enable them to address those flaws sincerely should become integral to formation. When human, relational and emotional problems appear, those accompanying seminarians during their formation must notice it and help such students to open to trained psychologists who know the ethos of formation. It is not enough to be pious in the chapel to become a priest. It is also necessary that this relationship with God be positively embodied in everyday life.

Unreasonable expectation on the candidates to priesthood either from those accompanying them in formation or from their superiors can be counter-productive. Many seminarians are preoccupied with the question "Will I be promoted to priesthood?" They want to convince their superiors that they are suitable and to achieve this, they can go to any extent to pretend what they are not. In India, the fear of annual report is wide-spread. Seminarians, whose companions in the secular world have already become responsible adults, unfortunately tend to be infantile and learn to be subservient to become priests by any means. They let themselves be treated like children and this goes along well especially if those accompanying them have paternalistic attitude. It curbs their responsibility. As they are so used to take orders from superiors and obey to please them, when they become priests and are entrusted with power and responsibility they begin to abuse them even sexually. It is important that those accompanying the seminarians in formation realize that they are entrusted with normal human persons and not extraordinary saints. They will surely have flaws that will have to be addressed but without exaggerating them. The interpersonal adult to adult accompaniment is what offers them the ability to grasp what is happening in the other and to build relationship with God. The true ability of transformation is possible only in a conducive atmosphere of freedom with responsibility.

According to Isabelle Mäder (2017), there is need for compulsory psychological examination during formation. Its success implies the freedom to submit to it. She pleads for a year of internship in a social institution before the year of discernment. It would help to observe the candidate, to see how he behaves when it comes to working with other people, including women, to confront authority and the laxity of the environment. An interesting alternative in the Indian context could be to reinstate the practice of what is known as free regency when the seminarians will work one year to have the experience of life outside seminary. In the past, it was successful and has made an impact in the formation and it may be desirably and necessary to revisit this practice. It is even more important now as the seminary formation at present reflects the model of formation in seclusion while in the post-Vatican era we do not want to divorce the world in which we live and evolve.

An idealized image of priesthood is dangerous. The priest is not a kind of superman above the fray. This is the great danger of spiritualism: the rejection of the body and denial of emotional affectivity. The priest is not pure spirits hovering in the air; he has a body and has emotional needs. Neglecting this reality can lead to all sorts of drifts. Ringlet suggests that every priest should have a prior immersion in learning a profession either manual or intellectual to have "enough layman in himself." For this, the Church must have the courage not to play the number game when it comes to the vocation to priesthood, which may dwindle but that should not matter because the Church needs to move away from the undue emphasis on clericalism. Ringlet goes a step further inviting the Church to reconsider the practice of Celibacy while accepting the meaningfulness of this practice if it is a choice that is freely made after a long personal journey. However, we must be realistic enough to acknowledge that abolition of obligatory celibacy would not solve all the problems associated with sexual abuse in the Church.

## Conclusion

Finally, we should evolve a reasonable financial structure in each diocese that would not only prevent misappropriation of parish funds but enables every priest to have a sense of financial security. Though priesthood is not a profession but a call to service, priests cannot be made dependent on the mercies of others to have his needs met. My suggestion is that a priest should be paid a reasonable amount every month – like a school teacher for example – and have strict mechanism in place that no priest has unchecked access to parish funds. This is not difficult to do. In fact, in many European countries and in the US this system is in place even if they are not perfect. All that we need is good will and sincere effort to work out a mechanism that is suitable for us. I urge those of us who have passed out from here to initiate a healthy dialogue with respective bishops and those Papalite bishops can set a new trend in this regard.

Let us remember the challenging words from the Papal Seminary Anthem: "O Mother of thousand sons, sent forth with hearts aflame the poor, the week and the oppressed to serve in Jesus' name."

## Reference

Fraser, Nancy and Axel Honneth. *Redistribution or Recognition: A Political-Philosophical Exchange*. London: Verso, 2003

Honneth, Axel. "Integrity and Disrespect: Principles of a Conception of Morality Based on the Theory of Recognition". *Political Theory*, 20:2 (1992): 187-201

Mäder, Isabelle. "Lorsque le bergerest un loup". https://abus-sexuels.cath.ch/5-lavenir/ (accessed on 7 October 2018).

Ringlet, Gabriel. "Les conceptions 'dangereuses' de la sexualité". Online video clip. *You tube*. 12 March 2018. Web. 7 October 2018.

Taylor, Charles. "The Politics of Recognition". *Multiculturalism: Examining the Politics of Recognition*. Ed. Amy Gutmann. Princeton: Princeton University Press. 1994: 25-73

16

# Reading the Parish as Sacred Page

**Paul Thelakat**

In 1256, St Thomas Aquinas was appointed as magister sacraepaginae (Master of the Sacred Page), the highest University post of the middle Ages. It clearly denoted three responsibilities: Legere, disputare, praedicare - to read, to dispute and to preach. 'The starry heavens above and the moral law within' are to be read and interpreted. There is the scientific reading of the visible and the sensible, but philosophy, poetics and religion look behind life. The reading of the interiority does not render sciences, but a horizon of values of life. What emerges is "differential observation of human life and practice."[1] "It is not how things are in the world that is mystical, but that it exists."[2] "The aspects of things that are most important for us are hidden because of their simplicity and familiarity. (One is unable to notice something – because it is always before one's eyes.) The real foundations of his inquiry do not strike a person at all. And this means: we fail to be struck by what, once seen, is most striking and most powerful."[3] Wittgenstein therefore distinguishes between showing in the sense of representational language and showing, to "climb up the ladder" to a right view of the world. So preaching things seen by the eyes and things seen by the eyes of the soul. Language endeavours to say things that cannot be put into words in an empirical way, we finally have to end the project of explaining the world – yet not without satisfying his own "longing for the transcendent"... "The work of art is the object seen sub specie aeternitatis; and the good life is the world seen sub specie aeternitatis. This is the connexion between art and ethics."[4]

## 1. The Christian Priest as Reader of the Word and Nature

A Christian priest is not a ritual poojari or the Levitical priest of the Old Testament, but a priest of the nature of Christ the eternal priest. He has to lead the people of God like Moses, perceiving the heavens and the interiority. The priest has the duty not only of reading, discussing and preaching the sacred scripture of the Holy Bible but also of catering to the spatio-temporal segment, which is the parish the "sacra pagina." Up to 17th century, the two books theory remained in the Western mind-set. Alan of Lille of twelfth century wrote, "Omnis mundi creatura quasi librumet picture nobis est et speculum" (The whole world is like a book and a picture of us, and a mirror).[5] The words of Anthony the Abbot in third century probably give the first example of hermitage: "My book is the created nature, a one always at my disposal whenever I want to read God's words."[6] St. Augustine said: "Some people in order to discover God, read a book. But there is a great book: the very appearance of created things. Look above and below, note, read. God whom you want to discover, did not make the letters with ink; he put in front of your eyes the very things that he made. Can you ask for a louder voice than that?"[7]

Maximus writes: "The natural law, as if it were a book, holds and sustains the harmony of the whole of the universe. Material bodies are like the book's characters and syllables; they are like the first basic elements nearer to us, but allow only a partial knowledge. Yet such a book has also more general and universal words, more distant from us, whose knowledge is more subtle and difficult to reach. The same divine Logos who wrote these words with wisdom, is like embodied in them in an ineffable and inexpressible way. He reveals himself completely through these words; but after their careful reading, we can only reach the knowledge that he is, because he is none of those particular things. It is gathering with reverence all these different manifestations of his, that we are led toward a unique and coherent representation of the truth, and he makes himself known to us as Creator, by analogy from the visible, created world."[8] The primary elements of the physical world are like the alphabets of a language. There is semiotic structure in the world. The following quote by Georges Lemaître the originator of the Big Bang theory seems, in this respect, quite impressive: "Both of them, (the believing scientist and the non-believing scientist) endeavour to decipher the palimpsest of nature, in which the traces of the various stages of the long evolution of the world are overlaid on one another and confused. The believer has perhaps the advantage of knowing that the enigma has a solution, that the underlying writing is, when all is said and done, the work of an intelligent being, therefore that the problem raised by nature has been raised in order to be solved, and that its difficulty is doubtless proportionate to the present or future capacity of mankind. That will not give him, perhaps, new resources in his investigation, but it will contribute to maintaining in him a healthy optimism without which a sustained effort cannot be kept up for long."[9]

## 2. Reading Poetically and Theologically

Reading the parish involves knowing the parish, its present with the issue at stake and the problems faced. Reading implies statistical evaluations, which involve predictions that are retro-dictions, for example how many children will be born in the parish in the coming year and how many vocations will become available. If the statistical average of vocations does not happen, the foundations of vocation are shaking. In 2015, the Ernakulam-Angamlay archdiocese of Kerala had 109218 Catholic families from which there were 1742 priests and 74 brothers and 6781 nuns. The priests nuns ratio was 1:4, but now when there are 735 seminarians, we have only 210 aspirants to convents. Something terrible is happening to the ground of vocation to convents. This empirical assessment calls for a deconstructive procedure that will be called for in the pastoral planning of the parish. It also implies that the parish is read also as palimpsest, with its layers of past, the reading of the under-writings. The parish is to be read poetically and theologically. The future is foreseen and invented. Poet tells stories of tomorrow and theologian invents the holy language. Language in which the origin speaks is essentially prophetic. The priest must hear and utter the voice that God had lent to the silent agony, a voice to the plundered poor. It is a form of living, a crossing point of God and man. Let God rage in the prophet's words.

## 3. A Present in the Ferment

There is a sense of life as a divine drama into which we are invited lies at the heart of the theology of Hans Urs von Balthasar. The liturgy is the divine play enacted in the church and community. The enactment of the life, passion, death resurrection of Jesus in liturgy shown not to enslave Christians to a historical lie of scapegoat mechanism but to reveal and to orient all human beings to the truth of human existence in relation to the transcendent. Balthasar believed that all Christians could engage in a kind of mysticism of ordinary life and thus become "contemplatives in action." In the flux of becoming there is the churning of the Spirit.

The leader of the Christian community has to read it not as a solipsistic one but as a community of voices merging and becoming one. It is not a tower of Babel. To be for oneself means still to be forthcoming, to cease being forthcoming, to prove to be already complete here, means to die spiritually. It has to be a celebrative "fusion of horizons" to describe understanding. "All understanding is a fusion of horizons"[10] Gadamer describes the event of understanding in relation "consensus" and "agreement." He asserts that "to understand means to come to an understanding with each other. Understanding is primarily agreement."11 Monologue manages without the other, and therefore to some degree materializes all reality. It pretends to be the ultimate word. It closes down the represented world and represented persons.[12]

'God's incarnation perfects the whole ontology and aesthetics of created Being.'[13] The special concern of aesthetics, and, on the other hand, a properly theological aesthetics, there is a moment of differentiation that cannot be overlooked: 'It is only when such a this-worldly aesthetics does not fit revelation's transcendent form that we suddenly come to an astonished halt and conscientiously decline to continue on that path.'[14] The leader's reading is not only of the meaning of the empirical events but also the changes that happen and why of the changes. It is not simple seeing, but is also foreseeing, the prophetic insight of the future and the stories of tomorrow. Von Balthasar puts it this way in the Theo-Drama: "the precious form points to the ground and origin behind … . What emerges as self-evident at privileged moments – particularly in erotic and agapeic love – is … the fact that ... the very uniqueness of the individual being causes the indivisible uniqueness of Being to shine forth with peculiar clarity."[15] All of a sudden, revelation is demonstrated not to be a mere set of historical events, but a present in ferment. It becomes apparent that one can have no real idea of the 'truth' of this revelation until one is caught up in it, relinquishing one's claim to neutrality. "The saints," as von Balthasar observes, "have always been on guard against such an attitude, and immersed themselves in the actual events of revelation."[16] The Church composes the Scriptures "as the spontaneous expression of its experience of the in-breaking of absolute love"[17] In the action or drama of salvation history takes place in the parish, the Son offers no technical copy or static icon of the Father – it is in the boundless obedience of the Son that the boundless self-giving love of the Father appears. Every Christian becomes an edition of the Scripture in the communion of saints in the becoming of the parish.

## Notes

1. Matthias Kroß, *Klarheitals Selbstzweck, Wittgenstein* über *Philosophie, Religion, Ethik und Gewissheit*, Berlin 1993, p. 65.
2. L. Wittgenstein, *Tractatus logico-philosophicus*, transl. by David F. Pears and Brian McGuinness, introd.by Bertrand Russell, London: Routledge & Kegan Paul 1961, rev. ed. 1963, 6. 44.
3. Wittgenstein, *Philosophical Investigations*, ed. by G.E.M. Anscombe and G.H. von Wright, transl. by G.E.M. Anscombe, Oxford, § 129. 1953: Basil Blackwell.
4. Wittgenstein, *Notebooks 1914-1916*, ed. by Gertrude Elizabeth M. Anscombe and G.H. von Wright, transl. by Gertrude Elizabeth Margret Anscombe. Oxford 1961: Basil Blackwell, 7.10.16
5. *Philosophical Investigations*, 210, 579.
6. Reported by Socrates Scholasticus, *Historia Ecclesiastica* IV, 23, (PG 67, 518).

7. *Sermones,* 68, 6 (PLS 2, 505).
8. *Ambigua*10 (PG 91, 1129 A)
9. O. Godart, M. Heller, "Les relations entre la science et la foi chez Georges Lemaître," *Pontificia Academia Scientiarum, Commentarii,* vol. III, no. 21, p. 11, quoted in John Paul II, Discourse to the Pontifical Academy of Sciences, November 10, 1979, in *Osservatore Romano*, English week edition, November 26, 1979, p. 10.
10. Gadamer, Hans-George, *Truth and Method.* New York: Crossroad, 1975, p. 302.
11. Ibid., p. 180.
12. M. M Bakhtin, *Problems of Dostoevsky's Poetics,* Caryl Emerson, edt. and trans, Minneapolis: University of Minnesota Press, 1997, p. 292-293.
13. Balthaser, *The Glory of the Lord, A Theological Aesthetics*, Volume 1: Seeing the Form, translated by Erasmo Leiva-Merikakis, edited by Joseph Fessioand John Riches, San Francisco, CA: Ignatius Press, 1983, p. 28.
14. Ibid., p. 37.
15. Balthasar, *Theo-Drama: Theological Dramatic Theory: Volume 2, Dramatis Personae: Man in God*, translated by Graham Harrison, San Francisco, CA: Ignatius Press, 1990, p. 22.
16. Balthasar, *Explorations in Theology I: The Word Made Flesh*, translated by A.V. Littledale with Alexander Dru, San Francisco, CA: Ignatius Press, 1989, p. 205.
17. Balthasar, *The Glory of the Lord, A Theological Aesthetics.* Volume 7: Theology: The New Covenant, translated by Brian McNeil , Edinburgh: T. & T. Clark, 1989, pp. 97, 100.

17

# Interfacing of Science and Religion in the 21$^{st}$ Century: Not an Option, but an Obligation

**S. Stephen Jayard**

Science and Religion are two powerful enterprises in the modern world. Whether or not, one is fascinated by science or attracted by any religious ideology, one cannot ignore these two power-houses in human society. As science advances in an unprecedented manner one might sometimes think that religion and faith in God may slowly be rendered unwanted or redundant. We are often led to think that science, as it gets more and more nuanced and intricate, it can answer almost any question that humanity faces. But serious reflections on the nature of science and its claims reveal that science has its own limits and limitations, and it is not necessarily opposed to religion or faith in God. Similarly, followers of religion have also to realize that religions are vulnerable to misuses and abuses. Religions need to be open to interact and learn from one another. There are several common platforms that can bring science and religion together, by which humanity can be enriched. This essay, after clarifying the basic notions of science and religion, presents a brief historical background and different models of science-religion dialogue; then it elaborates on the notion of limits and limitations of science to show that there is a need for Science-Religion dialogue and that science and religion need to be open and humble enough to learn from one another.

## 1. Science-Religion Dialogue

**What is Science?** Science is traditionally understood as a totally rational enterprise, based on observations and experiments. Their results are unbiased and objective. Such an abstract understanding of science does not recognize the actual features of science. It is actually a profession where *individuals* work together in order to increase human knowledge, remove ignorance, and solve day-to-day problems of our lives. Since it is concerned with *individuals*, which automatically involves their and the society's goals, desires, interests, motivations and values; since it aims at solving *practical problems*, humans have to be taken seriously, their day-to-day concerns and well-being play an important role in the scientific enterprise. Therefore, it is obvious that science can't just be an ideal or theoretical enterprise, where only experts are involved in an abstract ideal world.

**What is Religion?** To define religion is not an easy task; it involves diverse dimensions - sociological, psychological, anthropological, naturalistic and spiritual. It can be generally understood as a system of beliefs and practices which are fundamentally centered on a transcendent Reality, which can be seen as a personal or impersonal; it aims to provide humans with ultimate meaning and purpose to life. In the Postmodern sense it is understood as follows: Religion "is a personal experience in the processes of human life. It is love of God, not love of religion".[1] In a wider sense religion does not confine itself only to the institutionalized forms of religious practices; rather it refers to the spiritual experience, in the sense, that one experiences a connection with the Impossible and Unlimited. Realizing our human limitedness", or the sense of achievement in spite of our shortcomings, is also a spiritual experience. In that sense, even an atheist can have spiritual experience.[2]

**What is Science-Religion Dialogue?** – It is an academic exercise to pave the way for a better world and humanity, by trying to bring together the recent advancements of the contemporary science and the noblest and deepest insights of religions, with the tools of the latest progress and awareness obtained in philosophy (especially, Philosophy of Science). It aims at harmoniously unifying the fundamental elements of matter and spirit, the human and the divine, the values and the technology, the scientific achievements and the deepest longing for meaningfulness in life.

**Some Efforts towards This Dialogue:** A German group was founded by Adolf Picht in Heidelberg to explore the possibilities of bringing science and religion together. The Dutch Atomium, a legacy of Dipler (1948) and the Institute for Theological Encounter with Science and Technology (ITEST, 1969), in St. Louis, U.S.A are a few of the significant developments in this regard. Templeton foundation in the USA (1972) has done remarkable work in taking the move further – several publications every year, meritorious awards for successful work in this type of research, number of international conferences all over the world are some of the major activities of the Foundation. The biannual conferences conducted by the European Society for the Study of Science and Theology (ESSSAT, 2000) are also noteworthy. The Association of Science, Society and Religion (ASSR) was established at Jnana-Deepa Vidyapeeth (JDV), the Pontifical Institute of Philosophy and Theology, the largest Seminary in India, in 1998. In 2000, the Indian Institute of Science and Religion (IISR) was also started in JDV, Pune; however it now functions in Delhi, under the able guidance of its founder-Director, Prof. Job Kozhamthadam, SJ.

**Why this Dialogue?** – The interaction between science and religion has been there for centuries. The thinkers of the ancient Greek Philosophy, from the time of Pythagoras (6th Century BC) or even before, were both philosophers and scientists. In the ancient Greek Philosophy there was no difference between science and philosophy; Aristotle, known as a philosophers, made contributions to Astronomy and Cosmology. Till the 19th century, science was known as 'natural philosophy' and those were doing science, knows as 'natural philosopher'; only in 1833 Whewell coined the term 'science and scientist'. Historical studies on scientific developments by Reijer Hooykas3 and Eugene Klaaren4 show clear religious roots of modern science.

In the 12th century, Thomas Aquinas integrated Aristotelian Physics and Christian Theology; and this was powerful till the 17th century. The geocentric worldview of the Aristotelian system went very well with the Biblical understanding of creation, keeping humans as the pinnacle of the whole of creation, and the earth at the centre of the universe. The Copernican proposal of heliocentrism, and the subsequent scientific developments at the hands of Galileo and Kepler and the mathematical accuracy of Newton's theories were projected as the rivalries or the denial of the Biblical teachings on creation. Interestingly, Galileo did not find any conflict between scientific findings and religious beliefs, as the Bible is not meant for scientific facts but it aims at truths that are beyond the reach of reason. His famous saying: the Bible teaches us how to go to heaven, and not how the heavens go.[5] Newtonian mechanics introduced material reductionism and determinism very strongly in every domain of humanity. Everything in nature and human society was seen in terms of matter, motion and force. However Newton had no problem with religion and in fact he brought in God to explain the orderliness of the planetary movements.

The 19th century science saw many breakthroughs in the world of physics (like the theories of optics, electromagnetism and thermodynamics), chemistry (like the atomic theory, periodic table) and biology (like theory of evolution).

The most crucial challenge came from Darwin's *The Origin of Species* (1859), which challenged the supremacy of humans. More than the heliocentric view, this disturbed humans, because it displaced them to the periphery; humans were no more seen to be special, as the crown of the creation, but a product of the long evolution from the smaller creatures. Since natural selection could explain the evolution of life, including human life, religious beliefs were thought to be unnecessary or misleading. Several theologians reacted vehemently condemning the scientific endeavours. This tensed situation led to the 'warfare' scenario between science and religion. Deeper studies in the theory of evolution and the more informed interpretation of the Biblical versions of creation make it clear that there is no real conflict between Darwin's evolution and religion. Vested interests projected Darwin to be an atheist and disproved the existence of God and so on, but it was not the real case.

Stephen J. Gould argues that "Darwin did not use evolution to promote atheism, or to maintain that no concept of God could ever be squared with the structure of nature. Rather he argued that nature's factuality, as read within the magisterium of science, could not resolve, or even specify, the existence or character of God, the ultimate meaning of life, the proper foundations of morality, or any other question within the different magisterium or religion."[6] In a letter to Asa Gray, Darwin himself confessed: "I had no intention to write atheistically. But I own that I cannot see as plainly as others do, and as I should wish to do, evidence of design and beneficence on all sides of us. There seems to me too much misery in the world... On the other hand, I cannot anyhow be contented to view this wonderful universe, and especially the nature of man, and to conclude that everything is the result of brute force. I am inclined to look at everything as resulting from designed laws, with the details, whether good or bad, left to the working out of what we may call chance."[7] At another time, he clarified even more clearly: "In my most extreme fluctuations I have never been an atheist in the sense of denying the existence of God... (There is) the extreme difficulty or rather the impossibility of conceiving this immense and wonderful universe, including man, with his capacity for looking backwards, and far into futurity, as the result of blind chance or necessity. When thus reflecting I feel compelled to look to a First Cause having an intelligent mind in some degree analogous to that of man, as I desire to be called a theist."[8]

Further, the period of the Enlightenment and Modernity saw religion as the enemy of science; even ridiculed religion. On the other hand, people becoming aware of the shortcomings of science and technology; they are not only not solving problems of humanity, but also creating newer ones: the invention of atomic energy and weapons, the ethical issues arising from the break-through in the world of biomedicines, the ecological issues with the increase of global warming, the pollution due to the boom in the industrial and transportation arena, the strange diseases and mysterious fevers that we face today – are some of the burning issues that have to be urgently addressed. People realize that they have become the victims of the one-sided growth of science and technology. The need for making science morally bound for the total welfare and the holistic developments of humanity is strongly felt today. As the only conscious beings, or at least as of our present knowledge reveals, we have the duty to save the environment.

## 2. Four Models of the Relationship between Science and Religion

With the close study of the interaction between science and religion, Ian Barbour proposed four models:[9]

**Conflict Model:** It is the outcome of the extreme positions held by science and religion, namely, Biblical Literalism and Scientific Materialism. Since both are the diametric opposite levels, it is not possible to combine both, and for instance, one cannot be a believer in God and in the Theory of Evolution, because the evidence of the theory of evolution goes against every aspect of faith in God. Both are in a constant conflict, as there is nothing common between them. (Major proponents of this model: Carl Sagan, Jacques Monod, Edward O. Wilson, Stephen Hawking, Daniel Dennet, Richard Dawkins and so on.).

**Independence Model:** There is no conflict, and at the same time, there is no any complementary relation either, between science and religion. Since the subject matter, the realms of inquiry and methodologies drastically differ, there is no question of any conflict; the strict compartmentalization of the two disciplines maintains and reaffirms their distinctive and unique nature. (Major proponent of this model: Karl Barth).

**Dialogue Model:** A more constructive approach; it encourages dialogue and integration between them, avoiding conflation or total segregation. While preserving the differences, it focuses on the points of possible relationship and aspects of similarities. The borders and frontiers of science can open up to the issues of religion; those phenomena at this threshold cannot be explained by science alone. In the past, religious and philosophical reflections are said to have contributed to the scientific understanding of the origin and evolution of the universe. (Major Proponents of this model: Karl Rahner, David Tracy, Thomas Torrance, John Polkinghorne, Arthur Peacocke, Pannenbergetc)

**Integration Model:** It looks for more substantial type of relationship between science and religion, than the dialogue model. Both are mutually enriching by more extensive and orderly partnership; Religion can positively help science in many ways in their great adventures of exploration into the deeper realities of the world (Major Proponents of this model: Copernicus, Kepler, Galileo, Newton, Paul Davies and so on)

Modern science has its roots in philosophy and religious thoughts. Davies argues, "Science emerged from medieval Europe, under the twin influence of

Greek philosophy and the Judeo-Christian thought.[10] Many of the founders of modern science did not find any conflict between science and religion; in fact, most of them were deeply religious minded, like Copernicus, Descartes, Galileo, Leibniz, Newton etc. Kepler believed that astronomers were priests of the Almighty; they were the ministers of the Book of Nature (the deed of God), while the priests of religion were the ministers of the Book of Scripture (the Word of God). Newton wrote more on theology than on optics. In his letter to the Bavarian chancellor Hans Georg Herwart von Hohenburg, he says: "since astronomers are priest of Almighty God with respect to the book of Nature, we should concern ourselves not with the praise of our cleverness but with the glory of God."[11] Newton in his letter to Richard Bentley, Bishop of Worcester, explaining his motivation for writing his masterpiece *thePrincipia*, namely he has a strong religious objective: "When I wrote my treatise about our system, I had an eye upon such principles as might work with considering men for the belief of a Deity; and nothing can rejoice me more than to find it useful for that purpose."[12]

## 3. Involvement of the Church in the Growth of Science

Though it is generally believed that the Church was a hindrance to the growth and developments of science, it is not completely true. Many Church men and women were experts in the fields of science; for instance, Pope Sylvester (999-1003) had incomparable scientific knowledge; he was acutely intelligent; he was the leading mathematician and astronomer in the 'dark ages'. He was the first Christian to teach Mathematics using the nine Arabic numerals and zero, which he called 'Hindu numerals'; using these new numerals, he devised an abacus, or counting board, which mimics the algorithms used today for computing; so it can be called 'the first computer'. He was the tutor of the future king of France, and two future Holy Roman Emperors. Pope John Paul II too happily acknowledged the great contributions of Pope Sylvester II.

Significant contributions were made by the Jesuits to the growth of science and Mathematics in the modern times; they are known as 'the scientific order of Catholicism'. The research by a world-famous historian of science, George Sarton, reveals that "One cannot talk about mathematics in the 16th and 17th centuries without seeing a Jesuit at every corner".13Poggendorf in his *Dictionnaire des Sciences Exactes*, from antiquity to 1863, lists 8847 scientists; of these 10% are priests and religious; a good number of them are Jesuits. Dhruv Raina, a historian and philosopher of science, points out that "Between the years 1600 and 1773, ... Jesuit scientists had authored more than 4000 published works, about 600 journal articles appeared after 1700, and about 1000 manuscripts were available. The Society's known publications include 6000 scientific works covering areas such as Aristotelian natural philosophy, medicine, philosophy, astronomy, and mathematics."[14]

Pope John Paul expressed his desire that theologians, scientists and historians must collaborate together to work towards fruitful harmony of science and faith, Church and world; he frankly acknowledged the need to correct the mistakes of the Church done in the past.[15] Further, he was also convinced that "Science can purify religion from error and superstition: religion can purify science from idolatry and false absolutes. Each can draw the other into a wider world, a world in which both can flourish."[16] However, both science and religion cannot lose their autonomy or distinctness: "The Church does not propose that science should become religion. On the contrary, unity always presupposes the diversity and the integrity of its elements... A unity in which one of the elements is reduced to the other is destructive, false in its promises of harmony, and ruinous of the integrity of its components. We are asked to become one, we are not asked to become each other."[17]

## Conclusion

With all these reflections upon the limits and limitations of science one can easily be convinced of the need for science to interact with other domains of knowledge, including Philosophy and Theology. Religion plays an important role in the lives of human beings, whether or not, one is a follower of any religion. As both enterprises of science and religion are very powerful and influential we need to take them very seriously for a holistic life. Science may not need religion and religion may not need science, as Fritjof Capra puts it, but we humans need both for our comprehensive lives.[18]

Science has its own weakness and greatness and that is what makes science interesting and inevitable for humans; weakness because it is the inadequacy of science, and greatness because, in spite of such shortcoming science is still the *best* (though not *perfect*!) knowledge enterprise that the humans have. Science needs to enter into partnership with other disciplines in its investigations of reality. Thus, Science and Religion dialogue is *not an option, but an obligation; it is not choice but a compulsion; it is not a desire, but a demand.* Science-Religion dialogue is, thus, urgent and necessary. The collaboration between science and religion is not an encroachment on one another's turf, but a great mutual help to enrich humanity and cosmos. The words of the following thinkers, who are spearheading the cause of Science-Religion dialogue are very pertinent and promising: *N. Whitehead:* "When we consider what religion is for mankind, and what science is, it is no exaggeration to say that the future course of history depends upon this generation as to the relations between them."[19]; Ralph Waldo Emerson: "The religion that is afraid of science dishonours God and commits suicide"[20]; and Paul Davies: "Science offers a surer path to God than religion."[21]

If science stops caricaturing religion and religion ceases to alienate science, if science is open to inter-disciplinary approaches, including religion and philosophy, and if religions stop their claims for superiority over the claim of comprehending the ultimate reality, both can get mutually enriched by the interaction. It is apt to end our discussion with the words of optimism by Prof. Job Kozhamthadam: "Thanks to the different recent developments in religious and scientific circles, they seem to be willing to talk to each other, respectfully and creatively. In some ways the dialogue has already started. Let us hope that it will not be too long before they come together to forge a more dynamic partnership to work for the betterment and enrichment of our world"[22] and the whole of humanity and the natural environment are to be enriched by this.

## Notes

1. Joe Arun, SJ, "The Post-modern God: Ways of Being Religious in the Postmodern World", in *Vidyajyoti*: *Journal of Theological Reflection,* Vol. 73 (2009), 564-580, 570.
2. Warren Nelson Nevius, *Religion as Experience and Truth: An Introduction to the Philosophy of Religion*, (London: Westminster Press, 1941).
3. R. Hooykaas, *Religion and the Rise of the Modern Science* (Scotish Academic Press, 1973).
4. Eugene Klaaren, *Religious Origins of Modern Science* (Grand Rapids, Michigan: Wm. B. Erdmans, 1978).
5. See: http://www.oratoriosanfilippo.org/galileo-baronio-english.pdf. Accessed on 5 Feb, 2019.
6. S. J. Gould, *Rocks of the Ages: Science and Religion in the Fullness of Life* (New York: The Library of Contemporary Thought, 1999), 192.
7. Quoted by S. J. Gould, Ibid., 35-36.
8. Francis Darwin, ed., *Life and Letter of Charles Darwin* (New York: D. Appleton, 1887), 1:274, 275.
9. G. Ian Barobour, *Issues in Science and Religion* (New Jersey: Prentice Hall Inc., 1966); *Religion and Science* (London: SCM Press Ltd., 1998); *When Science Meets Religion*: *Enemies, Strangers or Partners*? (New York: Paulist Press, 1995).
10. Paul Davies, "The Mind of God," in *Physics and Our View of the World*, ed., Jan Hilgvoord (Cambridge: Cambridge University Press, 1994), 231.
11. Kepler's letter written to Herwart, on March 25, 1958, in *Gesammelte Werke*, ed. W. von Dyck, Max Caspar, F. Hammer and V. Bialas (Munich, 1937-), Volume XIII, no. 91, II:182-184.
12. H. S. Thayer (ed), *Newton's Philosophy of Nature* (New York: Hafner Press, 1953), p. 46.
13 George Sarton, "An Appeal for the Republication in Book Form of R. Bosman's Studies,", *ISIS* 40(1949), 3-6.
14. Dhruv Raina, "French Jesuits in India", *Economic and Political Weekly* (January 30, 1999), PE-30.
15. John Paull II, Acta ApostolicaeSedis, 71(1979), 1464-1465, tr. in *The Pope Speaks*, 25(1980), 106.
16. Robert Russell, William R. Stoeger, and George V. Coyne, SJ, eds., Physics, Philosophy and Theology: A Common Quest for Understanding (Vatican City: Vatican Observatory Publications, 1988), M13.
17. Ibid., M8.

18. See: https://en.wikiquote.org/wiki/Fritjof_Capra. Accessed on 4 March, 2018.
19. A. N. Whitehead, *Science and the Modern World*, (New York: Simon and Schuster, 1983) p. 181.
20. See: https://harpers.org/blog/2008/03/emerson-science-and-religion/ Accessed on 20 January, 2016.
21. Paul Davies, *God and the New Physics* (New York: Simon and Schuster, 1983), the cover page.
22. Job Kozhamthadam, "The Changing Face of Science-Christianity Dialogue", in Job Kozhamthadam, ed, *Science, Technology and Values: Science-Religion Dialogue in a Multi-Religious World* (Pune: ASSR Publications, Jnana-Deepa Vidyapeeth, 2003), 3-34, 30.

18

# Rediscovering the Spirituality of Indian Christians in a Pluri-Religious Context

**Stephen Chundamthadam SJ**

## Introduction

Spirituality is closely associated with culture, dogmas, faith in God, worldview and life style. Hinduism, Buddhism and other religions in India contributed greatly to the shaping of the culture, traditions and spirituality of India. Indian spirituality emphasises the importance of the ways of liberation, uniqueness of the goal, single mindedness and continuous pursuit and liberation as the ultimate goal. Christians in India mostly follow Western spirituality characterized by dogmas, liturgical ceremonies and rituals. The foundation of Christian spirituality is the life and teachings of Jesus, the Kingdom values and the teachings of the Church. Being Indian Christians, our spirituality should be solidly founded on Jesus spirituality and at the same time should be able to integrate the positive elements from the spiritual traditions of India. This paper is an attempt to rediscover and elaborate on a spirituality for Christians suited to the Indian pluri-religious context.

## 1. Understanding Spirituality

In the Indian languages there is no equivalent term for 'spirituality' but we have a term '*dharma*' which includes a wider and complex set of meaning aiming at maintaining individual and social order. The terms *moksa* in Hinduism and *nirvana* in Buddhism denote final liberation through a 'thorough transformation' of the self. In that sense, perhaps these terms are closer to spirituality as it is used in the West. In the Western understanding the term "Spiritual" is defined as "of or pertaining to, affecting or concerning, the spirit or higher moral qualities, especially as regarded in a religious aspect."[1] Though the term spirituality was not used in India till the latter part of the 19th Century, spiritual opposed to worldly and higher moral qualities in the religious aspect were relevant in the Indian traditions. Ursula King observes, "Admiration for 'Indian Spirituality' in this form was originally not something indigenous to Indian culture. Ideals expressed by the notion of 'spirituality' were an integral part of the Hindu tradition and this taken for granted. It was only in a dialectic situation, from a standpoint of contrast, that this 'spirituality' could suddenly come to prominence."[2]

## 2. Indian Contribution to World Spirituality

In their understanding of Indian philososophy, the British and German orientalists, based on their study and research on the Vedas and Upanishads, highlighted 'Indian spirituality' against the material world view of the West. In course of time the admiration of the Western scholars to Indian spirituality was appropriated by Indian thinkers like Raja Rammohun Roy, Keshab Chandra Sen, Bankim Chandra Chatterjee, Swami Vivekananda and Sri Aurobindo who were prominent among the pioneers in this line of thinking. These thinkers believed that India has to learn and integrate many aspects of the Western culture while the West has to imbibe the spirituality of India. Swami Vivekananda said, "We should give our ancient spirituality and culture and get in return Western science and technology."[3] Vivekananda's attempt was to stir the spirit of Indians to be the spiritual leaders of the world. He said, "Up India and conquer the world with your spirituality!"

Sr. Nivedita (Margaret Elizabeth Noble) the foremost disciple of Vivekananda was disillusioned with the Western culture devoid of spirituality and accepted Indian spirituality. Referring to Nivedita's search for genuine spirituality Ursula King wrote: "The searching questions of an educated young woman of the late nineteenth century, disillusioned with the West, thus found a personal answer in Indian spirituality which she accepted much more unquestioningly."4 Mrs. Annie Besant was of the opinion that "India's future is as a spiritual nation, as the teacher of the world in spiritual truth."5 From the beginning of the twentieth century many Western seekers enthusiastically accepted Indian spirituality as a way of life and a means of liberation.

Indian spirituality consists of a number of religious traditions, ethical values and practical disciplines oriented to God experience and final liberation. It cannot be reduced to any single tradition but is a way of life. According to Jordan Aumann:[6]

> In its widest sense, spirituality refers to any religious or ethical value that is concretized as an attitude or spirit from which one's actions proceed. This concept of spirituality is not restricted to any particular religion; it applies to any person who has a belief in the divine transcendent power and fashions a life-style according to one's religious conviction. In this context, one can speak of Zen Buddhist, Jewish and Muslim Spirituality as well as Christian Spirituality.

Among the spiritual classics of India the Bhagavad Gita is the most important one.

## 3. The Spirituality of the Bagavad Gita

The spiritual inquiry in the Bhagavad Gita, termed as 'yoga' is presented through the struggles and agonies of Arjuna the disciple of Lord Krishna. When Arjuna found himself in a crisis situation, first he thought that he was capable of solving the crisis but soon he realized his helplessness. This realization made him humble and open to seek the guidance of Lord Krishna. His genuine search for liberation is the main theme of the text. Arjuna represents all sincere seekers who aspire for liberation from the struggles of life and final liberation from repeated births and deaths. Liberation is possible only when one leads a life according to the divine will and plan which are revealed through the scriptures and enlightened persons. In the Gita, the author presents three ways of liberation, i.e., the way of action (*karma marga*), the way of devotion (*bhakti marga*), the way of knowledge (*jnana marga*). There is a fourth way of liberation known as the way of disciplined life (*rajamarga*). One cannot say that a particular way is superior to other ways. One way may be predominant at one stage later it may change or two ways may function as complementary. This division of ways of liberation is based on the mental aptitude of persons.

## 4. Ethical Living and Detachment in Spiritual Pursuit

The Buddhist way of liberation, though indebted to Hindu spiritual tradition, focused more on 'desireless existence' as the means of liberation. The early Buddhist monks wandered around experiencing homelessness and solitude. A monk is expected to live by begging and possess nothing personal except his/her habit and the alms bowl. However, the monastery is entitled to possess land, house, and other property. Buddhist spirituality based on the four noble truths and meditation aims at developing a desireless, detached human existence leading to nirvana. The Sikh spirituality is based on the fundamental principles of service (*seva*), chanting (*kirtan*) and meditation (*japa*). Based on the five great vows (*mahavrtas*) and ethical principles the Jains seek liberation from the earthly existence. Non-violence, even to plants and trees, is the most important principle for them because they accept the existence of soul even in the material objects. Parsis in India developed a spirituality based on the golden principle good thought, good words and good deeds and service to the supreme Lord Ahura Mazdah. Islamic spirituality is based on the strong faith in the one God (Allah) and in his messenger prophet Muhammad. Pilgrimage to Makkah (hajj), fasting during the month of Ramdan (sawm), alms giving (zakat), five times ritual prayer (salat) and holy war (jihad) are the five fundamental principles of Islam.

## 5. Christian Spirituality

The people of the Old Testament experienced God as a mystery and considered God as the Supreme. Jesus event shifted the focus from the other worldly God to God in our midst (Immanual). Christian spirituality is partaking in the Christ event (life, passion, death and resurrection of Jesus) through personalization of Christ mystery and his Abba experience. In this sense spirituality is a life of total detachment lived in the awareness of the all-pervading spirit to do the will of God. Christian spirituality, based on the kingdom values of love, forgiveness, compassion, suffering and *koinonia*, is a life of committed response in faith to God revealing himself in the person of Christ and inviting us to the ultimate goal of liberation, salvation and communion with him. The Church as the continuation of the mission of Jesus is the custodian of faith and spirituality of the faithful. The spirituality which Christianity developed based on the life and teachings of Jesus Christ invites the faithful to partake in the Jesus event through contemplation and ethical living. For centuries, the monastic contemplative spirituality was prominent in Christian spirituality. Contemplation in Christian tradition involves two factors, i.e., the way of affirmation, way of light (*kataphatic*) and the way of negation (*apophatic*). The desert fathers lived a life of total detachment from the world and dependence on God's providence. The concept of contemplation in Action by St. Ignatius of Loyola; Contemplation and action of Thomas Merton a Cistercian Monk, etc., are guide lines for the faithful in the Christian spirituality.

## 6. The Church's Approach to Indian Spirituality

We, the Christians in India, have a right and responsibility to integrate the positive elements found in other traditions in India. The Vatican II exhorted its members, we are expected "to learn by sincere and patient dialogue what treasures a bountiful God has distributed among the nations of the earth" (*AG* 11). The Church fathers in the Vat II was in clear admiration for the ancient Indian Spiritual traditions.

> In Hinduism, men explore the divine mystery and express it both in the limitless riches of myth and accurately defined insights of philosophy. They seek relief from the trials of the present life by ascetical practices, profound meditation and recourse to God in confidence and love.... Let Christians, while witnessing to their own faith and way of life,

> acknowledge, preserve and encourage the spiritual and moral truths found among non-Christians also their social life and culture (Vat. II, *Nostra Aetate no. 2).*

The Catholic Church is not against what is true and holy in other religions. She has a high regard for the manner of life and conduct, the precepts and the doctrines of the other religions. Vatican Council teaches: "Seeds of the Word lie hidden in these cultural and religious traditions of people," and these have to be respected. (*AG*.11), since "they are precious elements of religion and humanity" (*GS*. 92). Whatever truth and grace are to be found among the nations is a sort of secret presence of God, because, "doubtless, the Holy Spirit was already at work in the world before Christ was glorified." (*AG*.9). In *PerfecteCaritatis* we read, "The manner of living, praying, and working should be suitably adapted everywhere, but especially in mission territories, to the requirements of the culture and to the social and economic circumstances. (*P. C.* no. 3). Vatican II challenges us to ask ourselves sincerely before God, whether their way of life is a witness to the Gospel in a way suited to the character and condition of the people. (*AG* n. 40, also see *AG* n. 18, *LG* n. 46). Culture, tradition and belief system play an important role in the formation of any spirituality, including ours.

## 7. Popes on Other Religions and Cultures

Popes through their official teachings on various occasion encouraged the faithful to be sensitive to other spiritual traditions. Pope Pius XII in his "*Constitution Apostolica de Sacro Monialium" wrote:*[7]

> Let not the Gospel, on being introduced into a new land, destroy or extinguish whatever its people possess that is naturally good, just or beautiful. For, the Church, when she calls people to a higher culture and a better way of life under the inspiration of Christian religion, does not act like one who recklessly cuts down and uproots a thriving forest. No, she grafts a good scion upon the wild stock that it may bear a crop of more delicious fruits.

Pope John XXIII in his allocution to the General Board of the Pontifical Missionary Association, said:[8]

> When they find shining before them the light of a higher culture, missionaries do not ignore it, they help their brethren to transcend and complete it by welcoming the great revelation of the eternal Word of the Father who has scattered sparks of His truth among all nations and awaits from them glowing flames by a voluntary acceptance of His message... As Christ assumed a real nature, so too, the Church takes to herself the fullness of all that is genuinely human, wherever and however she find it and transforms it into a source of spiritual energy.

Pope Paul VI in 1964, during the Eucharistic Congress in Bombay, addressing the non-Christian Religious Leaders said: "Yours is a land of ancient culture, the cradle of great religions, the home of a nation that has sought God with a relentless desire in deep meditation and silence and in hymns of fervent devotion."

Pope John Paul II on 2nd February, 1986 addressing the representatives of Religion in Delhi affirmed:

> Integral human development requires a spiritual vision of man – that man is a pilgrim of the Absolute, travelling toward a goal, seeking the face of God. From this spiritual vision of man comes the strength to persevere in the cause, as well as the clarity of thought needed to find concrete solutions to man's problems. From it comes an indomitable spirit to win for each man and woman the rightful place in this world (To the representatives of religions, Delhi, 2nd Feb. 1986).

These popes through their official teachings, interactions with representatives and heads of other religions and prayer meetings have encouraged the faithful to develop a culture of respect and dialogue with other faiths and cultures. We, the Indian Christians are called not only to respect the other spiritual traditions but to integrate the positive elements found in other cultures and traditions. This call is all the more important in the pluri-religious context of India.

## 8. The Spirit beyond the Boundaries

The Indian Theological Association in its Statement during the 14th Annual Meeting at Ishvani Kendra, Pune said:[9]

> Spirituality is the inner dynamism of the Spirit or the Shakti, that energizes men and women to develop their ability for depth-awareness of reality, which is liberating, transforming, integrating and humanizing. It supposes a vision and constantly reviews and renews that vision. In order to be relevant in our religiously pluralistic country, every authentic spirituality must be contextual, liberative, inter-religious and holistic, that is, not constrained by the boundaries of major or minor living traditions and ultimately focused on the secular and the human.

Spirituality also proposes a set of practices (*sadhana*) coming from an underlying theory – adopted more or less spontaneously by some people which lead them to their perfection. In this process, spiritualities cross the boundaries of religious allegiances, although they generally flourish especially in the climate of one or more religions.[10]

The document continued:11

> We feel that our search for such a spirituality, authentically Indian and truly Christian, could give a new dynamism to the Christian community,

and help to build bridges of understanding and cooperation among the different religious communities of our country. We are convinced that Christians have to foster more and more those forms of spirituality which are connatural to the culture of the land. This will in no way dilute the Christian commitment. On the contrary it could make it deeper and more alive, and, at the same time, help Christians to overcome many obstacles in their interaction with people of other religions.

## 9. Some of the Main Characteristics of Indian Christian Spirituality

Indian Christian Spirituality is a faith response to the spirit revealed in the Indian social, cultural and religious context. Western spirituality is eschatological whereas Indian spirituality is universal and liberation oriented. Indian spirituality with its capacity to adapt, grow and incorporate other elements and trends takes an inclusive approach. Indian Christian spirituality has to imbibe this spirit of inclusiveness and openness to the Spirit working in and through other spiritual traditions. Following are some of the main characteristics of Indian Christian spirituality:

1. *Life in the awareness of the transforming presence of the Sprit:* The Spirit is present and active in all the spiritual traditions cutting across religious and cultures. No single religion can claim the exclusive possession of the working of the Spirit in the pluri-religious context of India. The spirit is working in and through various spiritual traditions. Indian Christian Spirituality, in order to be vibrant, has to be dynamically open to the guidance of the spirit by acknowledging, promoting and integrating thc positive elements from other spiritual traditions.

2. *Ascetical lifc as a way to salvation*: Christianity in India is inseparably associated with hierarchical structure, meaningless rituals and ceremonies, institutional and economic power and political influence. Because of these Christianity failed to represent the Kingdom values, which was the guiding principle in the life and ministry of Jesus. The Church in some parts of India doesn't represent the Christ who was poor and the friend of the marginalized. If only the Christians follow the master who didn't have a place to lie down and who went through villages and towns proclaiming the good news, we could easily dialogue with the ascctical traditions in Hinduism and Buddhism. Because these two spiritual traditions are well known for their austere life style and ascetical practices as means of liberation.

3. *Partaking in the Abba experience of Jesus:* The turning point in the life of Jesus was his Abba experience which led him to intense prayer and fasting in the desert. The spirituality of the desert fathers and the others who lived in solitude and prayer was an attempt to partake in the Abba experience of Jesus. The monastic spiritual tradition in Christianity was faithful to Jesus'

spirituality. But the organized church in course of time deviated from the path of Jesus and failed to communicate the spirituality of Jesus to the faithful.

4. *Deep loyalty to the church*: Swami Abhishiktananda was a Christian *sanyasi* who had the Advaitic experience of non-duality and the Christian experience of the inner mystery of the living God. "In his person," says Sara Grant "the advaitic experience of no-duality and the Christian experience of the inner mystery of the living God fused at the end into a transcendent unity in which the rich complexity of his life and personality were not destroyed but integrated into a wonderfully harmonious whole." (*Lord of the Dance*, 1987 p. 59). He was extremely simple in his life style suited to a *sanyasi,* he had deep loyalty to the church even at the point of misunderstanding and criticism. Throughout his life he exhibited extraordinary loyalty to the Church and its mission.

5. *Contemplative life and action*. Abhikshiktananda was fully aware of the need for deeply contemplative prayer for all in the church. In connection with his vision of a "pilot seminary" for priests, he stressed the need for understanding from within the contemplative heart of Hindu India, so that they will be able to contribute to the deeper understanding of the mystery of Christ which would flower into an authentically Indian and Christian contemplative life, liturgy and theology. In 1969 Swami wrote to his sister referring to the National Seminar: "The aim is the renewal of the Whole Church in India, and my role is to insist on the values of contemplation and on the integration of the deeper elements of Indian spirituality... If only I can give to the Christian world the honey I plunder in the Hindu world, and vice versa, however dislocating it may be at times, it is an immense joy all the same, and the solution of the antinomies which are turning both the world and the Church upside down!" (quoted by Sara Grant,1987 p.63). His attempt was to safeguard the contemplative goal in everything. He came to the awareness that the spirit is everywhere, in the depths of everything, inexorably immanent in all things.

6. *Spirituality is very closely associated with culture, worldview and life style:* Hinduism and other religions in their manifold strands, contributed greatly to the shaping of Indian culture, tradition and spirituality. Indian Christian spirituality is greatly indebted to all these spiritual traditions. Indian spirituality emphasizes the importance of the ways of liberation, uniqueness of the goal, single mindedness and continuous pursuit. Liberation is the ultimate goal of Indian spirituality. This implies self realization, freedom from the cycle of rebirth and death, union with the ultimate reality that is Brahman, experience of wholeness and fullness and being in harmony with the entire creation.

## Conclusion

Indian spiritual traditions, in general, value a life of total detachment, deep meditation in silence, surrender to God in extreme humility and respect and care for the other which includes the entire creation. The spirituality of Jesus was characterized by communion with the Father in deep prayer, total surrender to the will of God and commitment to the people of God particularly to the poor and the marginalized. The spirituality of Christians in India has to be rooted in the Abba experience of Jesus and enriched by the spiritual traditions of India. The spirituality of the 'disciples of Christ' in India should have some of these characteristics. Moreover, being Indians, we should integrate the positive elements from the Indian Spiritual traditions. Indian spiritual traditions, in general, value a life of total detachment, deep meditation in silence, surrender to God in extreme humility and respect and care for the other which includes the entire creation. Indian Christians, to be the genuine disciples of Christ, should imbibe the spirit and values of Indian spiritual traditions and live accordingly.

## Notes

1. Oxford English Dictionary 1970, vol. 10: 622.
2. Ursula King, *Indian Spirituality and Western Materialism* in Ideas for Action Series, New Delhi: Indian Social Institute 1985, p.4.
3. Gambhirananda. *History of the Ramakrishana Math and Mission Calcutta*: Advaita Ashram, 1957, p. 102
4. Ursula King, "Indian Spirituality and Western Materialism" in Ideas for Action series, New Delhi: Indian Social Institute 1985, p.12.
5. Annie Besant. *Essays and Addresses*, Vol. 4 (London: The Theosophical Publishing Society, 1913), 41.
6. Jordan Aumann, *Spiritual Theology* . London Sheed and Ward, 1979. P. 17
7. Pius XII, "Constitution Apostolica de Sacro Monialium", AAS 43 (1951) 6-7.
8. Pope John XXIII, Allocution to the General Board of the Pontifical Missionary Association, 16 May 1963, CML. 28 (1964) 60.
9. Indian Theological Association in its Statement during the 14th Annual Meeting 28-31 December, 1990 at Ishvani Kendra, Pune, *Word & Worship*, Vol. XXIV No. 3 March 1991, p. 103.
10. *Word & Worship*, Vol. XXIV No. 3 March 1991, p. 103.
11. *Word & Worship*, Vol. XXIV No. 3 March 1991, p. 104.

PART FOUR

# ROOTED IN INDIA: FAITHFULLY AND JOYFULLY

# 19

# The Church Open to the Rural People: The Church in Ahmednagar Area

**Michael Bansode**

The Catholic missionaries came with a burning zeal to Ahmednagar, Maharashtra, in the year 1831 to preach the Gospel as result of their own spiritual experience of God. Missionaries shared their personal experiences of missionary activity bringing people to the faith in Jesus Christ and in the establishing of churches. In line with this endeavour today the Ahmednagar mission is a flourishing one in Maharashtra. It is also closely connected to Papal Seminary.

Therefore, I would like to provide you a comprehensive understanding of evangelizing or mission. Today missionaries face a few more challenges in this mission. The first challenge, the phenomenon of modernisation is a real challenge, but along with it, come the phenomena of urbanization, new technology, secularization, cultural and religious pluralism.

Evangelisation is a complex process, i.e. the renewal of humanity, witness, explicit proclamation, entry into the community, acceptance of signs, apostolic initiative. (EN 24) Today we need to to rejuvenate the great mission work of the foreign missionaries in Ahmednagar.

The concept 'mission' can be traced back to God's activity *ad extra* which is always through Christ (Eph 1: 4). This divine activity *ad extra* can be termed as '*missio Dei.*'[1] The root notion of mission is 'sending.'

## The Biblical Understanding of Mission: Old and New Testament

Selection of Israel as the chosen people is not a rejection of the other nations, rather only as a model and example, to be prophet and priest to all the nations. Moses was the first missionary of whom we have any knowledge.[2] The New Testament understanding of mission centred on the Great Commission (Mt 28: 16-20) making God's abiding presence among all people. This message is evidently and obviously a universal one, with special focus on the Gentiles as evidenced by the Acts of the Apostles.

## The Church Understanding of Mission: Vatican II and Post-Vatican II

This mission was entrusted to the Church at Pentecost, rendering the Church missionary by its very nature. Vatican II came up with documents: *Ad Gentes (which holds that the Church is missionary by its very nature)*,[3] Evangelii Nuntiandi (which affirms that the task of evangelizing all people constitutes the essential mission of the Church),4 andRedemptoris Missio (re-emphasizing the command of the Risen Lord, "Make disciples of all nations"). It is in the Trinitarian communion that the Church lives, moves and has its being. This has been brought into sharp focus by Pope John Paul II, in his apostolic exhortation Ecclesia in Asia.

Therefore I would like to deal with the historical and political formation of Ahmednagar, the early history of Christianity and the protestant influence and the difficulties which the Catholic Church faced with regard to evangelisation. It also focuses on the Jesuits, who laid the foundations and spearheaded the growth of Christianity in Ahmednagar for over 165 years.[5]

## 1. Christianity in Ahmednagar

Ahmednagar District has held an important position for Christians in Maharashtra. Right from the early 19th century, it has been a great centre for Protestant-Christian activities such as medical, charitable, social and developmental works. The most outstanding monument of Christian involvement in the educational field is the founding of Ahmednagar College, a college affiliated to the Poona University.[6]

Pope Gregory XVI issued his famous *Padroado*[7] by which evangelizers could be sent from Europe. Without prior permission from the civil authorities they were allowed to go and preach the Gospel in India. It was presumed that it was impossible for the *Padroado* clergy alone to spread the faith in the Indian subcontinent effectively. Thus, though Portugal claimed spiritual monopoly over the whole subcontinent, *propaganda-fide*[8] priests were sent to those parts in which the *padroado* had no effective existence.[9]

After the order of the sacred Congregation of *Propaganda-fide* in 1869, to appoint missionaries in every mission for the conversion of people around, opportunities were sought in Ahmednagar. "In the next few years some *dalits* were converted in and around Ahmednagar through the efforts of Bishop Meurin, and Fr. Weniger, a military chaplain.

It is important to note here that the initial thrust of the missionaries was to work for the conversion of the *Brahmins* who, as priests and *Vedic* scholars, dominated the entire Hindu society. This approach was advocated by many and the missionaries did try their best to get acess to the *Brahmins*. But the *Brahmins* and the higher castes were not receptive to the Christian doctrine of brotherhood of all people and advocating equality to all, as it went against the *Chaturvarnas* based on the idea of inequality that gave them a higher rank and dominance over the lower castes.[10]

So against this background, the conversion movement of the low caste who were open to receive the message of Christ in Ahmednagar was a great opening for the Jesuit missionaries.

**Early History of Christianity:** On 12th August 1803, Lord Wellesley, defeated Tipu Sultan of Mysore. He further attacked Ahmednagar and established the British rule by conquering the forts and the city from the *Marathas*.11 Protestantism in Ahmednagar had its beginning in 1812 when a small group of students of Williams College in Massachusetts decided under the shelter of haystack to establish a foreign mission.

"They landed in Bombay in 1812 as missionaries of the American Board of Commissioners for Foreign Missions. They sought their way to Ahmednagar in the same year and carried on with social work till 1830."[12] After few decades their mission work flourished so much that the local people acknowledged their missionary as well as social work and designated their mission as the Jerusalem of Maharashtra.[13]

**The Roman Catholics:** The Catholic Mission started its missionary works in Ahmednagar in 1831.[14] There was also a Catholic priest present at St. John's Catholic Church, Bhingar15 in Ahmednagar, as a chaplain for the British military.16 Records show that Fr. Antonio de Cruz, a Portuguese diocesan priest performed the first baptism in 1831.

From 1833 to 1852 the mission Ahmednagar was looked after by the Portuguese diocesan priests.17 From 1852 to 1854 it was cared for by the Italian Discalced Carmelite Fathers who operated under the Bombay Missions. From 1854 onwards the Jesuits took over.

**The Protestant Influence:** The American Marathi Mission (AMM) started the missionary process forty years before the Catholics. The AMM opened schools and institutions in the vernacular. "The first school that pioneered efforts in the field of women's education was named 'Clare Bruce High School' and was opened in 1838. In 1882, another school was built for the education of boys. The first Teachers' Training College in Maharashtra, 'Union Training College,' was 1864."18 The opening up of education to all classes of society produced many Marathi authors and poets. Many text books were written by the missionaries and locals educated by these missionaries.[19]

Fr. Thomas Stephens, the first English Jesuit to come to Goa, wrote the Catholic classic *Kristapurana* in the Marathi language. Due to composing difficulties, unfortunately, he used the Roman script.[20] In spite of being published in 1619 it came to prominence only in 1956 after Shantaram P. Bandelu, a Protestant from Ahmednagar, rewrote the *Kristapurana* using the *Devnagari* script.[21] Soon the Marathi speaking colleges included essays from the *Kristapurana* in their syllabus and acknowledged it as one of the great classics of Marathi literature.[22] Salvation Army started the 'Evangeline Booth Hospital' in 1939. This hospital has till date been serving the poor and sick of the area.[23]

## 2. Indian Pioneers of Evangelization

The conversion of some high caste *Brahmins* encouraged other high caste youth such as Vishnu Bhaskar Karmarkar to embrace Christianity in 1853, a promising Khoja Muslim to embrace Christianity. The most notable person, KrishnaraoSangale, a leading Marathi hymn writer and a pioneer in the indigenization of Christian music embraced Christianity. Narayan Tilak, Laxmibai Tilak, PanditaRamabai and Bhasker Hiwale also embraced Christianity.[24] In the early decades of the mission, conversion from humbler castes like dalits took place oftener.

**Narayan Vaman Tilak and Laxmibai Narayan Tilak:** Narayan Vaman Tilak was born in 1862 at Karazgaon, in Ratnagiri in Maharashtra in a Hindu Chitpavan*Brahmin* family.[25] During the period of 1869-1873, he studied in the town of Kalyan near Bombay and primarily studied Sanskrit literature during the next four years in the town of Nashik. He was married to Laxmibai. Laxmibai had no formal schooling. However, through her husband Tilak's encouragement, she learned to read and write Marathi. She further mastered the language to the extent of later writing her autobiography, *SmrutiChitre*, which today is considered to be an autobiographical masterpiece in Marathi.[26]

On accepting Christianity, Tilak lived in Ahmednagar and served the church as a preacher for about 24 years right until his death in 1919. Tilak experienced Christ as the Great Mother. A devotee in his relationship with Christ, he experienced all fine qualities of a beloved Mother in and through Christ. Tilak was an earnest seeker after spiritual enlightenment, and found in Christ the perfect *Guru*. He thus experienced Christ as the great Mother and the *Guru*.[27]

Tilak a Marathi Christian poet was convinced that the Christian Gospel needed to be communicated to Indians in Indian spiritual expressions and forms.[28] His noted masterpiece is the *Kristayan* which is based on the life of Christ.[29] In 1842 while in Ahmednagar he founded the Marathi magazine

*Dnyanodaya***.** Today it has already completed more than 160 years of existence and is the oldest surviving Marathi publication. It is still being published from Ahmednagar.[30] He performed his missionary activities in the Ahmednagar region with the AMM for twenty one years. He taught in the Ahmednagar Theological Seminary. He helped Pandita Ramabai in her translation of the New Testament. Tilak composed over a hundred Christian devotional songs in Marathi in the *abhanga* form. In 1909 he also commenced composition of the epical *Khristayan*. He was able to complete only 11 Cantos while the rest of the Cantos (12-74) were completed by his wife Laxmibai and the last one (75th Canto) was completed by their son Devadat.[31]

**Bhaskar Pandurang Hiwale:** In 1882, Rev. James Smith the AMM's missionary started the first higher secondary school for all category of students. The mission High school's building was a historical palace. This same palace was later converted into the Ahmednagar College in 1887. But for many reasons the concept of college came to an end. It is only after 60 years which means in 1947 that Rev. Dr. Bhaskar Pandurang Hivale, a local from Ahmednagar felt the need of establishing a college at Ahmednagar.[32]

The Ahmednagar College began in this mission, as a Christian Minority institution. It was the first centre for higher education committed to liberal humanist ideals and has been renowned for its role in social justice initiatives.

## 3. The Jesuit Mission of Ahmednagar

The arrival of one of the co-founders, the zealous missionary and model St. Francis Xavier only laid emphasis on the same. In 1542 before Xavier landed in Goa, the Franciscans were firmly established there. However after Francis Xavier, many Jesuits of different nationalities followed in his footsteps and walked all over the Indian mission soil.[33] "The German Jesuits who were sent to India in 1854. They had made significant contributions around the globe."[34] It was on 2nd August 1854 that the Jesuit General, Fr. Beckx, entrusted the Bombay-Pune mission to the German Province. The mission work in Ahmednagar district is called Marathi mission in the Pune Diocese and today covered an area of 1,50,000 sq. km.[35] It started in Kendal an insignificant village about thirty kilometres from Ahmednagar.

**The Need of Catechists:** A catechist had to come from among the people, had to know the language, customs and mentality and had to be the suitable link between the people and the missionaries, who were in the initial stage exclusively foreigners. Fortunately individuals with these requisites were found in the Ahmednagar District and they were trained.

**Growth and Achievement:** Among the missionaries who worked in this region, Fr. Maximilian Zinser is easily one of the most outstanding. This great man was a *Jnana Yogi*, a *Bhakti Yogi* and a *Karma Yogi* all rolled in one. A devout and dedicated missionary, Fr. Maximilian Zinser is particularly remembered for his mastery of the Marathi language. Not only did he teach Marathi in the first Catholic school of Ahmednagar at Sangamner, but he also wrote three grammar books in Marathi and became the first Catholic priest to translate the New Testament from Greek into Marathi.[36]

Catholic literature was promoted in Ahmednagar right from the early years. The magazine '*Niropya*' was born in April 1903. The centenarian *Niropya* ranks third in the list of longest surviving publications in the Marathi language,[37] this Magazine is circulated till date.

Another great missionary, Fr. Pius Geisel S.J, made St. Ignatius's motto: 'All for the greater glory of God,' a personal philosophy, built the first hospital in Shrirampur. This visionary priest, seeing the total non-availability of medical facilities at the time, chose to build a hospital in Shrirampur because of its central location in the district (1953). The Sisters of Charity of St. Anne took over the administration of the Hospital in 1989.[38] The Hospital at Shevgaon is another achievement for the Jesuits. Besides, there are many dispensaries in the district run by the different sister congregations who were all initially invited by the Jesuit fathers.

The following mission stations opened: Kendal (1878); Valan (1889), Sangamner (1892) and Rahata (1910). New stations were opened during the following years at: Tilaknagar (1953), Ghodegaon (1961), Shevgaon (1963), Pathardi (1966) Rahuri (1969) and Shrirampur (1982).[39]

**The Catholic Marathi Mission:** The Papal Bull issued in Rome in 1861 granted permission for the conversion of the natives.[40] Officially it was in 1878 that the Catholic Marathi Mission began."[41]

**Catholic Diocese of Nashik:** The Diocese of Poona was established in 1887 and exactly 100 years later in 1987 His Holiness Pope John Paul II erected the Catholic Diocese of Nashik. It consisted of five districts, at that time the total Catholic population of this diocese was about 71,000.[42]

During the last hundred years, in this diocese a majority of the converts to Christianity have been that of the scheduled caste origin. Due to their acceptance of Christianity, the Christians are either mostly excluded from Government assistance.

In the Ahmednagar district there was a time when all the parishes were in the hands of the Jesuits. Today the work load is divided because a good number of native priests has joined the diocese. The appointment of Rt Rev Thomas Bhalerao as Bishop gave the missions of Ahmednagar a marvellous boost.

## Conclusion

The history of the Ahmednagar is rich in its diversity. Its historical and political importance gives us a perspective in which the missionary work put in has an added significance. Today the Ahmednagar District is booming with schools and colleges carrying the torch of the Christian mission far and wide.

The Catholic community in this area seems to have made a considerable amount of progress both spiritually as well as economically. Today there are many local religious and priests working in the place, covering almost all the areas of life. I am confident that this Church will be able contribute towards a better Maharashtra and India!

## Notes

1. A Latin Christian theological term that can be translated as the, "mission of God," or the "sending of God." Cf. Joseph Mappilaparambil, "A Paradigm Shift in Church's Outlook on Mission," in *Be My Witnesses,* (eds.) Jose Varickasseril and Mathew Kariapuram, (Shillong: Vendrame Institute Publications, 2001), p. 102.
2. Cf. Harold Henry, *The Missionary Message of the Old Testament,* (London: Kingsgate, 1944), p. 15
3. Cf. Paul VI, *Ad Gentes*, n.2.
4. Cf. Paul VI, *Evangelii Nuntiandi*, n. 15.
5. Cf. Lawrie Ferrao, *Reise*, (Mumbai: Printania Offset Pvt. Ltd., 2004), p. 34.
6. Cf. Matthew Lederle, "Only God Makes Things Grow," in *Smarnika,* (ed.) William Falcao, (Ahmednagar, 1986), p. 2.
7. *Padroado* is the Portuguese word for patronage. It implied both rights and duties. The chief right was that of nominating candidates to all the usual ecclesiastical offices in the region, where the king was patron. The Holy See granted this right to the Kings of Portugal in the 15th and 16th centuries as a reward for their sustained efforts in providing men and money to evangelize the countries of Africa and Asia. This right carried with it the corresponding obligation of spreading the Christian faith and that of establishing and maintaining the Church in the area in question. Cf. Joseph Thekkedath, *History of Christianity in India*, p.414.
8. *Propaganda Fide*: Since its establishment in 1622 the Congregation of *Propaganda fide* in Rome has been used by the Holy See for evangelization in mission territories. Its guidelines on procedures for enculturation were mainly concerned with the missionary situation in Asia but they were applicable universally. Cf. Josef Metzler and George Kottuppallil, "Mission History of Asia and Pacific Region," in *following Christ in Mission,* (eds.) et al, Sebastian Karotemprel, (Bombay: Pauline Publications, 1995), p. 178.
9. Cf. Joseph Velinkar, *German Jesuits on the West Coast of India*, (Pune: Marg Prakashan, 2005), p. 10.
10. Cf. Jadhav, *Evangelization as Community Building*, p. 121.
11. Cf. Nagarkar, *Glimpses of Ahmednagar,* p. 45.
12. Vijaya Punekar, "Dnyanodayachya Panantun Maharashtrachya Prabhodhanacha Magova," in *Dnyanoday,* Sudhir Sharma (ed.), (Ahmednagar: Dnyanoday Trust, 1997), pp. 55-57.
13. Cf. Punekar, "DnyanodayachyaPanantunMaharashtrachyaPrabhodhanachaMagova," in *Dnyanoday,* p. 72.
14. David, *Mission: Cross-Culture Encounter and Change in Western India,*p. 42.
15. One of the oldest churches in Ahmednagar is St. John the Baptist Church, at Bhingar, established in 1833. The present Parish Church was built in 1851. Ten years later, the residence was set up in the same campus by the Jesuits. In the early years of parish, the

Capuchins were in charge, and later the diocesan priests took charge. The Jesuits followed them and took care of the parish for 130 years. In 1986, the Bishop of Pune, Rt. Rev. Valerian D'Souza, entrusted the pastoral care of St. John's Parish to the Salesians of Don Bosco. During these past 30 years, Salesian work has rapidly spread across the Nagar *Taluka*, and has contributed to the spiritual growth and the socio-economic development of the people in several villages. Cf. Rodrigues, "Bhingar," in *Memory*, p. 154.

16. Cf. Matthew Thalanany, *St. John the Baptist Bhingar,* (June, 1986) Source: House Archive, (Ahmednagar, 1986), p. 8.
17. Cf. Nigrel, "Ahmednagar," in *Memory*, p. 156.
18. Gazetteers of the Ahmednagar Precedence *Ahmednagar District*, p. 140.
19. Cf. David, *Mission: Cross-Culture Encounter and Change in Western India,* p. 60.
20. Cf. Ruth Hivale, *AmacheKrithrthSahajivan,* (Pune: Vidharb Marathwada Book Company, 1968), p. 142.
21. Cf. CamilParkhe, *Contribution of Christian Missionaries in India*, (Anand: Gujarat Sahitya Prakash, 2007), p. 160.
22. Hivale, *AmacheKrithrthSahajivan,* p. 142.
23. Cf. Hivale, *AmacheKrithrthSahajivan,* p. 178.
24. Cf. Clerk A., *American Marathi Mission Report*, p. 36.
25. Cf. Joseph Barnabas, *Christian Witness,* (Ahmednagar: Dnyanoday Trust, 1960), p. 10.
26. Cf. Hans Staffner, *Dialogue Stimulating Contacts with Hindus,* (Anand: Gujarat Sahitya Prakash, 1993), p. 157.
27. Cf. Robin Boyd, *An Introduction to Indian Christian Theology,* (Delhi: ISPCK, 2004), p. 115.
28. Cf. Falcao, "Christology in the Writings of Narayan Vaman Tilak," in *Jeevadhara,* p.223.
29. Cf. Tilak and Devdatt Tilak, *SampurnaSmrutichitra,* p. 480.
30. Cf. Parkhe, *Contribution of Christian Missionaries in India*, p. 153.
31. Laxmibai Tilak and Devdatt Tilak, *SampurnaSmrutichitra,* pp. 480-482.
32. Cf. Dharmadhikari, *Ase Hote Nagar*, p. 53.
33. Cf. Lederle, "Only God Makes Things Grow," in *Smaranika,* p. 2.
34. Velinkar, *German Jesuits on the West Coast of India*, p. 4.
35. Cf. Lokhande, "Pune Jesuit Mission and Catechists in the Ahmednagar District: Reminiscences, Appraisal and Perspectives," pp. 72-73.
36. Lawrie Ferrao, *Reise*, p. 21.
37. Cf. Parkhe, *Contribution of Christian Missionaries in India*, p. 153. It may be recalled that Fr BhausahebSansare SJ, the present Rector, Papal Seminary, is the currend editor of this journal.
38. Cf. Lokhande, *Mission Missionary and Me,* p. 135. It may be noted that Fr Geisel is one of the founding fathers of Papal Seminry, Pune (1955).
39. Cf. Velinkar, *German Jesuits on the West Coast of India*, p. 86.
40. The mission work in the Ahmednagar district is called Marathi mission in the Pune Diocese. Cf. Lokhande, "Pune Jesuit Mission and Catechists in the Ahmednagar District: Reminiscences, Appraisal and Perspectives," p. 73.
41. Rodrigues, "Bhingar," in *Memory*, p. 154.
42. Cf. The Catholic Bishops Conference of India, *The Catholic Directory of India 2013,* (Bangalore: Claretian Publications, 2013), p. 1487.

# 20

# The Miniscule Presence of Catholics in Jammu-Kashmir: A Small Signpost of Love and Compassion

**J. Charles Davis & A. Soosai Nathan**

## Introduction: The Rich Heritage of Kashmir

Kashmir was once known for its unique culture, beauty and heritage, but today its problems are militancy and terrorism. "If there is a paradise on earth, it is this, it is this, it is this,"[1] said the Moghul emperor Jahangir referring to Kashmir. For the ordinary people of India, Kashmir was, as Asghar Ali Engineer comments, "nothing more than a beautiful tourist spot which they aspire to visit at least once in their life-time. It was paradise on earth."[2] This land of exuberant natural beauty has people who have their own needs, aspirations and dreams for peace, prosperity and progress.

The social ethos and cultural practices of India and Kashmir had common features during the rule over Kashmir of the Mughals (1589-1753), the Sikhs (1819-1846) and the Dogras (1846-1947).[3] Kashmir Sufism was reconcilable with the common milieu and spiritual attitudes of Kashmiri Hindus, who followed a *Shaivite* cult very similar to Islamic monotheism. The Sufi virtues of contemplation, asceticism, renunciation, abstinence, simplicity and coexistence were common to Hinduism and Buddhism. The *Kashmiriyat,* the sense of being a Kashmiri, is basically ethnic not religious.4 It is the socio-cultural tradition evolved over thousands of years in Kashmir. Kashmiri Hindus and Muslims are a real inheritors and essential part of this tradition. It is because of these virtues embedded in the psyche of the Kashmiri people that there was no bloodshed, no intolerance and no communal riots during Partition in 1947 when the rest of sub-continent was filled with communalism and fanaticism. That is the reason, why someone recited the *Rishis'* (Sufi) saying during the Independence days:

> We are the progeny of the same parents,
> Then why should we differ?
> Let Hindus and Muslims together adore God alone.
> We came to this world like partners
> We ought to share our joys and sorrows together.[5]

## 1. The Present State of Jammu and Kashmir

By the logic of the Two-Nation Theory of the Partition in 1947 the Princely State of Kashmir, with a Muslim majority population should have gone to Pakistan. Jinnah tried to persuade the Hindu Maharajah Hari Singh, who was the then ruler of Kashmir. This failed. He then sent in tribal raiders to seize Kashmir by force within eight weeks of Partition and after them regular Pakistani troops. Hence, the Maharajah had to seek military help from the Indian Dominion. The Maharajah said, "In view of the great emergency of the situation, I have no option but to ask for help from the Indian Dominion, which was not possible without my State acceding to the Dominion of India."[6] The majority of the people of Kashmir also wished the same as they feared theocratic rigid rule under Pakistan and threw in their lot with India because "India was *secular* and *democratic.*"[7] Thus, the Maharaja signed the Instrument of Accession to the Indian Dominion on October 27, 1947 according to which he ceded only three subjects, namely, Defence, External Affairs and Communications.8 M.J. Akbar feels that there are two Kashmir problems, which are predominantly political:[9]

> The first began on 15 August 1947 when India and Pakistan became realities without the state of Jammu and Kashmir becoming a part of either.
>
> The second problem actually began in the month of June in 1984. The critical decision was the unsavoury sabotage of Farooq Abdullah's government by a Delhi government more concerned with power than democracy. Suddenly the mood in the Valley began to sour. Kashmir had come into India because of the promise of secularism and democracy; secularism was in tatters, by any token; and now democracy had been brutalised.

Today, political instability tied with religious antagonisms caused the Kashmiri Hindus to flee to other parts of India and escalated cross-border terrorism in the 90s forcing an extreme presence of military forces. Since then more than 50,000 people have lost their lives. Schools, colleges and universities are often closed due to bomb blasts and threats. Fear rules the day. Political will is the answer to bring permanent peace to the war-stricken state of Jammu and Kashmir, where there are different political orientations:[10]

> In Indian-controlled Kashmir, there are three distinct political orientations in this fundamental sense – *pro-independence* (the preference of a decisive majority in the Valley and of a sizeable minority in the Jammu region), pro-India (the preference of a majority in Jammu as well as in Ladakh and of a small minority in the Valley), and *pro-Pakistan* (the preference of a relatively small minority in the Valley and an even smaller one in Jammu). ….in Pakistani-controlled areas, I believe two major and fundamentally different political orientations exist there as well – *loyalty to Pakistan* and support for the '*third option' of independence*."

## 2. The Presence of Catholicism in Jammu and Kashmir

In 1880 the Vicariate of Punjab was created, by separating Agra Vicariate and forming into a Vicariate. Since then, the Mill Hill Missionary Society of London, began the missionary activity in Kashmir. On 6 July 1887 a new Prefecture of Kafiristan and Kashmir was created out of the Diocese of Lahore with Msgr. Ignatius Brouwer MHM as the first Prefect Apostolic on July 13, 1888 and Rawalpindi as the headquarters. The prefecture comprised of Rawalpindi, Northern Punjab, North West Frontier Province, Kashmir and Ladakh. The Jammu region was entrusted to the Belgian Capuchins. After the partition of India in August 1947 communication problems due to the continued tensed political situation between India and Pakistan forced Vatican to erect the Apostolic Prefecture of Kashmir and Jammu o January 17, 1952 with Msgr. George Shank MHM as the first Prefect Apostolic and Srinagar as the headquarters. In July 1963, the Prefecture Apostolic of Jammu and Kashmir received Msgr. Baerkamp as the successor. On May 14, 1968, the territory was reconstituted and renamed as the Prefecture of Jammu and Kashmir. The Prefecture comprised the districts of Kashmir and Ladakh till then part of the Rawalpindi diocese and the districts of Jammu and Poonch which belonged to the diocese of Lahore. On the retirement of Msgr. Baerkamp, the Prefecture was entrusted to the Indian Capuchins by the Holy See. Msgr. Hippolytus Kunnunkal OFM. Cap. of St. Joseph Province, India, was appointed the first Indian Prefect Apostolic.

The Capuchin Fathers Wilfred Mubarak and Peter Celestine were pro-prefects till 1986. Raising the Prefecture to the rank of a Diocese on 10 April 1986, the Holy See appointed Msgr. Hippolytus Kunnunkal as the first Bishop of Jammu-Srinagar.[11] His consecration took place in Rome on 29 June 1986. On September 7, 1986 Bishop Hippolytus was installed at St. Mary's Cathedral in Jammu Cantonment. The Diocesan curia which was in Srinagar since 1952 was shifted to the Bishop's House attached to St. Mary's Cathedral on 23 December, 1986. Bishop Hippolytus gave a solid foundation to the mission creating many institutions in the fields of pastoral, education, social and health ministries and inviting simultaneously many congregations of men and women to cater to the needs of the people. The Capuchin missionary Dr. Peter Celestine Elampassery was appointed the second Bishop of Jammu-Srinagar on 7 May 1998. Under his leadership, the diocese expanded the mission and service centres. On 3 December 2014 the diocesan priest Fr. Ivan Pereira was appointed the third Bishop. The missionaries have made steady progress in the field of evangelization, education and development, and continues to be a Christian witness in Jammu and Kashmir. The service of Irish Presentation sisters through education and of Franciscans Missionaries of Mary in health sector in Baramulla deserves a special mention for their fearless presence and relentless service for more than a century despite political instabilities and the killing of six people including the 29-year-old Spanish nun Sister Maria Teresalina Joaquina de Sánchez FMM during the tribal attack on 27 October 1947.

## 3. The Ministry of the Contemporary Church in Jammu and Kashmir

There are about 42 Parishes and Missions, 52 Diocesan Priests, 20 Religious Priests, 200 Religious Sisters, 18000 Catholics, 40 schools and a few health and social institutions. The priorities of the diocese are:

To be Living Witness to the Gospel Values.
Spiritual Formation of the Christian Faithful.
Charity for the Promotion of Development.
School Education with the Christian Virtues.
Socio-economic Development and Health Care.
Emergency Service to the Migrated and Replaced.
Partnering with other NGOs and Movements for Peace

At the heart of the Christianity is the quality of compassion. We believe in and worship a God whose external action is caused by the deep movements of his heart. Priests, sisters, catechists and laity volunteer to reach out in compassion and love to the displaced, to the uprooted, to the homeless. This is what exactly happened in 1999 when the Kargil War took place between India and Pakistan. Due to war, thousands of people in the border villages in Jammu region had to flee from their homes and the Catholic Social Service Society, the official body of the Diocese for social concern and social action, came to the aid of those internally displaced through relief and rehabilitation works. This society is known for its activities of empowerment of the poor and the marginalized, and especially in times of natural calamities. The Society has been consistently working towards capacitating the rural youth through vocational, entrepreneurial, and skill training programmes.

Education seems to be the best means in this land of terrorism and instability. Majority of the priests and sisters in the diocese are doggedly engaged in witnessing to the Gospel values of love and peace through imparting good education to the children of the Himalayan State, especially to those in the rural areas.

## Conclusion

As Bishop Hippolytus recalled, "the government as well as people of other faiths have an open mind and respect for the Catholic Church and its various activities. It is a special blessing that religious minded people of other faiths look upon priests and religious as men and women of God." The people of the state have always welcomed the services of the Church and appreciate the missionaries for what they receive through education, medical care and relief. The diocese situated at the foot of the Himalayas makes a steady progress in spite of the difficulties and struggles amidst the problems like terrorism. During the past 100 years there has been a real sharing of love and joy through education, health care, relief, etc. to the people in this mission. It is indeed an evangelisation without conversion. The people of the state value the charitable work and respect the Christian missionaries for the tremendous work done to them without which there may have been a real problem, especially in the field of education.

## Notes

1. "Paradise on Earth," *Maharashtra Herald*, Pune, Friday, 27 December, 1991, 5.
2. Asghar Ali Engineer (ed.), *Secular Crown on Fire: The Kashmir Problem* (Delhi: Ajanta Publications, 1991), 1. This was a special issue of *Islamic Perspective,* Vol. VI, No. 1 (1990).
3. Jagmohan, "Past, Present, Future," *Seminar* 392 (April 1992): 18.
4. Syed Shadbuddin, the Editor of *Muslim India* said this in an interview. See "Some Prominent Muslims Speak," *Manthan,* Vol.XVI, No. 3 (October-December 1995): 158.
5. Jagmohan, "Past, Present, Future," 19.
6. Ibid., 16.
7. Asghar Ali Engineer (ed.), *Secular Crown on Fire*, 8.
8. The terms and conditions of Accession were subsequently incorporated in Article 370 of the Constitution of India, which was adopted on November 26, 1949 and came into force on January 26, 1950. see Teja Singh, "Restoration of Autonomy to Jammu and Kashmir," *Mainstream,* 17.
9. M.J. Akbar, "The Second Problem," *Seminar* 392 (April 1992): 15.
10. Sumantra Bose, "Kashmir: Sources of Conflict, Dimensions of Peace," *Economic and Political Weekly,* Vol. XXXIV, No. 13 (March 27-April 2, 1999): 762.
11. It may be mentioned that a special scholarship in memory of Rt Rev Bishop Hippolytus Kunnunkal OFM Cap was inaugurated for the students of Papal Seminary by Mr Rony George (Director, Chaitanya Institute for Mental Health), Pune, on the day of the academic seminar, November 8, 2018.

21

# The Hope of a Tiny Minority: The Challenges and Prospects of the Catholic Church in Gujarat

**Joseph Mattam SJ**

## Introduction: The Land and the People

Gujarat came into existence as a separate state only in 1960, but its history is closely linked to the Indus Valley civilization. It is blessed by many gods and goddesses: Kali in the East, Kunteshwar Mahadev in the South, Amba Mata in the North, Dwarka of Lord Krishna and Somnath in the West. Though it is the land of the Mahatma and is dotted with temples and shrines, it is notorious for its communal outbursts and violence and is still deeply casteist; untouchability is still practiced in many subtle ways, especially in the rural areas.

The population of Gujarat (nearly 50 million) consists of some 315 castes, intermediate castes, Scheduled Castes and Scheduled Tribes. One classification puts the Hindus at 89.54 per cent, Muslims 8.53 percent, Jains 1.37 per cent, Christians 0.28 per cent, Sikhs 0.07 per cent, Buddhists 0.02 per cent, other religions/no religions 0.09 per cent. The Scheduled Castes are said to be 7.15 per cent, and Scheduled Tribes 14.22 per cent.

This article looks at the challenges and promises that this tiny minority of the Christians in Gujarat faces.

## 1. History of the Catholic Church in Gujarat

The foundation of the Ahmedabad Mission was laid, unknown to themselves, by the Daughters of the Cross at Bandra when a few Gujarati Vankarsfrom the present-day Kheda district, working in their convent, were baptized there in 1891. In 1893 Bishop Dalhoff of Bombay sent Father Manuel Gomes to Gujarat. Those baptized in Bandra provided a good contact point and with their help Father Gomes baptized 18 boys in 1893. From 1894, the German Jesuits came to Anand and despite opposition from the caste people, opened new stations in Kheda district, and saw to the training of catechists and started many schools for Vankar children who had till then no schooling.

In 1914, Father Zurhausen founded the Anand Credit Cooperative Society, which became the economic backbone of the Christian community. When the First World War broke out the growth of the mission was arrested by the internment of the German Jesuits. The Aragon province of the Society of Jesus took over the Mission; Father Grau landed at Anand in 1921. The mission grew steadily, and in 1933, the Ahmedabad Mission was separated from Bombay as an independent ecclesiastical unit under the leadership of Father J. Vilallonga, SJ.

The Church entered the modern period from 1934, when under the able leadership of Father Vilallonga, S.J. the mission grew rapidly. The period 1934-1949 may be considered a period of mass conversion among the Vankars. The number of Catholics in 1934 was 8,884, whereas in 1949 there were 26,970. A combination of various circumstances helped this process. The missionaries too were often ill-treated and humiliated along with the Vankars.

One of the major events of this period is the founding of the first religious congregation of women in Gujarat. The *Little Daughters of Saint Francis Xavier* (LD) was founded in 1936. The number of educational institutions also increased significantly during this period; by 1942 there were 208.

In 1948, the Ahmedabad Mission was entrusted to the Castille Orientale Jesuit province headed by F. Arellano who sent to Gujarat as many as 65 young Jesuits in four years before he himself joined them. On May 31, 1949, the late Edwin Pinto, SJ, was appointed the first bishop of the newly established diocese of Ahmedabad. From 1955, there is a decline in the new baptismal entries. One of the major reasons for this decline is the State regulation which makes baptized SCs ineligible for the special privileges available to non-Christian SCs.

For nearly seven decades all the missionary efforts were concentrated in Kheda. Given the universal nature of the Church, it was felt that being present only to the Vankars, a mere 2 to 3 per cent of the total population, was not justified. Already in 1949, the missionaries had resolved to go out to other groups as well; it became a reality only in the sixties.

In I960, missionary work was started in South Gujarat from the Bharuch centre. Bharuch, Surat, Valsad and the Dangs districts were eventually contacted and work was done among the various groups of Tribals, mainly the Vasavas, Gamits, Kokanasand Chaudhrys. The work developed fast, and the Baroda diocese was carved out of Bombay in 1966, with the late Ignatius D'Souza as its first bishop.

In 1962, the Sabarkantha mission among the GarasiaTribals was opened. There too scarcity and famine conditions spread all over the region and the work of the Fathers was much appreciated. In 1964 starts the mission to the caste Hindus in Mehsana district and the Majiranas in Banaskantha district. This was indeed a new approach in the sense that people were not taken out of their caste, but while preserving their caste way of life and customs, they had to reject the high-low categorization of people and all discrimination on the basis of caste. In spite of opposition from within and outside the Church, the community has grown steadily.

In the seventies Saurashtra was entrusted to the Carmelites of Mary Immaculate (CMI). They began schools, various social activities, and eventually in 1977 that region became the Rajkot diocese with the late Jonas Thaliath as the first bishop. After the CMIs came the SDBs, SVDs and SFX priests and a number of congregations of women religious.

One of the major achievements of the modern period has been the training of diocesan priests, especially in Ahmedabad, Gandhinagar and Baroda dioceses which have a sizable number of diocesan priests and seminarians.

Religious, both male and female, and priestly vocations from Gujarat have been on the increase since some years. The area of inculturation, especially in architecture and forms of worship, has been attended to with creditable success.

## 2. The Gujarat Church before and after Vatican II

Working exclusively with the Vankar community, the Kheda mission remained active and growing up to the fifties. With the mid-fifties the expansion came to a halt. About this period of the mission, one often hears the complaint that the early missionaries were concerned only with 'saving souls' or making 'rice Christians'. This accusation is not at all justified. It is true that they did help the people when there was a famine or a calamity, and there might have been conversions following such a calamity. But they did much more than that. Already in 1914, we find Father Zurhausen opposing the caste people for destroying the windows of the Vankar School and *forcing them to apologize; enabling the Vankars to have windows in their* houses facing the caste locality (Suria, 1990:144 ff). Their eagerness to start schools to educate Vankar children, especially girls, was geared to fighting injustice and helping the development of the people. Defense of the rights of the people was one of the main reasons for the rapid growth of the mission in the first half of the century.

Already in the late fifties a shift was made from relief to developmental activities to empower the people to be shapers of their own future, through conscientization and organization for unity and self-reliance. Some of the activities undertaken with this objective are: food for work; irrigation projects (wells, pumps, etc.); loans of seeds, fertilizers, buffaloes; dairy cooperatives; village farmers' association, developing the habit of saving; income generating projects for women, *mahilamandals*to make them self reliant and to organize them; slum dwellers' housing and educational projects;income generating projects;soil conservation; water-shed management; education, etc. Various camps tried to raise the consciousness of the people through social analysis about their rights and about injustice done to them. The Behavioural Science Centre (BSC) in Ahmedabadtook up rural education, especially in Adivasi areas.Theyalso took up a study of the Dairy Milk Cooperatives in South Gujarat. Through Trained Village Workers (TVWs) they have been ableto help these cooperatives. Another undertaking of the BSC is cooperative social forestry, which provides regular income. These cooperatives have trained people to expresstheiropinions in public, to gain self-respect, to fight for their rights and to become self-reliant. *The Rajpipla Free Legal Aid Centre* worked with the villagers in the Rajpipla area. *The Modasa Free Legal Aid* activities have helped many Tribals to regain their lost land, have given them courage and enabled them to stand up for their rights. The *Asha Deep Youth Centre* at Vidyanagar too, has done much to conscientize the Kheda youth. Thepolice and the moneyed class are not allowed to go scot-free afterharming the poor, as in former days.

Another major change in the post-Vatican II period is the re-introduction of high schools, especially for poorer children in villages. Another major change has been the efforts of some of the priests, especially in South Gujarat, to get to know the people, their culture and languages (very different from Gujarati). They also insist on lengthy training period for the catechumens. Fr Raymond Chauhan, S.J. has produced grammar books and dictionaries for a number of south Gujarat dialects which do not have any written literature.

## 3. The Impact of the Church on Gujarat

In Gujarat with just 0.28 per cent of Christians made up mostly of SCs and STs who do not carry much weight in society, it is too much to expect any great impact. However, there are a few areas where the Church has made some impact.

The Church is recognized as being with the poor and the victims of society. This has been acknowledged from the very beginning, so much so that people used to wonder what the priests saw in this despised class of SCs (Lobo, 1991: 18 ff).Those who are not afflicted by the cancer of caste—the upper caste people—are criticizing conversions, not because they are interested in the welfare of the 'untouchables', but because such conversions will deprive them of free servants. So, those who oppose the Church here do so because she is with the poor, and her work is affecting the status quo, for when the people became Christians and are educated, resist exploitation and demand theirrights.

The Catholic schools have projected an image not only of good performance, but also of dedication, honesty, and a system without bribes. The Christians, in general, are recognized as hard working, reliable and trustworthy; the ethos of honesty among Christiansin general is recognized. The spirit of cooperation and hard work is spreading in the villages where there are Christians.

The correspondence course, though rather recent, is having a great impact on the people. Each year, more than 2,000 inquirers receivethe message of Christ and the centre receives very beautifultestimonials of how this message has touched their lives. Many correspondents ask for further information about Jesus and theyexpress a desire to serve the poor.

At least, someChristians have consciously rejected the *varna* ideology, and itseffects are being felt at least in Kheda district. The stage of fright and flight has now given way to fearless affirmation of theirVankar identity with dignity and a readiness to challenge the higher castes.

On the cultural front, the contribution of the Spanish born Father C. Valles, SJ, is well-acknowledged by all. He has won the highest awards in Gujarati literature and is one of the most read authors in Gujarat. The Gujarati translation of the Bible has been applauded by eminent literary critics as a major contribution to Gujarati literature. There are also Catholic novelists and poets like IgnasMacwan and Joseph Kavi whose contribution is recognized in the literary circles. One of them has also won the Sahitya Academy award.

In South Gujarat, though not numerous, the Church is a force that cannot be overlooked. In the tribal areas it has helped the people to free themselves from the fear of evil spirits, and many have begun to relate to God as a loving Father.

## 4. Evangelization: Obstacles and Challenges

The so called high caste people resort to various means to hamper the work of the Church. They would term conversion as 'denationalization' since Christianity is considered by some as foreign. The real fear, however, is that when the depressed classes awaken and fight for 'social and economic equality' and, when the Tribals who were leading a 'secluded and peaceful life for centuries in the hilly forest areas, almost at the periphery of the mainstream of Indian nationalism', join hands with others in demanding their rights and stand for the cause of human freedom, they will be a force to reckon with.

Hinduization of the SCs and the STs is another challenge that the Gujarat Church faces. All over the state, there is a planned campaign to convince the Tribals and SCs that they are Hindus. Hindu festivals are celebrated by all these in an unprecedented manner. The unjust government discrimination against the baptized SCs is a serious deterrent for them in exercising their free choice of Christ.

The Church as it is today is still too clerical, and the whole Church does not feel itself the evangelizer.

Officially, the universal Church has moved to ecumenism and wider ecumenism, yet the Church in Gujarat is still following the older pattern of indifference, if not opposition, at least with regard to others, except in very limited cases. One can understand that the Kheda Christians would find it hard to enter into dialogue with Hindus who have been a source of much suffering to their community; even with other Christians there are problems.

Still another obstacle to evangelization is the crisis of faith and motivation among the over-busy clerics. Not a few hold that the younger generation of religious and priests are reluctant to carry on with direct evangelization work. Theologically too, there are confusions as to the need and goal of evangelization if people are saved in their own religions.

There have been very creditable efforts at inculturation in architecture, liturgy, food habits, and also at entering into the myths and world-view of Tribals and Dalits. More needs to be done. But an area where we have defaulted is in our solidarity with the people we work with. Our life-style, mode of travel, food habits, our confusing efficiency with apostolic effectiveness, etc., convey the impression that we are not men/women of God. Older generations still reminisce about the earlier missionaries who walked or cycled to the villages, spent the nights there sharing the meagre food of the people, and compare their attitude with the present-day culture of jeeps we have adopted.

## 5. Looking Ahead

The Catholic community seems to have come of age with the laity awakening to their responsibility in the Church. There is a serious questioning of the leadership by the people. Though at times these questionings may be due to personal grievances, by and large, there is a growing awareness of mutual accountability. Most of the churches built in tribal area are the work of the people and according to their own style; they celebrate Christian feasts in line with their own genius and culture. They have the New Testament in some of their languages even if there be no other written works in these dialects. Increase in vocation to the priesthood and religious life augurs well for the future. The growing number of diocesan clergy and the arrival of other groups of men and women religious offer better chances for consolidation of the work done and further expansion.

We are, in a sense, at the crossroads—we can live in the past, glorifying ourselves on what had been done, and carry on with clericalism, leading to further deepening of anti-clericalism which is already rather strong and will do great harm. The BSC in Ahmedabad has proved that handing over leadership roles to the laity is possible and necessary.

An aspect that augurs well for the Church in Gujarat is the diversity of Christians in the state: we have here the Vankars, Tribals of the south and the north, Christians from caste groups and non-Gujaratisresiding in Gujarat. Each of these has its own specific contribution to make to the self-understanding of the Church, its inculturation and mission in spreading the Gospel.

A major contribution the Church in Gujarat can make to the whole Church is the matter of discovering one's self-identity. Forced by circumstances, people have come to look at themselves the way others see them: as lower and higher, pure and impure, etc., and identify themselves with that image. This is unchristian. Here, we are forced to question the value system which is based on equating the person with what he/she has, does, and appears to be. This has to be radically rejected in order to come to a deeper source of self-identity. You are what God has made you: God's child, empowered to be creative, free and to love as God loves (Mt 5:43 ff). We Christians will have to consciously reject the *vama*ideology and deal with all as equals, brothers/sisters, work with others in a spirit of cooperation, sharing, etc.

Therefore, there is the necessity of a death and resurrection: dying to elements that have become irrelevant, like clericalism, the acceptance of the value system of the world, allowing ourselves to be exploited, and the acceptance of doctrinal formulae as the whole of Christian life. We need to emerge, be born again with a fresh outlook: viewing and accepting all as equals before God, all as recipients of the mission given by Christ and as agents for the spread of the Gospel, giving greater importance to families. A lot more energy will need to be spent on forming good families and making them carriers of the Good News. Evangelization is understood in terms of the Kingdom (Mattam 1988: 359ff).The whole community of believers is the agent of this proclamation by word and deed, and its concern is the building up of communities of love, freedom and justice. Hence, we readily join hands with all those who are working for the same goal though with different names. We address ourselves to the most needy, oppressed and neglected, not just to prospective converts. It is to announce Jesus, not just as a truth to be believed in, but as one who is with them in their struggle for a better humanity, for a more just society of sharing and caring. In this view, though numerical expansion is not our primary concern, we would not be opposed to baptism if it means the celebration of one's acceptance of Christ and his ways, of one's conversion (Mattam, 1988: 450 ff). The fact that already for some years we do not limit our work to the Christians or prospective converts, but reach out to all the needy holds great promise to forge a unity of the needy on the basis of their being needy, and not on the basis of caste or creed.

One of the areas requiring keener attention is the dialogue with people of other faiths, so that, first of all, prejudices are removed and, secondly, we can work together with them for a better Gujarat for all its people, and not just for a few.

## Conclusion

One may conclude that the Church in Gujarat, though still very small in number and beset with many difficulties, is full of hope for the future, for, we stand with the Spirit of God renewing the face of the whole earth in God's own unforeseeable and inscrutable ways. God will not spare us conflicts and trials, but we are confident of God's strengthening presence in all of us (Lk 12:11-12). Death to our own limited, selfish interests will be the channel for the Spirit's unlimited work and of his using us as his instruments for the bringing about of the Kingdom of God.

# 22

# The Tribal Church in Jharkhand: Building Communities of Love and Justice

**Arjen Tete SJ**

## Introduction

The involvement of the Church in the lives of the Adivasis in Jharkhand has witnessed some hostile reactions recently. Undoubtedly, some people perceive the presence of the Church as a boon for the progress and prosperity for the Adivasis. They underscore the way the Church has extricated the Adivasis from the abyss of illiteracy, superstition and primitiveness and propelled them to the portals of modernity. Others, including the current state administration, view the Church as a curse holding it responsible for the perpetuation of poverty among the Adivasis. The state legislature has recently passed the anti-conversion law. Consequently, the Christians are being harassed, heckled, and hounded. The government of Jharkhand has been intimidating the Church accusing its institutions of diverting their foreign donations for religious conversions. Highlighting the Church's commitment to liberation and empowerment of the Adivasis right from its arrival in Chotanagpur as well as acknowledging its limitations this paper explores the task of the Church in Jharkhand during these challenging times and suggests the way the leaders of the Church could form themselves to minister effectively to the people of God.

## 1. The Origin and Growth of the Church in Jharkhand

Christianity came to Chotanagpur first through the Gossner Evangelical Lutheran (GEL) Mission from Berlin in 1845. Within a short span of 1845 to

1920 six different missions came there representing different Churches. Apart from GEL, the Anglican Mission, also known as Society for Propagation of Faith (SPG), the Roman Catholic Mission, the United Free Church of Scotland, the Dublin University Mission and the Seventh Day Adventist (SDA) established their Churches. Considering it to be a "fertile" ground for mission and conversion many more Churches came there in later times. Each of these Churches has made significant contributions towards empowerment of the Adivasi communities.

The origin of the Chotanagpur Roman Catholic Mission dates back to July 1869 when Fr. Auguste Stockman, the first Jesuit, came to Chaibasa from Calcutta where ten years earlier in 1859 the first two Belgian and one English Jesuit missionaries had begun the Bengal Mission. Fr. Stockman's work among the Ho Adivasis was not very successful. Hence, he moved to Ranchi in 1875. The arrival of Fr. Constant Lievens in 1885 gave real impetus to the Mission. Subsequently, the Loreto Sisters came from Ireland in 1890, the Daughters of St. Anne in 1897 and the Ursuline Sisters of Tildonk, Belgium in 1903.[1] The Mission grew rapidly. On account of its rapid growth, by decree of the Holy See, 25th May 1927, the Archdiocese of Calcutta was divided. Rev. Louis Van Hoeck was installed as the first Catholic Bishop of Ranchi. Rev. Oscar Sevrin succeeded him in 1934 and remained in the office for 18 years. Spearheaded by these farsighted Bishops, massive expansion of Primary and Middle School Education brought about deepening of faith. A limited Christian group grew into a progressive Adivasi community.

Three social processes – Hinduisation, Islamization and colonization – were at work among the Adivasis before the arrival of the Christian missionaries. The Hinduisation of the Adivasi chiefs and the establishment of larger Muslim kingdom were breaking down the Adivasi institutions and systems. With the introduction of the *jagirdari* (service grants) system, the Muslims rulers paved the way for the emergence of outsiders as middlemen. The process of colonization expedited the process initiated by the Muslim rulers. The rapacious exploitation and brutality of control over the Adivasis accelerated with the introduction of Zamindari System by the British to collect revenue.[2] The revenue collectors, mostly outsiders (*dikus*) from North Bihar, sucked the blood and sweat of the Adivasis and turned them pale. The Adivasis were used for exploitative labour in their own lands in Chotanagpur or in the tea gardens in Assam.

Seeing the plight of the Adivasis, Fr. Lievens learnt the local language, studied land laws and defended the distressed Adivasis in the court against the landlords. He creatively combined social justice to the conventional method of missionaries. This new method liberated the Adivasis from the shackles of superstitious beliefs and the landlords. Fr. Lievens' legal help and solidarity with the afflicted resulted in the massive growth of the Catholic converts.

Similarly, with the expert advice and help from German Catholic Missionary Fr. John Baptiste Hoffmann to the Government, the Chotanagpur Tenancy Act (CNT) was passed in 1908 according to which non-Adivasis could not possess the Adivasi land. Fr. Hoffmann also created the Chotanagpur Cooperative Society in 1910 which helped the Adivasis economically to be free from the clutches of the moneylenders. The beginnings of the Chotanagpur Roman Catholic Mission were marked by compassion, creativity, concern for the poor and their spiritual need. Hence, Christianity in Chotanagpur emerged as a mass movement.

Despite their empowering work among the Adivasis, the early missionaries of Chotanagpur have been criticized for being selective in providing help to the people. It is said that catechumens who did not care to be baptized and who did not prepare to receive the Holy Communion were not granted loans from Roman Catholic Cooperative Bank. Fr. Lievens, too, has been criticized for demanding conversion of the whole village in exchange of legal help from him. The missionaries thus seemed to have given confusing signals to the Adivasis. They seemed to have stressed on the one hand "spiritual" reasons for conversion and demanded collective conversion for secular benefits on the other.

Withstanding such criticisms, the Church in Jharkhand has grown and matured in a relatively short time. Since the advent of Fr. Lievens to Chotanagpur in 1885, during the last 132 years, there have been 32 bishops, 4 Archbishops, 1 Cardinal consecrated from the Adivasi Christian community.[3] Innumerable priests have been ordained. Hundreds of men and women have joined different Religious Orders and have dedicated themselves from this community for the spread of the Gospel and service of Universal Church not only in India but also in different continents of the world. How did it happen? An apt answer to this may be the two following sentences from the pioneering missionaries: "If it is God's work, it will be realized (Fr. Lievens)," and "We did not fail, it was God's work (Fr. Hoffmann)."

Indeed, God's work and human cooperation seem to be going hand in hand! Speaking about the history and growth of the Adivasi Church in central India at the Asian Mission Congress in Chiang Mai, Thailand, on 20th October, 2006, Cardinal Telesphore Toppo, president of the Catholic Bishops' Conference of India, then, narrates an instance of the providence of God, thus: "In 1903 an Apostolic School was opened. A few years later, some candidates ready to do their Philosophical studies were sent to Kandy, the only Papal Seminary in the Indian Sub-continent. It was then that the famous Apostolic Delegate Mons. L.M. Zaleski (even though he was a great admirer of Fr. Constant Lievens), made this disparaging remark, "It will take a hundred years before we can even think of ordaining a tribal priest!" He forbade the Rector to admit the Adivasis. But providentially he added, "If the Archbishop of Kolkata wants to ordain them, then let him have his own seminary." Happily, the Holy Spirit inspired the Jesuit Archbishop of Kolkata to approach the Holy See, and thus St. Albert's Seminary, Ranchi was opened in 1914." This seminary has formed in 100 years thousands of priests. The seminary has been moving towards indigenization of theology and spirituality giving space for Christian reflection and articulation on Indian and Adivasi cultures in its annual journal *Sevartham*.

The Chotanagpur Mission has matured today and branched out in Jharkhand alone forming many dioceses: Ranchi, Gumla, Simdega, Khunti, Jamshedpur, Daltonganj, Hazaribag and Dumka.[4] This Mission was covering the present dayneighbouring states of Chhattisgarh, Odisha, West Bengal and Bihar as well. Hence, many dioceses like Jashpur, Raigarh, Ambikapur, Sambalpur, Rourkela, and Purnia are also its offshoots.

The Church leadership, in these dioceses, is in the hands of the Adivasis. As has been noted above, right from the beginning missionaries had a chain primary and secondary schools. Hence, thousands of Adivasis have received formal and informal education. Apart from priests and nuns, the Adivasi teachers, government officers, doctors, and lawyers, professionals in private organizations, administrators and village level social workers are engaged in nation building all over the country.

## 2. Some Significant Challenges

It is true that the Church in Jharkhand is no more a nascent Church. But right from the dawn of this century it has been facing some hostile challenges from within and without. In the following section we try to locate some of these challenges beginning with those coming from outside.

**Communalization:** The Hindutva strategy has been trying to depict the Adivasis as Hindus in the Adivasi dominated areas of Jharkhand. The intention is to gain from the polarization between Christian Adivasis and those who have been Hinduised or follow local faiths (Sarna Adivasis). In 2003, Sangh Pracharak and former Chief Minister of Jharkhand Babulal Marandi claimed that the Adivasis were Hindus and they worshipped Hindu Gods and Goddesses. He justified that "everyone who had links with the Sindhu Ghati (Sindhu Valley) was a Hindu because the word "Hindu" derives its meaning from Sindhu."[5] The present Jharkhand government had come up with a malign campaign, on August 11, 2017 in all the local dailies in the state, which attributed a quote to Mahatma Gandhi questioning Christian Missionaries for trying to convert the Adivasis. "If the missionaries felt that conversion to Christianity is the sole path to salvation, why don't they start with me or Mahadev Desai," the ad claimed Gandhi (Desai was Gandhi's personal secretary) to be saying. The advertisement was splashed a day before the state government tabled its anti-conversion bill in the Assembly. Nobody knows if Gandhi ever said this but government was using that to target missionaries. The aim was to spread hatred against Christian missionaries and divide the Adivasis on the basis of their faiths. The Sarna Adivasis organized a series of agitations against the Church and burnt the effigy of the Cardinal Toppo.

Bishop Theodore Mascarenhas, secretary-general of the Catholic Bishops Conference of India (CBCI), the apex body of Roman Catholics, the very next month appealed to Prime Minister Narendra Modi to curb the spread of hatred by [Jharkhand] Chief Minister Raghubar Das. In his strongly worded letter, Bishop Mascarenhas said that he was compelled to write to Modi as he was disturbed over the politics of hate unleashed in Jharkhand. He further said that Modi had personally campaigned before elections in Jharkhand in 2014 on the inclusive plank of *sab ka saath, sab ka vikas* that "made Raghubar Das the chief minister of the state," but Das had begun "vitriolic attacks against the Christian community." "If the chief minister is unable to control his ideological hatred, then it is time for him to go," he said. Communalization is a great challenge faced by the Church today.

**Colonization:** Within a decade of its creation in year 2000, the government of Jharkhand signed some 104 Memoranda of Understandings (MoUs) with the corporate houses. In order for the MoUs to translate into real money, the Adivasis need to be moved. But, to compulsorily acquire tribal land and turn it over to private mining corporations is illegal and unconstitutional under the Panchayat Extension to Schedules Areas (PESA) Act, 1996. Hence, the government of Jharkhand amended last year two laws—CNT and Santhal Pargana Tenancy (SPT) Acts—that guaranteed the protection of the Adivasi land used for agriculture. The government declared their land as non-agricultural and, since non-agricultural land does not come under the purview of protective legislation, the Adivasis could be deposed.

Promptly, the CBCI team headed by all India chairman of tribal affairs, Bishop Vincent Barwa, and Ranchi Archbishop Cardinal Telesphore Toppo met governor Draupadi Murmu requesting her not to ratify CNT-SPT Amendment Acts, approved by the state Assembly during the budget session. The Adivasi community stands divided over the Amendments. The Adivasi Christian community stands in support of the demand raised by Catholic Bishops. The Kendriya Sarna Samity, a socio-religious-cum-political outfit of the Adivasis took out a procession against the archbishop and Bishop Nirmal Minj and burned their effigies on M. G. Road, Ranchi. Polarization prevents Adivasi assertion, required to ensure they do not unite to oppose mines, the setting up of factories and exploitation of forests.

**Criminalization:** The government of Jharkhand has been treating Christians like criminals. The Church's effort to protect land is seen as a major reason for official hostility. The state-backed crackdown has begun on Christian missionaries in which the police have initiated a probe on several non-governmental organizations (NGOs) run by them for alleged misuse of foreign funds which they legitimately acquired under a Foreign Contribution Regulation Act (FCRA) license. The police action is a part of the ongoing harassment of Christian missionaries by the Raghubar Das-led BJP government in the state. It was also claimed that funds were being used to support the Pathalgadi Adivasi movement that seeks greater autonomy from both the federal and state governments. Christians were targeted for their faith and faced violent attacks, false accusations and arbitrary actions by various government functionaries. Once again, the bishops met the governor Draupadi Murmu, who is the representative of the Indian president, to report that the state government had used its Anti-Terrorist Squad (ATS) to probe Christian institutions.

In addition to these challenges coming from outside, the Church in Jharkhand is also facing trials from within. We can locate some of them as follows:

**Clericalism:** The temptation for parochialism, even though not prevalent, is present among the Jharkhand Church leaders. It has led to inordinate attachment to one's ethnic and linguistic groups. Ethnic feelings seem to grip the Church leaders in such a manner that "power, money, position" become matters of great importance. There was a time when the missionaries were sought after as "men of integrity and justice" to resolve Adivasis' justice issues. Today missionaries themselves seem to have fallen prey to these forces, thus curtailing their apostolic efficacy, vitality and solidarity with the laity.

**Corruption:** There are instances when Church leaders in Jharkhand have been in financial scandals. What has come to light as a modus operandi is that they run or support NGOs associated with family members or friends in a bid to profit from such endeavours. A few others have embroiled themselves in such scandals associating themselves with greedy caste people and working as their agents. In good faith or out of ignorance village people invest their hard-earned money only to be told that they have been swindled. It is true that an individual member gets snared but the Church as an institution loses its face.

**Class Consciousness:** The Church-run institutions have liberated and empowered the Adivasis but they have also promoted individual success at the cost of the community. Helped by modern education, the Adivasi Christians have gone in good number to metropolitan cities and have forgotten their roots. Streamlined with the mainstream people they consider themselves as of higher class. Consequently, villages continue to lag behind. Literacy, food security, modern gadgets and amenities might have increased in some places but the diminishing quality of faith and morals and growing violence pose serious challenge to the Church in Jharkhand.

Despite excellent works of liberation and empowerment by the Church in Jharkhand, the age old problems are still present today. The divide between the rural and urban, the rich and the poor, remains very much the same if not widened further. Agrarian distress, land alienation, massive unemployment, both in rural and suburban areas, are leading young Adivasi boys and girls, to migrate to the cities and are unwittingly getting caught in trafficking. Some have preferred to take up guns and have joined the Naxalite movements. The standard of education in government schools continues to be abysmal. Hence, the demand for opening good Christian schools continues. How does the Church in Jharkhand face these challenges is a relevant question.

## 3. Important Opportunities

It is not sufficient for the Church in Jharkhand and its leaders to be just "grief-gatherers." We have seen above how the Church leaders have responded promptly to some of the challenges coming from outside. Following the trajectory of their responses the Church in Jharkhand needs to be conscious, critical, creative and compassionate in creating an Adivasi community of love and justice.

**Community Building:** Christians account for just 4.3% of Jharkhand's population, Muslims 14.53% and Hindus 67.83%, according to the 2011Census. If the figure for Hindus is relatively low in comparison to many states, it is because 12.84% of the state's population counted themselves as followers of "Other Religions" who are primarily those of the Sarna faith. It is obvious that after decades of providing healthcare and education facilities, Christian missionaries have not managed to convert the Adivasis on a scale as is alleged.

It is an immediate need to oppose those who propagate communal hatred among the Adivasi communities in the name of religion. The Church in Jharkhand is passing through troubled times. As responsible citizens of this great nation, it is the duty of every Christian to uphold the Constitutional values of our country. The Adivasi Christians need to be on their guard not to let the dirty politics and selfish motives of antisocial elements permeate into their society and culture.

Christianity is not merely about administering and receiving of the sacraments or about going to heaven and avoiding hell. It is about creating a community of love (Mt 22:34-40). Like Fr. Lievens who studied law to help the Adivasis, the Church leaders today ought to know the Constitution of the country well. The Church leaders ought to make use of the pulpit to awaken and alert their flocks about more important issues staring them in the face like poverty, unemployment, livelihood, health, and education. The flocks need to be made aware of their rights. The Church leaders ought to promote unity and communal harmony among the Adivasis so that they can fulfill the spirit of self-rule, self-dignity and self-determination.

**Capacity Building:** The early missionaries of Chotanagpur radically opted for the poor. They were interested in the development of the Adivasis.

They advised them how to handle legal issues. Christian converts were emboldened and empowered to challenge the *Zamindars*. The landlords felt threatened and became hostile to Christians and missionaries. The Church in Jharkhand has been selflessly serving the marginalized through education, social action and various other ministries. The devil is trying to hinder its work today. Hence, Christians have to be strong in faith and in the teachings of Jesus Christ, and continue capacity building works for the poor. In the context of human rights abuses, land alienation, poverty, illiteracy, the Church in Jharkhand has the opportunity to be a prophetic voice of the voiceless. A prophet does not merely announce; he also denounces. The Church ought to give hope for holistic liberation.

Compassionate Church Leaders: The early missionaries of Chotanagpur were sympathetic listeners. They listened to the people and reinvented their method of approaching and answering to their questions and needs. They were contemplative, compassionate and creative. The contemporary situation of the Church in Jharkhand needs leaders who are spiritually alert to the grace and demands of the Spirit of God. It calls for a discernment that will make them listen to what the Spirit is telling them in the concrete life situation. Hence, a module of socio-cultural analysis could be integrated in all seminaries and the Church-run educational institutions and parishes in Jharkhand. Compassion demands that the Church leaders become sensitive to the sufferings of their people. It makes all brothers and sisters irrespective of community, creed, caste and class. In this process the Church leaders could also get rid of the baggage of clericalism.

Committed Action and Collaboration: Action without critical reflection can be disastrous activism. The Church leaders need to create networks with other Church bodies, the media, civil society and other secular forces to promote a pluralistic and inclusive society. Often our involvements tend to get confined to church structures and issues. So many people of goodwill including people of other religious traditions are co-labouring with us seeking a more just world. The Jharkhand Church leaders need to commit themselves in deep solidarity with the marginalized and collaborate with the forces that have taken up the causes of the poor participating in peoples' movements and dialoguing with secular thinkers.

## Conclusion

The paper has highlighted how the Chotanagpur Catholic Mission, begun in Ranchi, has affected the lives of the Adivasis. It has affirmed that the Church in Jharkhand has liberated and empowered the Adivasis from superstitious beliefs in the spirits and from the clutches of landlords. It has offered them an alternative faith for holistic liberation. Despite its extensive ministries of education and empowerment, the Church continues to face various challenges from within and without. Although alarming, these challenges open up new horizons and fresh possibilities for the Church. Being conscious of these challenges, the Church in Jharkhand and its leaders need to invigorate themselves to building communities of love and justice through compassion, collaboration and committed action.

## Notes

1. MarianusKujur and Sonajharia Minz, ed., *Indigenous People of India: Problems and Prospects* (New Delhi: Indian Social Institute, 2007), 303.
2. GladsonDungdung, *Whose Country is it Anyway?* (Kolkata: Adivaani, 2013), 20.
3. Agapit Tirkey, *The Liberator of Tribals: Short Biography of Servant God Father Constant Lievens, S.J.* (Ranchi: Ranchi Jesuits, 2014), 71.
4. Tirkey, *The Liberator of Tribals*, 71.
5. Dungdung, *Whose Country is it Anyway?,* 255.

# 23

# Whither Goes the Church in India? With Special Reference to the Church of Chotanagpur

**Shashi Minz**

How can the Church spread the message of love and Joy in India? What has Papal Seminary contributed to the growth of the Church in India? How can the future priests in India offer witness to the love of God to our people, both Christians and non-Christians?

In the light of my experiences as a woman belonging to the indigenous community of India, the Oraons, I, as a member of the Indian Customs and Central Excise and Narcotics, want to share my experiences and hopes with the readers. Since they flow from my heart, they may not be well-organized. They are anecdotal. They invite the readers to dream of an Indian Church that is inclusive, vibrant and joyful. The Word of God helped me through all difficulties and trials during my service. It was a great task to balance my home life with that of the bureaucracy.

## 1. Knowing Jesus

It was a wonderful and blessed experience to know that we have a Cardinal in our midst from our own community. When we heard the news of the appointment of the new Cardinal, the Oraon (Kurukh) ethos and pride rose higher. The octogenarian mother of the newly acclaimed Cardinal Rt Rev Telesphore Toppo was delighted and she shed tears of joy and thanked the Almighty God as she sat in her warm bed awaiting the special occasion. The Cardinal blessed as all when we met her on that auspicious day. The Cardinal's mother who was a centenarian was blessing us along with him. Hence today we have my great, great aunts Mata Cecelia and Mata Bernadette of the Daughters of Saint Anne, Ranchi, being beatified. They have given selfless service and have brought about a revolution in the homes of Chotanagpur with their service to the families of all the people in need along with the Ursuline nuns. They have been influenced by the Jesuit priests from the St Alberts Seminary, Ranchi who used to Celebrate Holy Mass for the Loretto nuns in Ranchi Doranda. Many more mothers in the states of Odisha, Chattisgarh and Jharkhand are delighted and blessed when they attend the ordination of their Santhal, Oraon, Munda, Ho, Kharia sons who have studied in the Papal Seminary, Pune.

It is also from the priests of Papal Seminary that Jesus is known to us personally. Their knowledge of the Good Lord and the Scriptures which they have received in this esteemed seminary which had its origin in Kandy (Ceylon, now Sri Lanka) is proclaimed to whole of Asia. The need of the hour is to ensure that persons from all backgrounds should be treated on equal footing, which is being done in this great Seminary.

## 2. Inspiring Personalities

There could be the temptation of promoting only one particular ritual church like Malankara rite mass or Latin mass or Kurukh,or Tamil mass or the Santhali mass. It is true that when we celebrate in our own culture and music and language Jesus really becomes personal and intimate. But we should also try to make Jesus widely relevant in our times as the great authors Michel Quoist and Anthony de Mello SJ have done through their books on Prayer, Contemplation and Awareness.[1] The book, *Song of the Bird* has helped many to mend broken homes and hearts especially in the lives of the laity in a secular country. Going beyond Syro-Malabar, Kurukh, Santhali, Bengali or Kannada Church, we should think in terms of a United Church of India. Only then can we survive in our beloved India. We need to reach out to every Indian in the countryside with the Word of God in the local language and promote Jesus in the culture of the place. Surely the Word of God translated in every language, is the need of the hour. I recall how Fr. Camille Bulcke SJ, from Ranchi, a Belgian scholar of Hindi did a marvelous work of translating the Bible into Hindi.[2] He showed the way to embrace the language of the place where one is at work. The whole of North India has benefitted by this translation of the *Pavitra Bible*.

Similarly, we find Mother Teresa of Calcutta speaking in Bengali despite being a part of the Irish congregation of Loreto nuns whose English was impeccable. Obviously, every language and culture should be promoted and given equal importance, especially in a place like the Papal Seminary, which has a wide spectrum of our nation representing every nook and corner of India.

## 3. The Future of the Church

I am glad to note that the Seminarians affirm their individual identity and at the same time go beyond. It is encouraging to note that after their training and formation in Papal Seminary they take the Word of God to all parts of the world and proclaim it faithfully and creatively. It is little wonder that the Congregation of The Missionaries of Charity attracts so many young men and women from all social and religious backgrounds to study, pray and worship the living Risen Lord. They go out in service of the poorest of the poor, picking up newborn children from the garbage and nurturing them back to life. Despite shortages of incubators, they look after the aged, the lepers and even the HIV patients.

The Papalites (those who have studied in Papal Seminary) promote and proclaim the Kingdom of God by believing in and worshipping the Risen Lord, whose personal encounter they experience in the depths of their hearts. By celebrating the Jubilee of its existence in India, we are acknowledging the selflesss service of many Papalites practically in all fields. The alumni have been successful in finding Jesus in their fellow human beings whom they are called upon to serve. In this context, Bishop Charles Soreng SJ and I had the chance to visit various Retreat Centres like Potta Ashram in Kerala, Tabor Ashram in Mumbai, Divine Mercy Centre in Faridabad and other Centres in Jamshedpur, Hazaribagh. These centres are doing marvelous job in deepening the faith of the people, and the source of their origin may be the Papal Seminary where they have been introduced to the worship of the living Christ, besides working for the good cause of building His Kingdom on earth.

## 4. Dialogue as Way of Life

At the same time, we need to pay special attention to the multi-religious experience of India. I had a refreshing experience of being immersed in flowing water of the Haridwar and had a healing experience during Kumbh Mela in Allahabad and Nashik, where I was posted in the Indian Revenue Service under various capacities. It was Fr Francis D'sa SJ[3] who opened my eyes to the multi-cultural religious experience. We used to meet every year as representatives from different religions and the sharing was truly enrichening.

We also need to be open to the world of business, politics and science. This realization was garnered very successfully by Rev Fr Job Kozhamthadam, a famous Jesuit scholar of Science and Cosmology, topper of Physics in St Xavier's College, Ranchi. It is through his various conferences and books, which opened for me a new way of relating to science and religion. I was very much impressed by his openness to scientific theories and how he related them to the religious insights.[4] I was happy to meet many enlightened clergy and scientists from all occupations, medical as well as pure science and cosmologists of different parts of the world. I understood that they were open to other religions and to the world and together we launched into the exploration of the unchartered paths of our Universe!

Exposure of the students of the Papal Seminary to the visiting faculty from Louvain the Marquette University, USA, Georgetown University and other Universities including, Oxford and Cambridge, have given us so many learned scholars like Rt Rev Phillip Ekka SJ and several others. Such priests, who have lived their committed lives, lead the faithful to the true faith. They inspire us to thank and worship the Living God in true spirit rather than confining ourselves to the stereotype of written prayers. They invite us to experience the liberating power of the Word of God, which has the power to heal, liberate and free us from all the bondages. They lead us to a life that is "fully human and fully divine."

## Conclusion: A Heart to Love and Forgive

Inspired by these great priests and scholars who are connected to Papal Seminary, we need a Church that can dance like David the sinner. We can sing the song of forgiveness, since we have been washed clean by the precious blood of Jesus. We can experience true miracles as Jesus did. I recall the great storm, Phalin, in October 2013, which battered the shores of Odisha and Andhra Pradesh. It was our fervent prayers that the storm should not devastate Bhubaneshwar and the Port of Paradeep. As assured by Jesus, people of our age shall work greater miracles than the ones done by Jesus. Such is the power in the holy name of Jesus our Eternal Saviour and Brother. We are going to inherit his wealth on Earth as it is in Heaven. Unfortunately thePhalin storm caused great harm to nuns of Missionary Sisters of Charity in Behrampur, who were taking care of over eighty lepers. They were left with no resources for their survival. I am grateful to God that together with MrsDugli Nayak, wife of an IAS officer, who was the former Rajya Sabha MP, we reached them the supplies even before the state government understood the emergency need.

I wish and pray that formation houses like Papal Seminary, where sanctity and blessings of the Lord prevail, enable the future Church leaders who have eyes to see and ears to hear and a heart to love and forgive.

## Notes

1. I have been much impressed by the writings of Anthony de Mello and Michel Quoist. Anthony "Tony" de Mello was an Indian Jesuit priest and psychotherapist. A spiritual teacher, writer, and public speaker, De Mello wrote several books on spirituality and led many people to a new experience of God through retreats and conferences. De Mello, Anthony. *The Prayer of the Frog: A Book of Story Meditations*. [Gujarat, India]: [Gujarat Sahitya Prakash], 2003. De Mello, Anthony. *One Minute Nonsense*. Anand, India: Gujarat Sahitya Prakash, 1998. Mello, Anthony De. *One Minute Wisdom*. New York: Image, 2013. Michel Quoist, was a French Catholic priest, theologian and writer, most known for his

bestselling book, Prayers of Life, first published in French in 1954. See Quoist, Michel. *Pathways of Prayer*. Windsor: Wilton 65, 2003. Quoist, Michel. *With open heart*. Dublin: Gill and Macmillan, 1983. It may be noted that Mrs Shashi Minz is using the term Papal Seminary as an umbrella term, including its sister institutes, Jnana-Deepa Vidyapeeth and De Nobili Colleges [The Editor]

2. Camille Bulcke was a Belgian Jesuit missionary in India, who attained pre-eminence in the Hindi language and came to be known as "India's most famous Christian Hindi scholar" Details could be found in Sundaram, V. Lawrence. *Jesuit Profiles: Some Eminent Jesuits of South Asia*. Anand, India: Gujarat Sahitya Prakash, 1991.
3. See the book in his honour. Amaladass, Anand and Rosario Rocha (Eds). *Crossing the Borders: Essays in Honour of Francis X. D'Sa on the Occasion of His 65th Birthday*. Chennai: Satya Nilayam Publications, 2001.
4. Kozhamthadam, Job. *Contemporary Science and Religion in Dialogue: Challenges and Opportunities*. Pune, India: ASSR Publications, 2002.

24

# Towards an Effective Telugu Catholic Mission: Possibilities and Promises

**Jayaraju Ghattamaneni SJ**

## Introduction

Telugu Catholic Church has a remarkable history of missions. With her humble and hard beginnings in small villages, she is now grown into 13 dioceses and the Christians making 1.34% of the state population. The early missionaries in Telugu land made use of every opportunity available and faced every challenge bearing the Gospel of Jesus as their strength and Jesus as their leader. They effectively contributed to socio-cultural-economic spheres of Telugu people.

In contemporary times, Telugu Catholic Mission and the pastors encounter new challenges and opportunities demanding retrospection and a renewal to be effective in their mission. This confrontation demands that Telugu Church revisits the authenticity of her mission to relearn the forgotten paths and to revitalize her effectiveness. With this task at hand, in this paper I analyze present challenges and opportunities and recommend alternatives for Telugu Catholic Church to be authentic, relevant and effective.

## 1. Geographical and Demographical Note on Telugu Sates

Andhra Desa becomes the first state declared in India under the State reorganization act on 1 November 1956 based on common spoken language *Telugu.* Geographically, it is bound by Orissa, Chattisgarh, Maharastra in North, Karnataka in the West and Tamilanadu in South and the Bay of Bengal on the East. The total population is 8.46 Crores (approximately).[1]

United Andhra Pradesh is divided and a new state of Telangana was bifurcated on 2 June, 2014 with still Hyderabad as common capital for both the states[2] and Amaravati as new capital in making for Andhra Pradesh. Now, Andhra Pradesh Population is 5.36 Crores and Telanganna Population is 3.96 Crores.[3] Though the states had been bifurcated, the catholic church still remains united by only changing the name of the Bishops' council from APBC (Andhra Pradesh Bishops Council, October 16, 1954)4 to TCBC (Telugu Catholic Bishops' Council). The Ecclesiastical Region of Telugu Catholic Bishops' Council (TCBC) comprises of two Archdioceses of Hyderabad and Visakhapatnam, and 11 other Dioceses.[5] The Christians in Telugu States make 1.35% of the total Population. The international demographic scholars associated with the Church estimate the numbers are higher than what are being reported in the censuses.[6] Aloysius Jesurajan (1971) says: "Although she (Telugu Church) is small, her numbers are few, yet she can go about her task of announcing Christ with great courage, determination and confidence."[7] That courage and determination of spreading Christ is evident in her substantial growth in a short span of period.

## 2. Challenges as Opportunities

Every challenge is a stepping stone towards an opportunity. Throughout the history and in contemporary times, Telugu Catholic Church continues to face challenges. Now, I shall explore the challenges from which arise the opportunities for retrospection and renewal.

## A Call to Become Untiring Missionary

Fr. A. Kroot MHM in his introduction to the *History of Telugu Christians,* Trichinopoly, 1910, refers to the year 1598 as the date of 'the attempt to bring Christianity to the Telugus.' Christianity reached Andhra Pradesh on different levels, as historian Sebastian explains: "The origin of Christianity in the Telugu country can be traced back to the beginning of the 16th Century."[8] The spread of Christianity is obviously the combined effort of many congregations.

The Theatines, namely Francisco Manco (- d.14 August, 1646 at Bimilipatnam), accompanied by an Indian priest sent by the Arch Bishop of Goa, went to Bijapur in December 1640. From there, he went to the Kingdom of Golconda.[9] The Augustinians worked at Golconda and Masulipatnam. They left the mission in 1663.[10] The Capuchins from 1786 attended to the Telugu Christians who fled from the persecution of Tippu Sultan and settled in the districts of Madras.[11] On 20 September 1696, Peter Paul Palma, a Carmelite was appointed Vicar Apostolic of the Great Moghul Empire. During this period the Vicars made periodic journeys to Golconda and Bijapur. Under Carmelite Vicars Apostolic, the Theatines and the Augustinian's worked among the Telugus. These times there was 'mass movement' of conversions among the

Telugus in the present day Kurnool, Nellore and Bellary dioceses.[12] Arch Bishop Thomas Pothacamury said, "The Society of Jesus toiled in full strength till 1764, and later, with diminished numbers till 1773 when the suppression of the Society was promulgated in the Malabar, Carnatic and Madurai Mission."[13] On 3 September 1710, Pierre Mauduit set out on a journey to Telugu speaking country up to Punganuru (Cradle of Telugu Christianity). He baptized a widow, three children and a young man, all velamas.14 Fr. Clement of Bonnad of French Foreign Missionaries of Paris (MEP) gave fresh impetus by his arrival at Phirangipuram on 20 December 1827. The first band of missionaries from St. Joseph' Society of the Sacred Heart for Foreign Missions (MHM) arrived at Madras on 7 December 1875. They arrived at their promised land 'Northern part of the Madras diocese' on 28 December 1875.15

Having inspired by these missionaries' zeal to spread the Gospel in unknown territories, facing ordeal of the times (transportation, climate, language, culture), the Catholics and the clergy and religious require to move out of the comfort zones to seek the untapped lands crying for helping hand. It is time for the Church in Andhra Pradesh to reflect seriously and act upon the Lord's words: "The harvest is abundant, but the labourers are few; so, ask the master of the harvest to send out labourers for his harvest" (Mt. 9:37). However, there are 1981 (1381+600) religious men and vast number of religious women (running 388 institutes). Catholic Church should know that they have harvest and labourers but in need of hard-working labourers. The challenge is the need for missionary zeal to explore new missions and to work together and to frame visions united (clergy and religious)

## Shepherding in Service

Amidst the inexplicable opposition from within and internal drive (ecclesiastical commitment) to build bridge between universal Church and the local Church, to be a shepherd is a herculean task.

The conversation between Peter and Jesus: Feed my lambs, tend my sheep and Feed my sheep (John 21: 15-17) reminds the responsibility of Shepherds. Lumen Gentium clearly highlights the responsibility of Bishops as 'guardians of the word of God'. Pope Francis calls the Shepherds to have 'the smell of the sheep' but the stench of the shepherd keeping the sheep scattered, lost in wild pastures. Hans India reports, "Bishop...prevented from performing mass."[16] National Catholic Report holds the title, "Married Catholic Bishop faces court case for embezzlement."[17] *Telanganna Today*, a local newspaper carries, "Protest in front of ...Bishop's Residence" over swindling of 150 crores.[18] There are many more issues evident within the Catholic communities.

Christus Dominus reminds every shepherd and the clergy that 'a diocese is a portion of the people of God which is entrusted to a bishop to be shepherded by him with the cooperation of the presbytery."[19] Bishops are then called to "be good shepherds who know their sheep and whose sheep know them."[20] They should manifest their concern for everyone, no matter what their age, condition, or nationality, be they natives, strangers, or foreigners.[21]

The challenge for the shepherds is to concentrate on guarding the word of God, not properties; to Serve people but not power. Shepherding is not an individual task but a responsibility shared with the presbytery and the faithful.

## Updating/Upgrading Seminaries and formation

Pope Francis when he met new bishops from mission territories at the Vatican on September 8, 2018 said, "We cannot respond to the challenges we have regarding them without updating our processes of selection, accompaniment, evaluation." Pope Francis address to the Plenary of Congregation for the Clergy (2 October 2014) said that those in formation are "uncut diamonds to be formed both patiently and carefully, respecting the conscience of the individual, so that they may shine among the People of God."[22] Formation is 'journey of discipleship'. Seminaries should form missionary disciples who are in love with the master and shepherds 'with the smell of the sheep'[23]

The Challenge is to form 'missionary' disciples in the seminaries and to broaden their way by establishing common seminaries for the Religious and the clergy or regular interaction between clergy and religious in formation.

## Beyond the Boundaries of Casteism: Anti-witness of the Clergy, Religious and Laity

One of the major challenges is a consistent and visible entertainment of caste issues with in the clergy and religious spheres of decision making. This is absolutely anti-witness to the Gospel. When Telugu people are looking at the leaders as the torch bearers towards emancipation from the social evils, it is saddening to see that the leaders seem to be playing an unhealthy role of perpetrating caste among the faithful.

The historical development of Telugu Catholic Church reminds that the development of the Catholic Church is not the hard work of a single caste or a single group but it is common endeavor towards embracing Christ for a better living. As long as this menace of caste remains the Telugu Church gropes in darkness because faith without living could never be a proper witness. Arch Bishop Prakash Mallavarapu reminds that 'in truth certain external practices like going to temples, taking prasadam and certain religious practices were left behind' but he asks " Do we find the change in thoughts that strengthen Christian faith and values? Was there a full transformation?" It seems that "being Christian we still hold on to practices of other religion" [ in Telugu: *Kraistavudaivuntu Samgamlohinduvunigavunnatlevundi].*[24] Catholic leaders do not leave an indelible mark? Either socially, culturally we are the same. It is time for the Telugu Catholic leaders to born anew amidst Telugu people, to be born in Christ. The challenge is to scrape off Caste from minds of the clergy and religious, to get rid of caste affinity.

## Empower the Young People: Go out, See and Call

Coming to the church, when I asked a youth to come to the church, he replied, "What is there for me?" They are looking out for an example. They are looking out for a faith that brings meaning to their lives. 80% of Catholic youth leave the Church. The Church needs to continuously ask 'why?' They are not mere physical workforce of a parish. They are the potential spiritual force of the Church. The church needs to accompany them to experience the love of Christ, in reality. The recent announcement by Pope Francis on commencement of Synod of Bishops in 2018 with the theme 'Youth, faith, Vocational Discernment' indicates the importance set aside for youth in the church. There are seven lakh jobless youth in Andhra Pradesh.[25] Unemployment is one of the key issues gaining steam ahead of Telangana Assembly elections (like Farmers crisis, land acquisition). Unorganized youth is yet another concern. Telugu Church manages 90 colleges and 523 high schools. Every year thousands of students pass from our colleges, do they leave well formed or ill-formed?

Synod on Young people is present invitation for the Telugu Catholic Church to respond and gear their educational institutes towards preparing men and women capable, skillful and responsible citizens. Dragging to meet the corporate competition should not water down our goal and charisms to strengthen the power of youth. The challenge is to listen and accompany young people.

## Subalterns Ask: Where is the Church? Where is the Priority?

### Farmers

A study of the social background of the Telugu Christians of the 18th century reveals that the majority of Telugu Roman Catholics came from two great communities of farmers.[26] According to NITI Aayog data, the economy of Telangana is mainly supported by agriculture, having overall 55.54 lakh farm holdings. Total number of villages in United Andhra Pradesh, according to Census 2011 is 16158. Andhra Pradesh Social Service Society caters to 2483 villages (6.5% of total number of villages). Kanchallaiah comments 'Why Modi government is for Sanyasis, not farmers?' Shall the Telugu Church too ask the same question?

### Women Empowerment

Look at the sisters run institutions (388) in the state, they are far outnumbered than any other institutes run either by clergy or religious. But, where is their role in decision making bodies of the Church. I appreciate the efforts of TCBC which a separate commission for women and which through social service centers builds self-help groups. But, this is not enough. Still, they lurk in silence.

In the first proposed project for communication apostolate in Andhra Pradesh in 1971, the organization of the center consists of 4 sisters out 6 staff [Sr. Ignatius JMJ (Editor), Srs. Attilia and Innocent (Corresponding Admin), Sr. Imelda C.A.N (Printing), Srs. Pearce and Secundina FMM (Reorientation)]. This kind of mindset has to be cultivated.

Andhra Pradesh stands fourth in sexual harassment cases; 463 minor victims in 994 rape cases reported in the year 2016.[27] The National Crime Records Bureau (NCRB)suggests that 16,362 cases of crime against women were reported in Andhra Pradesh last year when compared to 15,967 cases reported in 2015. When it comes to sexual harassment, Andhra Pradesh, with 1,305 cases, is behind only three States in the country. Andhra Pradesh recorded 193 dowry deaths as against 174 in 2015, apart from 31 women trafficking and 626 kidnapping and abduction of women cases last year. The death of engineering student Swapnika of Warangal, a victim of acid attack, brought to the fore the issue of safety of the fair sex.28 The data shows that Dalit women face sexual harassment frequently in the state. More than 300 women faced various degrees of sexual assault. More than 100 women were raped, while others were molested. As many as 21 women were stripped by the perpetrators in various places in AP too last year.[29]

Dalits are more vulnerable in AP than any other state in India. A state with more than 84 lakh Dalits, AP has the second largest rate of violence against Scheduled Castes in the country after Rajasthan, as per the population ratio.[30] Telangana also saw an increase in crime against Dalits in the last year. As many as 1,678 cases in which Dalits were victims were reported in the state in 2015.

Policy for Dalit Empowerment in the Catholic Church in India (8 December 2016) calls for 'metanoia' to have the mind of Christ (Phil 2.5ff) and 'networking with the people of good will.'[31] The challenge is to hear voices of the neglected and to respond to their cry for help having the mind of Jesus. Telugu mission to hold fast to the mission manifesto of Christ (Luke 4:18)

## 3. Local Literature: Towards Communicating the Gospel

New evangelization needs a new language. The document 'The priest and the Third Christin Millennuium' speaks about the necessity to adapt the terminology to the changing times.[32]

Internal migration and internal displacement and influence of technocratic education systems, the faithful are struggling to understand local language. If you speak in Telugu youngsters do not get it and when you speak in English, elders do not understand. Both the ways, the communication of the Gospel is at risk. Therefore, need to employ methods to familiarize people with Gospel in local languages.

Ignorance of people about Church teachings because there is no proper literature translated to local languages. Even if some of them are translated, they are not an easy reading for the common people. Therefore, like Fr. Jojaiah SJ who with humble efforts spread the Gospel through his simple but profound writings, making the teachings available at lesser cost to the people living in villages provides a potential possibility towards reaching the faithful. The challenge is to find ways to communicate Gospel effectively, to make translations easy and understandable and by continuing the work of literary contributions.

There are also many others which need a radical attention of Catholic mission like struggles of Tribals, Eccumenical movement (amidst mushrooming of independent charismatic groups and so on. These challenges too provide for Telugu Catholic Church to intensify her liberative mission.

## Conclusion

Pope Francis during the Mass celebrated for Deceased Cardinals and Bishops said that "For all of us, life is a constant call to *go forth*: We are always on the move, until we make our final journey." The journey of the Church in Telugu land is on the move. Every challenge creates an opportunity. The Papal auditorium has caption on this Jubilee occasion, "look back with gratitude and look forward with trust." Telugu Catholic church looks back and cherishes the hard work of missionaries. She looks forward to respond to the challenges which are opportunities placed before her to renew and revitalize her witness to the Gospel by moving forward with missionary zeal, shepherding with service, communing, scraping off caste from clergy and religious, raising prophetic voice and radical involvement in the issues of farmers, women, youth and strengthening interreligious bonds of togetherness by forming seminarians who think beyond reginal boundaries and beyond cultural clutches.

I conclude with hope from vision and action plan of APBC [TCBC now], "We commit ourselves anew to proclaim the Good News, the Gospel of Jesus Christ, by proclaiming the faith, hope and love of the message through our life style, institutions, mass media and communication."[33] This journey of facing challenges and turning them to opportunities of renewal and vitality will make Telugu Catholic mission transformative, liberative and effective.

## Notes

1. Census 2011, https://www.census2011.co.in/census/state/andhra+pradesh.html (accessed on 1 November 2018).
2. Here after, instead of mentioning the names of both the states Andhra Pradesh and Telugu States, I shall refer to them as Telugu States since the language spoken in both these states is *Telugu* (a certain portion in Telanganna speaks Urdu/Hindi which indicates the influence of the Nizam rule).
3. Census 2011, 'Population of Telangana,' http://indiapopulation2018.in/population-of-telangana-2018.html (accessed on 1 November 2018).
4. APBC takes its origin from the "Regional Episcopal Council of Andhra Pradesh" which was set up on October 16, 1954, http://www.apbc.in/about_us.html (accessed 31 October, 2018).
5. Refer to information Compiled by Dr. AnthonyrajThumma, Deputy Secretary of TCBC, Secunderabad, January 08, 2015.
6. Swarajya staff, 'Andhra-Telanganna Demographics: Christian Population down, SC population up,' https://swarajyamag.com/columns/andhra-telangana-demographics-christian-population-down-sc-population-up (accessed on 25 October, 2108)
7. Aloysius C. Jesurajan, S.J. *An Evaluation of the Communication Apostolate of Andhra Pradesh: A Case Study* (Secunderabad: The Catholic Information Center of Andhra Pradesh, November, 1971).
8. Jose Sebastian, *The Jesuit Carnatic Mission: A Foundation of Andhra Church* (Secunderabad: 2004), 44.
9. J. Puthuman SVD, *A Brief History of The Catholic Church in Andhra Pradesh* (Secunderabad: Jeevan Institute of Printing, 2011), 25.
10. Thanugundla Solomon, *The Structures of the Church in Andhra Pradesh* (Rome: Pontifical Urban University,1976), 63.
11. Ibid., 66.
12. J. Puthuman, 27.
13. An excerpt from writing of Archbishop Thomas Pothacamury. Refer to J. Puthuman, 29.
14. E. R. Hambaye, *History of Christianity in India* Vol.III (Bangalore: Church History Association of India, 1997), 311-334.
15. J. Puthuman, 29.
16. *The Hans India*, 'Bishop Prevented from performing mass,' (Jul 26,2018) http://www.thehansindia.com/posts/index/Andhra-Pradesh/2018-07-26/Bishop-G-Prasad-prevented-from-performing-mass/401064 (accessed on 30 October 2018).
17. Jose Kavi, *Matters India*, August 3,2018, https://www.ncronline.org/news/world/married-catholic-bishop-faces-court-case-embezzlement
18. *Telangana Today*, Sunday November 4, 2018, https://telanganatoday.com/protest-in-front-of-nalgonda-bishops-residence
19. *Christus Dominus* (Decree Concerning Pastoral office of Bishops in the Church, October 28, 1965),11.
20. Ibid., 16.
21. Ibid.

22. Pope Francis, Address to the Plenary of the Congregation for Clergy (3 October, 2014): *L'Osservatore Romano* 226 (4 October 2016), 8. *Pastorem Dabo Vobis* sets out an integrated vision of formation of future clerics in all dimensions: human, intellectual, Spiritual and Pastoral.
23. *Ratio Fundamentalis Institutionis Sacerdotalis*, The Gift of the Priestly Vocation, *L'Osservatore Romano*, 8 December 2016, 3.
24. Mallavarapu Prakash, 'Andhra TelanganalaloSreesabhaedurkontunnasamskrutulu', in *Lokaniki Nene Velugu*39/3 July-September 2016, 36-37.
25. Deccan Chronicle, " hopes of 7 lakh jobless youth shattered in Andhra Pradesh', published 16 October 2018, https://www.deccanchronicle.com/nation/current-affairs/161018/hopes-of-7-lakh-jobless-youth-shattered-in-andhra-pradesh.html (accessed on 25 October 2018).
26. Catholicism in Andhra Pradesh, https://en.wikipedia.org/wiki/Telugu_Christian (accessed on 25 Oct 2018).
27. Harish Gilai, http://www.newindianexpress.com/states/andhra-pradesh/2017/dec/01/andhra-pradesh-stands-fourth-in-sexual-harassment-cases-463-minor-victims-in-994-rape-cases-reporte-1715440.html, published 1 Dec 2017. Also refer to Dr. Shreematha Kumar Dash, 'Voilence against woman from Rural Andhra', in JIAFM 28/4 (2016): 184-186.
28. The Hindu 'Attrocities against women' https://www.thehindu.com/todays-paper/tp-national/tp-andhrapradesh/Atrocities-against-women/article16353974.ece, published January 19, 2009.
29. 'Dalits most vulnerable in AP than any other State in Southern India', https://www.deccanchronicle.com/nation/current-affairs/030916/dalits-most-vulnerable-in-andhra-pradesh-than-any-other-state-in-southern-india.html.
30. Ibid.
31. Policy of Dalit Empowerment in Catholic Church in India: An Ethical Imperative to build Inclusive Communities, 8th December 2016, no. 93.
32. J. Puthumana, 117. Refer also to document released by the Congregation for the Clergy, *The Priest and the Third Christian Millennium*, 14.
33. Vision and Action Plan of the Catholic Church in Andhra Pradesh, Hyderabad, 2000, no.4.

25

# Christianity in Goa: Entangled Pasts and the Possible Futures

**Victor Ferrão**

All history writing is rooted in a historiography which provides a surplus frame to its narrations. History of the Christianity in Goa is no different. There is also a surplus of historiographies that are employed to frame this past. Most historiographies serve the interest of the dominant class or a group. It is historiography that frames the surplus past or the plural past and in several ways is a negation of the past. It chooses the event, personages and perspectives that will fit into its historiographical frames and excludes, negate or discards that which conflicts and militates the interest of the dominant class. All history writing is therefore interest laden and privileges the present and future expectations of the dominant class. Perhaps, Hegel's view that teaches that determination is negation[1] might assist us to understand how the surplus past when framed into an order of things opened by a historiography selects some aspects and excludes other aspects of the past. Derrida has already shown us that this framing through exclusion can always be deconstructed and we can release several locked, expelled and hidden horizons, meanings, perspectives as well as bring to light events, persons, views etc., that are exiled from the narrations of history. This paper attempts to manifest the surplus that resides in our past in Goa as well as tries to open in the articulation of history of Christianity in Goa. The opening of the surplus can lay bear before us how it is narrowly closed in the articulation of our history in Goa, particularly the history of Christians. We then look at how the arrow of time that has led us to a point of this affliction and open other arrows of time that might offer us opportunities to manifest the lost voices, silenced ahistoricals, absented events, etc., that can be traced on other arrows of time irrupting out of the voids of our collective pasts . We opine that this other arrows of time may become salutary for our society.

## 1. Present Concerns Framing the Past

History is said to be the story of the victors. Besides, it was shown to be 'his' story. Thus history is accused of forgetting the story of the losers and the women. Michel Foucault has demonstrated that history privileges the present over the past. We can notice that history has objectified, silenced and framed Christians of Goa in several of its discourses.

### Outsidering Christians

Post-colonial historiography frames history of Christianity within the narrative of nationalism. Such a framing of our past forgets that nation was product of recent history. Nations were born after the treaty of Westphalia.[2] As such nationalism appears to be a borrowed idea. But it is employed to render Christianity as alien to our nation. Thus, history when determined through the lens of the nationalism leaves out anthropology, sociology, and religious history of our people.3 Christians who share biological kinship with other Goans, particularly the majority brethren then begin to look like outsiders. This outsidering or a negative determination of Goan Christian is socially engineered by forgetting their biology and religious history. It is like saying that we prefer coffee without cream to coffee without milk. Although, there is no real difference between coffee without milk and coffee without cream, but negative determination does mark a divide. Maybe the coffee without milk in this regard is the Christians. It means when we fix a lack in something, we perceive its reality differently. Christianity as lacking Indian-ness is such a negative determination which forgets the common biological, anthropological and even cultural ancestry of the Christians and frame them as outsiders based on religion. This framing of humans as merely religious beings is reductive and forgets there is an irreducibility of our past. Moreover it does its framing on the basis of the categories that had emergence in the recent past.

### Viewing our Past as a Hindu Past

Hinduism as a term has been a geographical ascription and originated outside of what we call the Hindu-fold of today. It became a catch all term for the Islamic rulers and was employed by the British colonizers who framed the plural cults and divine orientations of the people of country into abrahmic religious framework to assist them to administrate our people. Thus, we use the term Hinduism only in retrospection.[4] Now this novel determination of our people as Hindu became acceptable to most of our people only in the nineteenth century. This singularization of the plural past of our ancestors is another important means that stereotypes Goan Christians as outsiders. It also sees conversion as a betrayal of Hinduism when there was no such one universal Hindu religion at that time. This framing of the plural past as a one unitary Hindu past does epistemic violence to the plural pasts of our ancestors as well renders Goan Christians of today victims to the accesses of the Hindutva forces. One cannot trace the term Hindu in the first hundred years of Portuguese writings from India. The plural history of our people is placed in the order of things set by the ideologies that developed much after the conversion of several Goans to Christianity when Goans are said to have been converted from Hinduism. One can notice that in the narration of breaking down of the then temples of our ancestors, the said temples are also viewed as Hindu temples. We can at the most call these temples Hindu in retrospection. This means this era is like coffee without cream but historians in Goa seem to smell the coffee without cream as Hindu era. This often can create a false consciousness among the majority people that grave injustice was done to them in the past and can set in a loss recovery dynamism that traces surplus enjoyment in victimising the Catholics of today.

## Narrations of Conversions

There are plural narratives of the conversion of Christians in Goa.[5] The mainstream narrative claims that it was the Portuguese colonizers and the missionaries who brought Christianity to Goa. But there are alternate narratives that contest it. The discovery of the Greek cross, now kept in the museum in the seminary at Pilar has demonstrated that there were pre-Portuguese Christian settlements in Goa. Historians had admitted that such cross was a sign of Christian travellers through Goa in the past. But the sheer size of the cross has indicated that there was a somewhat permanent settlement of these pre-Portuguese Christians. Besides, conversion is seen as dark period where coercion, persecution, punishment and allurement were thought to be employed by the Portuguese to reap the harvest of the Souls for Christ. There is no doubt that the Portuguese entered Goa with a cross and a sword. But we cannot frame the past with categories that are alien to it and were developed at a later time. The narrative of forced conversion that abounds in the description of the conversion saga of the Catholics needs to be revisited. The narrative of forced conversion gains legitimacy by forgetting the role of the village communes or ganvkarias, Mazanias in the process of conversion.6 At a time when village communes were sovereign, the communitarian identity was the order of the day. There is another violence of framing of conversions as an attack on individual freedom. The modern free Cartesian subject was yet to be born in Goa and therefore conversions were more a result of mimetic desire that drew the masses to follow the decision of their Village elders. This might explain why we had mass conversions at that time.

## 2. Seeking Productive Semiosis

The order of things that has framed our history has not merely emerged out of conscious semantic resource. There is an asignifying dimension to it. The voids of the past may have ignited an idealised visions of the past and future which then might have triggered the desire to organise, code the semiolgical flows that have led to the articulation of history of Christianity in Goa in the shape and form that it has today.

### The Arrows of Time

Deleuze and Gauttari view unconscious not in the past as has been the case with most psychoanalyst, they see it as turned towards the future and in its screen see how it identifies the possibilities for the present . As such, they try to name it as machinic to drive home that it is not just semiotic but chiefly productive. This means that it is not just populated by images and words but is constituted by the mechanisms that generate or produce these images and words in the first place. In some way, we attempt to descend into the non-semiotic dimension of the unconscious. But paradoxically to articulate the meaning of it, we will need semiotic and semantic resources. This is the generative ground which Deleuze and Gauttaricalls the plane of consistency that opens various possibilities for semiotic and semantic structures to appear. This means we enter the non-semiotics sphere or force fields which may be regarded as the predecessor of the semiotic and semantic field that we all inhabit. These force fields have plural arrows of time and one that has reached our temporality is one that has irrupted out of this plurality. This journey backwards to open new possibilities for a future is viewed as sychizoanlysis by Deleuze and Gauttari.[7] The schizoanalysis will open the arrow of time that has brought us to this juncture and at the same time will open new possibilities for future by show other opportunities of riding other arrows of time. Hence, it would be important to enter the non-semantic or semiotic depths of our collective unconscious and examine how an arrow of time has led us to singularize a plural past in the destinies that has brought us to the articulation of histories of Christians of Goa.

### Semiological Flows

The semiological flows[8] that has acquired crystal forms in our present have emerged for the dynamics of force fields that lie beneath the organizations of those semiological flows. The framing of history of Christians have its roots not just into semiotic and semantic ancestries but has in the first place reached an organisation and formulation of the semiotics flows on the plane of consistency because of the play of the asignifying forces or energies in the force fields. It would be interesting to decode these force fields to disentangle the present from the stranglehold of sigualrization of our pasts and open up other possibilities of being Indians/ Goans today. This would open how several lines of flights and lines of dissidence are repressed and a sort of freezing of time is arrived for the present. This can loosen the fixations of the past and the present and open the future for us. It will dismantle kinds of power formations exhibited in our society. Our study can demonstrate how if we reverse the different encodings that are accepted as normal and natural by us, we might open other dimensions of our plural pasts that are forgotten. History is thus, ordered and bestowed verbal articulation from an imagined future that is deemed as salutary to the voids of the past. The voids of the past have led to the assemblages of the semiotic resources that organise and formalises the power formations that promise redemption from the shackles of the traumas and voids of the past.

## Visions of Future and the Semiological Flow

The voids of the past may generate force fields that we might understand through a system of algorithms that might account for the morpho-genetic changes that has led to the frames that articulate our pasts. The voids that we are looking for can be traced in colonial trauma, separation of conversion and the encounter of modernity. Colonization and the consequent conversion to Christianity and our encounter with modernity are ridden with profound complexity. But they have produced several voids that cannot be easily articulated. They have pushed us into what Lacan calls the register of the Real.[9] This fall into the Real of Lacan is a descent into the non-semiotic sphere which cannot be understood with our semiotic as well as semantic resources. This descent into the asignifying force field has triggered a dream future that produced assemblages that have organised the semiotic flows in our society which then organised or coded the power formations that acquire legitimacy today and write our history. Power is knowledge and hence, history follows the victor. This means the voids irrupting from colonization, Conversion and encounter with modernity had different arrows of time or possible futures. Perhaps the Hegelian analysis of the wound might assist us to understand how we rode an arrow of time and reached this point where we find ourselves. Hegel teaches that wound triggers us to imagine a golden past before it and directs our energies to enact it into the approaching future. The present that we are facing has arrived on the backs of the force fields that led the semiological flows to acquire crystallizations of the power formations that animate our society today. By understanding this dynamism, we may open other arrows of time to animate the force fields and the semiotic resources and open alternate timelines for power formations that might derail the present regimes of power and its discursive formations. This is means the timeline of the present power formations is arbitrary and can be dismantled to allow other alternative futures to emerge.

## 3. Opening Possible Futures

There are multiple potentialities in the voids of the pasts and visions of the future. The arrow of time that has arrived to us in the present is one that is laden with a sense of recovery of something precious that is thought to be lost under disruption of colonization, conversion and encounter with Modernity. We still have to deal with this sense of loss to find freedom from it. The sense of recovery is thought to be crystallizing in the Hindu singularity. But it is actually unmaking of the civilizational ethos of our country.

### Accepting the Surplus Aspect of Reality

The sensitivity to the surplus dimension of reality opens us to understand mystery in everything. There is always more in everything. We too are seeking surplus. This drive to surplus might have been described as restlessness by St. Augustine. He also rightly says that this restlessness only rests in God who is a mystery par excellence. Awareness of mystery calls us to embrace a humble epistemology. This humble epistemology can assist us to stay open to plural pasts that are framed and singularized by different power interests. Hence, we cannot Oepidalize as if there is no alternative outside the frame that has rendered Goan Christians as objects of history. Being anti-Oedipal would mean that we Goan Christians have the challenge to become subjects of our pasts and find our voice. This would mean instead of staying in an infantilized silence, it is for us to take charge of our past and code the semiological flows and semantic resources to open salutary present and future for all communities in Goa. This means Goan Christians have to ride the drive for surplus that seeks alternate pasts that have been excluded, hidden or exiled in the historiographies that articulated our history and have rendered us alien. This means we have let the asignifying force fields of the trauma of the past stimulate new multiple orders of ensignifiyingsemiological flows that would heal us and articulate inclusive futures emerging out of the dark cloud of the pasts.

### Seeking Therapy for the Wounds of the Past

There is no zero starting point to begin. We cannot go in the past and change it for us. But to let the past be past, we need to have courage, hope and healing. Our courage, hope and healing is in the awareness and acceptance of existence of multiple arrows of time that are flowing out of the voids of the past. The colonial disruption, the conversion and the encounter with modernity has opened several voids in our society and there are several arrows of time that irrupt through them but we have rode some force fields and resonated with the semiological flows and semantic resources that lead us to the kind of society we have today. The awareness of alternate arrows of time is indeed therapeutic. It gives us courage in the face of hopelessness. Here, we might remember George Agamen who said that thought is the courage of hopeleness.[10] It is in this acceptance of possibilities of other arrows and other possible futures that is courageous as it contains the refusal to Odepalize in the face of castrating and crippling fear that seem to point that our future is doomed. Riding the hope for an alternate future can become the first step to let such a future to come closer to us. The alternate destinies that we take the courage to think have the promise to heal the wounds of the past that and give us a salutary present.

## Embracing Otherness

Rejection of the trap to be the other of the same is profoundly emancipative. The drive to become like the other is called the mimetic desire. Scholars like Rene Girard have identified the mimetic desire as the cause of violence.[11] The other triggers a lack in us. The lack becomes object a that Lacans call the cause of our desire. We are naturally attracted to the economy of the same. The other becomes a mirror for us and we draw our standards of being from him/her. One can never shed over one's otherness and has to become the other of the same. Trapped in this logic of equivalence, we are destined to become copies and never can be our original self. Thus, there is a discursive production of the Goan Christian as the other of the same. We as Christians seem to have borrow sanskritized models of what is thought to be the most original way being Goan or Indian. In this manner, we end up becoming the other of the same as those that are regarded as original, pure and fully national provide bench marks for our imitation. This is why our subjected subject positions not allow us to be original. All copies are counterfeit and hence, a Christian is framed to become less of an Indian as a result of the discourses that populate our writing of history. Hence, it is important to reject these borrowed models and stick faithfully to our otherness or uniqueness that would enrich each of us and our country. Thus, we have the challenge to ride the waves or lines of flight that would open us to possible futures to be different and other and yet be an authentic Indian as well as Goan.

## Conclusion

Our study has exposed how writing of history is fixated and is afflicted by the trauma and pain of the past. This trauma and the voids of the past has nurtured a sense of loss and triggered a dynamism of recovery that has pushed the force fields of the asignification to swell into semiological flows that have crystallized into a the order of things that animate our society as well as lead our writing of history in Goa. This does not mean that we are to resign ourselves to the fate of being objects of history. There are alternate arrows of time irrupting from the voids of our past and can open new waves and flows that we can ride an open the lost pasts that are silenced so that we can enrich our being as both Goans and Christians in India.

## Notes

1. http://eprints.whiterose.ac.uk/97865/2/determination%20is%20negation%20paper%20 final.pdf accessed on 1-2-2019.
2. https://opus.lib.uts.edu.au/bitstream/10453/3289/1/2006006060.pdf accessed on 1-2-2019.
3. Victor Ferrao, *Being A Goan Christian*: *The Politics of Identity, Rift and Synthesis* (Panjim: Broadway Publishing House, 2011), 41-43.
4. Victor Ferrao, "Reversing, Displacing Ultranationalism" in Johnson J. Puthenpurakal (ed.), *Enhancing Our Home*: *Re-reading and Re-living Gandhian Thought* (Banglore: Asian Trading Corporation, 2016), 236-246.
5. Victor Ferrao, *Being A Goan Christian*, 92-105.
6. Luis de Assis Correia, *Goa through the Mist of History from 1000 BC-AD 1958*: *a Select Compilation of Goa'sGenesis* (Panjim: Grafica (Goa) Dourada, 2006), 160-162.
7. Gilles Deleuze and Fellix Gauttari, *Anti-Oedipus*: *Capitalism and Schizophrenia* (Minneapolis: University of Minnesota Press, 1983).
8. Felix Gauttari, *Machinic Unconscious*: *Essays In Schizoanalysis* (Los Angeles: Semiotext(e) 2011), 9-15.
9. https://www.sunypress.edu/pdf/61618.pdf accessed on 1-2-2019.
10. https://zizek.uk/the-courage-of-hopelessness/ accessed on 1-2-2019.
11. http://www.imitatio.org/brief-intro/ accessed on 1-2-2019.http://journal.psyart.org/wp-content/uploads/2014/08/PsyArt-2014-Article-18-R-Silhol.pdf accessed on 1-2-2019.

26

# Filled with Joy and Carried by Love: The Mission of the Church in North India

**Subhash Anand**

Pope Francis alerts us: "The disciple is ready to put his or her whole life on the line, even to accepting martyrdom, in bearing witness to Jesus Christ, yet the goal is not to make enemies but to see God's word accepted and its capacity for liberation and renewal revealed."[1] Sometimes the triumphalist way 'missionaries' go about evokes resentment. Hence mission today calls for honest and critical reflection.

## 1. The Context of Mission

### a. The Society in North India

Different seminars in the recent past have drawn our attention to the situation in the country: religious and cultural pluralism; massive poverty: malnutrition, inadequate health care; gender injustice and violence; fundamentalism leading to communal violence; superstitions: godmen and godwomen taking people for a ride; caste discrimination; anti-missionary ethos; anti-conversion bills. John Paul II's *Ecclesia in Asia* presents a similar picture for Asia at large.

### b. The Church in North India

Speakers after speakers at seminars have called for a preferential option for the poor, social activism against all forms of discrimination, inter-religious dialogue, inculturation, etc. *Ecclesia in Asia* calls for not only action on behalf of, but also for being with the poor. But we are disturbed by the return to pre-Vatican II neo-orthodoxy. Inculturation is superficial and inter-religious dialogue is a non-starter. Injustice against women continues to mar the Christian community. Now we have more and more institutions that bring in a lot of money. As a result, priests, bishops and even religious are moving away from the poor. In the past we had few priests, much work, but little money. Now we have many priests, plenty of money, but not much work. With all our opulence our uneducated and unorganized lay workers do not receive proper remuneration. The Church is becoming more and more cultic: new devotions, shrines, grottos, adoration chapels, glamourous celebrations, etc. The more cultic we become the greater the importance given to forms, less to values. Cult generates more fundamentalist thinking, less critical reflection; more superstition less the truth of the Gospel.

## 2. Mandate Missiology

Pope Francis says that "evangelization takes place in obedience to the missionary mandate of Jesus: 'Go therefore and make disciples of all nations…' (Mt 28: 19-20)."[2] Pope John Paul II was even more emphatic: "All the Evangelists, when they describe the risen Christ's meeting with his apostles, conclude with the 'missionary mandate'" (Mt 28:18-20; cf. Mk 16:15-18; Lk 24:46-49; Jn 20:21-23)."3

a. *Markan Mandate*: The original Mark does not have a mission mandate. The second ending (16: 9-20) was composed in the second century C.E. using Matthew and Luke. Those who read the text literally will insist on baptism. But I regret to say that baptizing people does not always really serve the community, but gives the 'missionary' a sense of achievement. The great missionary Paul was aware of this temptation (1 Cor 1: 14-16).

b. *Matthean Mandate:* Matthew's was largely a Jewish-Christian community. Matthew alone speaks of church and baptism, the Jewish *kāhāl* and circumcision. At that time some Jewish thinkers maintained that baptism was adequate substitute for baptism. Matthew's is a specific solution to a particular problem. We just cannot extrapolate it and make it a universal norm.

c. *Lukan Mandate:* Luke's Jesus ends with these words: "Thus it is written, that the Christ should suffer and on the third day rise from the dead, and that repentance and forgiveness of sins should be preached in his name to all nations, beginning from Jerusalem. You are witnesses of these things" (24: 46-48). This is a call for repentance with a view to the forgiveness of sins. The emphasis here is not on teaching but on bearing witness.

d. *Johannine Mandate:* In John, Jesus says: "Peace be with you. As the Father has sent me, even so I send you…Receive the Holy Spirit. If you forgive the sins of any, they are forgiven; if you retain the sins of any, they are retained" (Jn 20: 21-23). The person sent out on a mission is expected to behave like a judge who exercises this power to loosen or bind persons.? He historical Jesus did not want his disciples to be judges of other others. John's failure to specify how is this power exercised may serve as a Christian guideline. No community can claim that its was is *the* way.

e. *Mission as Mandate:* The mandate texts in the four Gospels do not come from the historical Jesus. Each writer reflects a particular point of view. Evangelization need not necessarily lead to baptism. Even the great missionary Paul emphatically stated: "Christ did not send me to baptize but to preach the gospel" (1 Cor 1: 17). In the Acts we have Apollos an unbaptized missionary. It is possible to have evangelization without sacramentalization.

Mandate missiology institutionalizes mission: mission is the task of some Christians. The others are called to pray and pay. This is a serious distortion of the Christian vocation. Every disciple of Jesus is called to be a missionary. He cannot be a Christian if he is not in some way the salt of the earth and the light of the world (Mt 5:1314).

The institutionalizing of mission is counterproductive. A bishop wants to develop his diocese. He gets help from a foreign mission funding agency. Many of his priests do not see eye to eye with him on this question. Hence, he mandates a senior priest to open a new 'mission' station in a particular district of his diocese. The priest accepts the job reluctantly. He buys some suitable land, encloses it with a strong wall, builds a presbytery and puts up a church, etc. Some poor people from the locality come to him. They think, and with good reasons, that he has plenty of money. They want to become Christians! They also hope that at least one of their sons will become a Christian missionary! This explains the many 'vocations' we find in new 'mission' stations.

John Paul II's Mandate missiology links the mission *Ad Gentes* to the creation of local churches. This is based on presuppositions that are being challenged by contemporary New Testament scholars.[4]

> The older blueprint supposition, by which Jesus had the church clearly in mind and had already planned its structure, sacraments, etc., has little or no textual support… In what are commonly accepted as historical memories from Jesus' ministry, he is singularly silent on foundational or structural issues. This is understandable, if we see Jesus interested not in founding a separate religion but in renewing Israel, which already had worship, priests, sacrifices—Jesus did not need to plan such structures.

Hence the goal of our mission cannot be the Church, which has a supreme head in Rome, a three-tiered cultic hierarchy, a ministerial priesthood, seven sacraments, etc. All these are later constructions. There was no need for Jesus to establish the Church as we understand it today. This was not necessary also because Jesus and even Paul expected the world to end very fast. Nor was it possible, unless we base ourselves on Docetistic Christology.

Mandate missiology cannot respond to the challenge posed by postmodern thought. Postmodernism is "incredulity towards meta-narratives: it rejects the 'great 'myths' of modernity: universality, perenniality and certainty."[5] Postmodern thinkers draw our attention to the plurality around us and make us aware of our being conditioned by many factors. Traditional mission theology is based on a meta-narrative: to be saved people need to be baptized and become members of the Church – the one sure way of salvation for all.

## 3. The Mission of Jesus

Jesus was a postmodern thinker. The best way to counter the challenge posed by postmodern thought is to return to Jesus himself. Over a hundred years ago, the French Biblical scholar, Loisy said, not without some regret: "Jesus came proclaiming the Kingdom, and what arrived was the Church."

### a. Content of the Mission

Jesus devoted his whole life to what he called the 'kingdom of God'. He "was not teaching a religious doctrine. He was proclaiming an event. People saw him as a prophet with a passion for a fuller life for everyone. His goal was not to perfect Jewish religion, but to hasten the coming of the long-awaited kingdom of God, which meant life, justice and peace."[6] Jesus was not a religious founder concerned about dogmas and rituals; but a profound religious guide, concerned about the quality of life.

For the kingdom of God to emerge, people must free themselves from the slavery of religion. God is a very loving Father: we can approach him directly. Hence, we do not need any intermediaries. The kingdom of God as the centre of our life and of our mission, challenges us, but makes us free. Religion provides us a sense of security often by generating fundamentalism and superstitions.

When the Church as an institution becomes our primary concern, then institutions dominate our horizon; and institutions can take many forms: ritual, legal, administrative, educational, etc. Institutions generate competition to gather as large a clientele as possible. Christians become people of rituals, often of rituals that have no meaning for us today. Rituals do not call for much moral integrity and intellectual depth. Rituals are centripetal: they tend to keep us within our compounds. Rituals are often based on a fundamentalist reading of the past, and a superstitions conception of the future. Like any human institution, the Church has its boundaries. Institutions tend to look to the past, often towards an imagined glorious past.

The Kingdom of God as a vision focusses on the integral development of creation. When it becomes our primary concern, values dominate our horizon. These values are the values of all humans; all humans need to cooperate to actualize then. Thus, the kingdom of God brings people together. We see each other not as competitors but as partners. Christians become people-centred; they learn to evaluate different aspects of their life with one norm: does this really serve God's kingdom: the integral development of all? The kingdom of God is a tensive reality: already and not yet. Hence, people gripped by it look to the future, with all its creative plurality. The Kingdom of God has no boundaries. It is not a human institution but God's gracious gift.

Mission always, but especially today, calls not only for moral integrity but also for intellectual depth: the ability to reflect, to critique and to contextualize. Without this critical reflection we remain superficial, complacent with the little things we do. For this reason, mission promotes critical reflection. Authentic missionaries try to enlighten people. Mission is centrifugal; it "takes the church beyond itself, into culture, into people's lives, beckoning it constantly to 'cross frontiers'."[7] The early disciples of Jesus were not sitting on chairs (*kathedra* → cathedral), but were people of the Way (*hodos*, Acts 9: 2); they did not follow a religion but the way of salvation (16: 17), the way of the Lord, the way of God (18: 25-26). Only later on were they called Christians (11:26). That is where the institutionalization of the mission of Jesus began. But the author of the Acts does not talk of Christianity, but continues to tell us about the Way (19: 9, 23; 22: 4; 24:14, 22). Only when we deconstruct Christianity will we find the Way back.

Mission is not doing something, but being a disciple of Jesus. Mission is *satyagraha*, an affirmation not of some truths, but an expression of Truth. Mission is authentic existence within a context.Rituals tend to block discernment. Of all Christians, the Catholics are the most ritual-bound. Rituals may make us loyal Catholics, but we may fail to be faithful disciples of Jesus.

The kingdom of God leads us to authentic religion. Jesus insists that compassion is greater than sacrifice (*thysia*, Mt 9: 13; 12: 7). Material help offered to the needy is liturgy (*leitourgia*, Phil 2: 17). For James "religion (*thrēskeia*) that is pure and undefiled before God and the Father is this: to visit orphans and widows in their affliction, and to keep oneself unstained from the world" (Jam 1: 27).

If, in spite of repeated proclamations, we have not taken the preferential option for the poor, the commitment to social and gender justice, our task of inter-religious dialogue and the imperative to inculturate our Christian life in India seriously, then one very important explanation is our neglect of the kingdom of God and our emphasis on *our* Church. We also noted that the religious life in India is distorted by fundamentalism and superstition and glamorized by consumer display. Once again, the main reason for this tragedy is the marginalization of the kingdom of God.

The Roman Catholic Church is the most organized religious denomination in the world. My struggle with organized religion convinces me that the more religion gets organized, the more it needs fundamentalism and superstition for its survival. This explains why people who represent religious establishments tend to feel uncomfortable in the company of creative and liberal thinkers. "All religious traditions seem to privilege compliance and stability over enquiry and dissent."8 Without that inner freedom to dissent—the absence of fundamentalism and superstition—we cannot effectively proclaim the kingdom of God. Without that inner freedom we may end up making people twice as bad as we are (Mt 23: 15).

### b. Jesus' Discovery of His Mission

Jesus repeatedly insist that he has seen the Father and so he is qualified to bear witness unto Him. (Jn 3: 11; 6: 46; 8: 38). Jesus is the primordial contemplative and his mission rises from that contemplation. In prayer the historical Jesus receives the mission to be the servant of Yahweh (Lk 3: 21), the mission to bring good news to the poor (Lk 4: 18). Through prayer Jesus chooses his co-workers; in prayer he discovers the cost of mission; in prayer he has a foretaste of the glory that will be his for being faithful to his mission (Lk 9: 28-36).

If mission springs from contemplation, then one conclusion is inevitable: only persons who share in the contemplative life of Jesus can share in his mission. One of the great tragedies of Christian history is the fact that we have institutionalized mission. This is a cogent proof that we have delinked mission from contemplation. When mission gets institutionalized it loses its credibility. Institutions can testify to our efficiency and to our capacity to raise funds. Their success is worldly success. Our institutions do not necessarily call for a deep commitment to Jesus. They may even serve to mask its absence!

## 4. Missionaries for North India

Paul was a zealous Jew. He thought that Jesus and all his disciples should be killed. But then something happened on the way to Damascus and his life took a right-about turn. It will be good for us to examine his life; because more than anything else, his life was his mission; and his mission was his life. For this I shall share with you some of reflections on the opening lines of Paul's letter to his beloved Philippians (Phil 1:3-11).

### a. Filled with Joy

Paul was a deeply joyful person. The man who travelled far and wide to proclaim Jesus was in prison when he wrote to the Philippians. Yet Paul begins his letter with these words: "I thank my God in all my remembrance of you, always in every prayer of mine for you all making my prayer with joy, thankful for your partnership in the gospel from the first day until now" (1:3-5). Two words – and expressions related to them – that come again and again in this letter are 'joy' and 'thank' (1: 18, 25; 2: 2, 18-17, 19, 28–29; 3: 1; 4: 1, 4, 6, 10). Paul is a deeply happy person, and he repeatedly invites the Philippians to share in his joy. The secret of Paul's joy in this adverse situation in his knowledge that his work is not his. It is the Father who begins the good work in the hearts of men, and it is the Father who brings it to completion (1: 6).

Pope Francis insists that our mission is the expression of the joy we experience in encountering the Risen Lord.[9] He is painfully aware that in our consumer world we may be satisfied with that superficial joy which results from instant gratification. Consumerism can bore us, and then we are joyless. "There are Christians whose lives seem like Lent without Easter."[10] There can be no mission without joy. "Consequently, an evangelizer must never look like someone who has just come back from a funeral!"[11] It is possible that in spite of all the comforts we have, we may not really be happy. Happiness is an inside thing.

### b. Carried by Love

If the Father sent Jesus because He loved us, then our being sent will be proved by our love for others. In the mandate model, 'mission' is possible without love. It is for this reason that mandate cannot be the foundation of our mission. Paul tells the Philippians: "God is my witness, how I yearn for you all with the affection of Christ Jesus" (v. 8). If this letter of Paul is full of the sentiments of joy, gratitude and tenderness, it is because he deeply loves the Philippians. But there is something more to it.

The love Paul has for the Philippians is not the love flowing from his heart. He is the channel of Christ's love for his flock. Paul lives, no it is Christ who lives in Paul (Gal 2: 20). He has no agenda of his own, neither conscious nor subconscious. Hence, the love Paul has for the Philippians is not only like the sacrificial love Jesus has for his Church (Eph 5: 25); it is also the love of Christ offered to his Church through the ministry of Paul. Through him Jesus loves his Church, and continues to give himself for her.

### c. Guided by Discernment

Paul was deeply upset when he learnt that some Jewish Christians refused to eat with the other Christians. He was angry when even Peter, followed the practice of the Jewish Christians (v. 12). Paul did not hesitate to publicly take him to task (v. 11). He was so annoyed by those Jewish Christians who insisted on circumcision even for the other Christians that he told them to get themselves castrated (5: 12). Yet the same Paul got Timothy circumcised (Acts

16: 3). Paul knew how to distinguish between a principle and its application. So too, he tells the Corinthians that they could eat any meat, provided they did not scandalize some who were not sufficiently enlightened (1 Cor 8: 7-8).

Paul wanted his Christian friends to be people of discernment, people who could think for themselves. Hence, he tells the Philippians: "And it is my prayer that your love may abound more and more, with knowledge and all discernment, so that you may approve what is excellent, and may be pure and blameless for the day of Christ" (Phi 1: 9-10). The mission of Jesus was to bring freedom to people and lead them to the Father. He did not make himself the centre of their lives and want them to be dependent on him.

### d. Rooted in Contemplation

Joy, love and discernment are the fruits of contemplation. Paul was a contemplative. The initial experience he had of the Risen Lord was deepened by a subsequent life of prayer.

> I must boast; there is nothing to be gained by it, but I will go on to visions and revelations of the Lord. I know a man in Christ who fourteen years ago was caught up to the third heaven—whether in the body or out of the body I do not know, God knows. And I know that this man was caught up into Paradise—whether in the body or out of the body I do not know, God knows–and he heard things that cannot be told, which man may not utter (2 Cor 12: 1–4).

Paul was able to love Jesus, to whose service he was called by the Father, and to give himself totally to his Church, because he had a life of intense prayer. He was a contemplative and that made him a far-sighted missionary, a missionary who was not satisfied with little things but who was constantly pressing forward, filled with the spirit of *magis*, longing to give as much as he could. Mission is not possible without contemplation.

The insistence on contemplation is significant for us in India, for two reasons. First, the Indian word for a witness is *sākṣin*, i.e., one who has eyes (*akṣa*). The idea suggested is that only when we have seen with our own eyes, can we bear witness with credibility. That is what mission is all about: sharing with others our experience of Jesus. This is what our country demands from us. This is also what people of our times expect of us. As Pope Paul VI puts it: "Modern man listens more willing to witnesses than to teachers, and if he does listen to teachers, it is because they are witnesses."[12] Here the Pope is speaking of the witness of life, but this witness of life demands a deep commitment to Jesus and his values, and it attains its maturity only when it is nourished by contemplation.

Secondly, our country has a long tradition of contemplation, a tradition that has nurtured great mystics. When we go through the history of missions in Europe, we see that those tribes who were evangelized by the monks of St. Benedict were all very primitive in their religiosity, in their culture, in their art. But for the last almost three thousand years India has presented the world with a tremendous mystical tradition. When the first European missionaries came to India they did not impress peoples with a very advanced religiosity. These could only be touched by persons who had within them a deep experience of God. Hence, it is not surprising that Pope John Paul II states: "My contact with representatives of the non-Christian spiritual traditions, particularly those of Asia, has confirmed me in the view that the future of mission depends to a great extent on contemplation."[13] This explains, perhaps tragically, why apart from a very small fraction, the bulk of Christians in North India and also in some parts of the South are from those communities who have other, down to earth needs to be taken care of: the Tribals and Dalits. This is not meant to be a disparaging remark, but a statement of facts. These people are marginalized. They have no say in our national life. Many of our missionaries, especially those linked with the colonial rulers, directed their missionary efforts towards these people and got a response from them.

Jesus was the prophet of the Kingdom of God. He did not establish any new religion, but he deconstructed religion. This explains why in "all the Gospels the chief priests are the most active opponents of Jesus." Today our mission is to redeem religion: free it from fundamentalism and superstition. Only then humans will be redeemed. The blind will see; they will find their way. They will not need others to lead them to their beloved Abba. Then they will be people with (*sa*) eyes (*akṣa*). They will be authentic witnesses (*sākṣin*) to the Kingdom of God.

To focus on the Kingdom, we will need to return to the *Jesus before Christianity*, the Jesus "as He was before He became enshrined in doctrine, dogma, and ritual, a man deeply involved with the real problems of His time, which are the real problems of our time as well." For this we will need to deconstruct Christianity, and move towards the religionless Christianity Bonhoeffer spoke about. This will mean that the Christian of the future will live by the inspiration from within. The Christian of the future will be a mystic or he will not exist at all. The call to contemplative life is addressed to all Christians. Through contemplation we listen to the Spirit of Jesus. We become Christians, walking the Way of Jesus. By becoming Christians, we become missionaries.

## Notes

1. *Evangelii Gaudium* (Post-Synodal Apostolic Exhortation: Proclamation of The Gospel in Today's World, November 2013), no. 24. In this document Pope Francis presents his views in the light of the XIII Ordinary General Assembly of the Synod of Bishops, 7-28 October 2012, The New Evangelization for the Transmission of the Christian Faith.
2. *Ibid., no.* 19.
3. *Redemptoris Missio* (On the permanent validity of the Church's missionary mandate, December 1990), No. 22.
4. Raymond E. Brown, Carolyn Osiek & Pheme Perkins, "Early Church", in Raymond E Brown, Joseph A. Fitzmyer& Roland E. Murphy (eds.), *The New Jerome Biblical Commentary*, Bangalore: Theological Publications in India, 2005, pp. 1338-1353, here p. 1339b-1340a. The scholars mentioned here are all Catholics. The book has a *Nihil obstat* and an *Imprimatur*.
5. Johnson J. Puthenpurackal, "Introduction", in Puthenpurackal, *A Siege of the Citadel of Reason*, pp. 8-13, here p. 8.
6. José Antonio Pagola, *Jesus: An Historical Approximation*, tr. Margaret Wilde, Bangalore: Theological Publications in India (TPI), 2013, p. 91.
7. Stephen B. Bevans & Roger P. Schroeder, *Constants in Context: A Theology of Mission for Today*, Bangalore: Claretian Pbs., 2005, p. 8.
8. Myron J. Pereira, Southasiajournal.Net/The-Tragic-Attraction-of-Fundamentalism; Accessed on 31-08-2018.
9. See *Evangelii Gaudium*, nos. 1-2.
10. *Ibid.*, no. 6.
11. *Ibid.*, no. 12.
12. *Evangelii Nuntiandi*, no. 41.
13. *Redemptoris Missio*, no. 91.

# CONCLUDING ARTICLES

# 27

# The Audacity of the Impossible Serving the Church and the Nation with Joy

**Kuruvilla Pandikattu SJ**

Confronted with the gigantic problems faced by our nation and the Church, what can we do? How can we creatively serve the Church in India? What is the role of faith in creating a better India and a better Church? What can we really hope for humanity? These are some of the questions we want to respond to in the contemporary context of the Indian Church.

During his last visit to Jabalpur February 20, 2017, Rev Arturo Sosa SJ, the Superior General of the Society of Jesus, expressed his "great desire to learn from you about India, the richness of its cultures that form this great nation and the challenges you face to make the Good News of Jesus Christ present in the hearts of its people and cultures."[1] He urged his listeners to be audacious even in impossible situations. He quoted Jesus saying to a worried father: Everything is possible to one who has faith (Mat 9:23).

Jesus is astonished because he encounters a faithless generation that is resigned to a co-existence with evil spirits, even with those of the mute and deaf.

Today we find it easy to list incidents that lead us to despair and defeat. Then is the time to search for the improbable and impossible. Acknowledging that often we bump into the question of having the audacity of the improbable and about going beyond what seems impossible.[2] It is in this context that Sosa urges us to have the faith of Mary who could affirm: "I am the handmaid of the Lord; may it be done unto me according to your word" (Lk 1:38)

In this article we describe briefly some of the challenges facing the Church and the world. Then we offer the traditional responses from Indian and Christian traditions. This is followed by the call of Pope Francis to achieve the impossible by committed faith, a theme dear to Arturo Sosa, the Superior General of the Society of Jesus. By evoking the past and remembering that we are all members of the earth community, the Pope urges us to achieve the impossible through faith, hope and charity. This I believe is the joyful task and creative experience of Christians in India.

## 1. Our Challenging Situation Today

The present situation we live both in India and the world is very complex and extremely delicate. I want to limit myself to three crucial issues we all confront, which makes living today very perilous and ambiguous.

***Migrants and Refugees:*** Let us imagine the fate and destiny of the many migrant and refugees who are forced to move out of their own place of origin. It is an estimated 258 million persons. During the period from 2000 to 2017, the total number of international migrants increased from 173 to 258 million people, an increase of 85 million (49 per cent). In 2015, 244 million people, or 3.3 per cent of the world's population, lived outside their country of origin.

The World Refugee Day (June 20, 2018) has seen the UN publish a damning new report stating that just 100,000 refugees were resettled by the international community in 2017, a year in which 2.9 million new asylum seekers were created as conflicts raged in Syria, Myanmar, the Democratic Republic of Congo and Sudan. It is sad that mostly the poor and uneducated people are the migrants and refugees.

***Neoliberal Economy and Religious Fanaticism:*** Similarly, the whole world, including the United States, Europe and India, is facing the dangerous mix of neoliberal economy and religious fanaticism.

Neoliberalism, ideology and policy model that emphasizes the value of free market competition, championing economic laissez-faire and the freedom of individuals against the regulative power of government. This leads to the rich becoming rich and poor left at the mercy of the powerful.

***Sixth Mass Extinction:*** The Holocene extinction is also known as the "sixth extinction", as it is possibly the sixth mass extinct event is a possibility confronting human beings in general. A "biological annihilation" of wildlife in recent decades means a sixth mass extinction in Earth's history is under way and is more severe than previously feared, according to research.

Scientists analysed both common and rare species and found billions of regional or local populations have been lost. They blame human overpopulation and overconsumption for the crisis and warn that it threatens the survival of human civilisation, with just a short window of time in which to act.[3]

## 2. Indian Responses: Jnana-Bhakti-Karma Margas

The response to this highly complex and unpredictable situation may be taken in terms of the traditional Indian triad, Jnana marga (knowledge leading to wisdom), Bhakti marga (love, devotion) and Karma marga (hard, committed and sustained work)!

***Jnana Marga:*** It is the way of the knowledge, of wisdom, the path of the sage or scholar. This path requires development of the intellect through the study of the religious scriptures and other sources of wisdom. The way of jnana marga or yoga is considered the most difficult and at the same time the most direct. It involves serious study and will appeal to those who are more intellectually inclined. Within the context of our Western religious traditions, "Kabalistic scholars, Jesuit priests, and Benedictine monks epitomize jnana yogis" writes Marra Corrico.[4] This path may be aptly symbolised by the head or brain.

From a Christian perspective Sosa adds: "we are convinced that the only wisdom is LOVE that comes from fully trusting in God and from opening our hearts and minds to the action of the Holy Spirit."[5]

***Bhakti Marga:*** It describes the path of devotion, symbolised by the heart. Seeing the divine in all of creation, bhakti yoga is a positive way to channel the emotions. The path of bhakti provides us with an opportunity to cultivate acceptance and tolerance for everyone we come into contact with.

Bhakti yogis express the devotional nature of their path in their every thought, word, and deed—whether they are taking out the trash or calming the anger of a loved one. Mahatma Gandhi and Martin Luther King, Jr., are prime examples of bhakti yogis. Through devotion leading to love (for God and fellow human beings), human beings have been able to transform themselves and the world.

***Karma Marga:*** The next branch is that of karma yoga or the path of service, and none of us can escape this pathway. The principle of karma yoga is that what we experience today is created by our actions in the past. Being aware of this, all of our present efforts become a way to consciously create a future that frees us from being bound by negativity and selfishness. Karma is the path of self-transcending action. We practice karma yoga whenever we perform our work and live our lives in a selfless fashion and as a way to serve others. This path may be symbolised by the hand (and feet).

The merciful "life and work of Mother Teresa epitomize the combination of the karma and bhakti yoga paths with devotional aspects of bhakti and the selfless service of karma yoga," writes Corrico.

## 3. Christian Responses: Faith, Hope and Charity

The triad of Hindu responses could be enriched by the trial of Christian response, in terms of Faith, Hope and Charity.

***Faith that Heals:*** To solve the problems facing us, we need to have faith in God, fellow human beings and nature. We also need in oneself and in other people. We need to believe with the guidance and assistance from God, we can solve the problems, both individually and collectively.[6]

***Hope that Leads:*** This hope for a better tomorrow is intrinsic to humans as the humanistic philosopher and democratic socialist Erich Fromm would hold. The hope that we Christians hold is one based on the promises of the loving God and does not reduce itself exclusively to life after death. It is a hope of the "already and not yet"[7] where we dream of a better future for the whole of humanity and the universe.

***Love that Lives:*** Finally, charity or love is the central Christian virtue that enables us to treat everyone, including our opponents, with love, compassion and tenderness, enabling us to work collectively for solutions facing our "common home."

When we respond thus, we become humble prophets of tender love, who radiates God's love and compassion to all the people. We remain open to the whole world and are willing to embrace this world, even when it is painful and problematic.[8]

## 4. Pope Francis: 'God Makes Impossible, Possible'

In a homily that Pope Francis gave in Milan on March 25, 2017, he encourages us to be people of hope and joy in our troubled times. He asks: Is it possible to live the joy of the Gospel today within our cities? Is Christian hope possible in this situation, here and now? How can God make the impossible possible?

"Nothing is impossible for God" (Luke 1:37): thus ends the Angel's answer to Mary. When we believe that everything depends on our capacities, on our strengths, on our myopic horizons, when, instead, we are ready to allow ourselves to be helped, to let ourselves be counseled, when we open ourselves to grace, it seems that the impossible begins to become possible," the Pope said.[9]

He referred to "the most important announcement of our history": the Annunciation to Mary (cf. Luke1: 26-38) – a dense passage, full of life, which I like to read in the light of another announcement: that of the birth of John the Baptist (cf. Luke1: 5-20). Two announcements that follow one another and that are united; two announcements that, when contrasted, show us what God gives us in His Son.

He contrasts the annunciation of John the Baptisthappened which took place in the liturgical ceremony at the Sanctuary of the Temple, while all the assembly is outside waiting with the Annunciation of Jesus, which took place in a lost place of Galilee, in a peripheral city and without a particularly good reputation (cf. John 1:46), in the anonymity of the home of a girl called Mary.

This contrast, according to the Pope, indicates that the new Temple of God, the new encounter of God with His people will take place in places that we generally do not expect, in the margins, in the periphery. There, they will meet, there they will encounter one another, God will become flesh there to walk together with us from the womb of His Mother. Now He will no longer be in a place reserved for a few while the majority remains outside in expectation. Nothing and no one will be indifferent to him, no situation will be deprived of His presence: the joy of Salvation began in the daily life of the home of a girl of Nazareth.

God Himself is the one who takes the initiative and chooses to insert Himself, as He did with Mary, in our homes, in our daily struggles, full of anxieties together with desires. And it is in fact within our cities, our schools and universities, squares and hospitals that the most beautiful announcement we can hear is fulfilled: "Rejoice, the Lord is with thee!"It is a joy that generates life, that generates hope, that is made flesh in the way we look at the morrow, in the attitude with which we look at others. It is a joy that becomes solidarity, hospitality, and mercy towards all.

Like Mary, we can also be at a loss and ask: "How will this come about"? There is serious concern about life, about work, about the family. There is speculation about the poor and about migrants; there is speculation about young people and about their future. All seems to be reduced to numbers, forgetting, on the other hand, that the daily life of so many families is tinged with precariousness and insecurity. While grief knocks at many doors, while so many young people grow dissatisfied due to the lack of real opportunities, concern abounds everywhere.

The dizzying rhythmto which we are subjected certainly seems to rob us of hope and of joy. The pressures and the impotence in face of so many situations seem to wither the mind and make us insensitive in face of the innumerable challenges. And, paradoxically, when everything is accelerated to build – in theory – a better society, in the end there is no time for anything or anyone. We lose time for the family, time for the community, we lose time for friendship, for solidarity and for remembering.

In face of Mary's bewilderment, in face of our bewilderment, there are three keys that the Angel offers us to help us to accept the mission that is entrusted to us. This could also help us to venture into the future guided by the Spirit of God and led by the love for our neighbours.

**Evoking the Memory:** The first thing the Angel does is to evoke the memory, thus opening Mary's present to the whole history of Salvation. He evokes the promise made to David as fruit of the Covenant with Jacob. Mary is daughter of the Covenant. We also are invited today to remember, to look at our past so as not to forget from where we came, so as not to forget our ancestors, our grandparents and all that they went through to come to where we are today. This land and its people have known the grief of two world wars and sometimes have seen their merited fame for industry and civilization polluted by unruly ambitions. The memory helps us not to remain prisoners of discourses that sow fractures and divisions as the only way to resolve conflicts. To evoke the memory is the best antidote to our disposition in face of the magical solutions of division and estrangement. Can we collectively evoke the memory of humanity and of the universe formed 13.8 billion years ago?

**Belonging to the People of God:** Memory enables Mary to appropriate her belonging to the People of God. It does us good to remember that we are members of the People of God! Made up of a thousand faces, histories, provenances, a multi-cultural and multi-ethnic people. This is one of our riches. It is a people called to welcome differences, to integrate them with respect and creativity and to celebrate the novelty that comes from others; it is a people that is not afraid to embrace the confines, the frontiers; it is a people that is not afraid to give hospitality to one in need because it knows that its Lord is present there. Can we reconnect ourselves to the story of humanity? And can we connect ourselves to other living beings and nature?

**The Possibility of the Impossible:** When we believe that everything depends on our capacities, on our strengths, on our myopic horizons, then things become difficult. On the other hand, when we are ready to allow ourselves to be helped, to let ourselves be counseled, when we open ourselves to grace, it seems that the impossible begins to become possible. "Overcoming sterile and divisive pessimism," we can open ourselves to God's initiative and become "signs of how fruitful a land can be that is not closed in its own ideas, in its limitations and in its capacities and opens to others," the Pope added. Can we relate to others, belonging to different religious, political and national identities and together strive for a community that is both inclusive and enabling?

The Pope reminds us that God continues to seek allies. He continues to seek men and women capable of believing, capable of remembering, of feeling part of His people to cooperate with the Spirit's creativity. God continues to tread our suburbs and streets. He pushes Himself in every place in search of hearts capable of listening to His invitation and make it become flesh here and now. Paraphrasing Saint Ambrose in his comment on this passage, we can say: God continues to seek hearts like Mary's, willing to believe even in altogether extraordinary conditions.

## Concluding Remarks: Enabling Intellectual, Moral and Spiritual Leaders

Inspired by the hope for the impossible as advocated by Jesuit Superior General Arturo Sosa and Pope Francis, we know that the challenge is great. But the assurance based on God's unconditional love is greater. Our response based on the Indian and Christian categories (wisdom, love and commitment with faith, hope and charity) enables us to be people of joy. It is the firm faith in God, creative commitment to His people and unwavering loyalty to "our common home" that drives us forward.

For this we need leaders who can turn information to knowledge and wisdom. Arturo Sosa adds: We need to "remember that all wisdom comes from the Lord. Wisdom is a gift and a temptation. It is a gift when we recognize its origin in God. It becomes a temptation when we are convinced of our own wisdom. Indeed, after a long intellectual formation we may feel that we have built up a store of wisdom. We do not any more feel the need to receive wisdom because we think we are able to create it. The danger is to confuse wisdom with knowledge. We can reach knowledge with our efforts."[10] Thus we need such wise leaders whose moral integrity is impeccable and who are willing to suffer for a cause larger than themselves. Leaders who are spiritually deep to be able to embrace everyone and everything with a passionate love and compassionate care.

Can we become such leaders who can collectively march ahead, in spite of setbacks and troubles? To a limited extent, Papal Seminary, Pune, has been able to achieve it through its committed formators and creative formees.

Thus following the triad of knowing, loving and acting based on faith, hope and charity, we can collectively achieve "the audacity of the improbable and even the impossible!" Thus we can make this world a safer place for humanity. It is fitting to end with a quotes from Pope Francis: "Yet all is not lost. Human beings, while capable of the worst, are also capable of rising above themselves, choosing again what is good, and making a new start, despite their mental and social conditioning. …I appeal to everyone throughout the world not to forget this dignity which is ours. No one has the right to take it from us" (LS 205).

That will enable the migrants and refugees to lead lives of dignity. That can provide us with economic system that serves human beings, especially the poor in the peripheries. That will enable religious people to encounter a compassionate God. That will possible help the humans and non-humans to flourish on this precious and perilous earth!

## Notes

1. Arturo Sosa SJ, Homily on February 20, 2017, given at Jabalpur, India. Accessed from http://sjweb.info/documents/assj/2017.02.20_7th_Monday_OT._Homily.pdf. All the sites for this article were accessed in February 2019.
2. This has been a question confronting us from the very beginning of General Congregation 36 of the Society of Jesus, that took place in October-November 2016.
3. Carrington, Damian. "Earth's Sixth Mass Extinction Event under Way, Scientists Warn | Environment | The Guardian," July 10, 2017. https://www.theguardian.com/environment/2017/jul/10/earths-sixth-mass-extinction-event-already-underway-scientists-warn.
4. Carrico, Mara. "The Branches of the Yoga Tree." Yoga Journal. Accessed February 13, 2019. https://www.yogajournal.com/practice/the-branches-of-yoga.
5. Sosa, 2017.
6. It may be noted that Jnana-Deepa Vidyapeeth, Pune, our sister-institute had its motto for 2018 as "Faith that heals and builds nations."
7. "Schonabernochnicht" ("already but not yet") is a theological or eschatological phrase, rich in insights, designating the relationship between this world and other world. 'Already fulfilled' and 'not yet consummated' ... und 'nochnichtvollendet' is how the German theologian Oscar Cullmann describe the dynamic relationship between our redemption and final salvation.
8. Purposely, I donot elaborate on this triad, not because it is unimportant, but because it is familiar to most of the readers.
9. Pope Francis. "'God Makes Impossible, Possible' (Pope's Homily in Milan)." *ZENIT*, March 25, 2017. https://zenit.org/articles/god-makes-impossible-possible-popes-homily-in-milan/. This whole section is based on this article.
10. Sosa, 2017.

28

# The Jesuit Apostolic Priorities for Today

**Kuruvilla Pandikattu SJ**

What has the Society of Jesus, which has been guiding the Home of Love, teach us in terms of setting our apostolic priorities? How far can we resonate ourselves with the priorities that the Jesuits have set for themselves? In this context, I want to reflect on the priorities that the Jesuits have set for the next ten years, with a view of setting our priorities both as individuals and as members of the Indian Church.

On Feb 19, 2019, the General of the Society of Jesus has revealed their Universal Apostolic Preferences (UAP) for the next 10 years. Venezuelan-born Jesuit Superior General Father Arturo Sosa, popularly known as the Black Pope, said the UAP would guide the Society of Jesus forward, inspired by the discernment of the spirits, concern for the excluded, care for the environment, and journeying with young people.[1]

In his letter addressed to the 15,536 Jesuits worldwide, Sosa elaborated on the four guiding principles. These include the promotion of discernment and spiritual exercises, walking with the excluded, accompanying the young in their journey and caring for our common home. These are the universal apostolic preferences set by the Society of Jesus for the next decade, 2019-2029.[2]

## Approved by the Holy Father

These preferences are officially approved by the Pope Francis, himself a Jesuit. The universal apostolic preferences of the Jesuits "are in harmony with the current apostolic priorities of the Church expressed through the ordinary magisterium of the Pope, the synods, the episcopal conferences, especially in the Apostolic Exhortation *Evangelii Gaudium*," the Pope emphasized in a letter addressed to the Jesuit General, Father Arturo Sosa on Feb 6, 2019.[1]

What has been undertaken, the Pontiff added, is a "dynamic discernment", not a "library or labour" process. Pope Francis stressed that the first UAP was "fundamental because it presupposes as a basic condition the relation of the Jesuit with the Lord, his personal and communitarian life of prayer and discernment." "Without this prayerful attitude, the rest will not function," he added in his official letter.2

## The Four Priorities

The apostolic preferences are the result of a process of discernment that lasted almost two years. It began with the General Congregation of the Jesuits in October 2016, that elected Fr Sosa as the 31st General of the Society of Jesus. Numerous meetings, discussions, group encounters, spiritual conversations and moments of prayerful discernment led to the selection of the preferences, which took two years in the making.

The UAP which deals with "four vital areas," inspire Jesuits "in their discernment and in apostolic planning," Sosa added. They are the points of reference, horizons and orientations for the entire Society of Jesus. They emphasize how Jesuits can "make better use of the means at their disposal to serve Christ's reconciling mission in the world." They are the Jesuits' response to the needs of the Church. These preferences were selected "through socio-political analysis, theological and pastoral reflection and discernment."[3]

### a. Promoting Discernment and *The Spiritual Exercises*

Illustrating these four apostolic preferences, Fr. Sosa told Vatican News that genuine discernment is a necessity for the Church today. The Spiritual Exercises, he added, are a preferential path for the Jesuits. It is also fundamental, as far as the exercises are concerned, to take the path of creativity. According to the Jesuit General, new forms must be found so that the exercises adapt to different groups, realities and contexts.

### b. Walking with the Poor and Those in the Peripharies

Walking with those who are discarded, said Father Sosa, means approaching the world of the poor and going to the suburbs to meet the people. "We want to take a path, he added, to promote social justice. "We want to promote a change in the economic, political and social structures that cause injustice. "We want to eliminate the scourge of abuse from the life of the Church and society," a drama that the Jesuit General said is manifest out in various forms, including in sexual abuse and abuse of power.

## c. Accompanying the Youth

According to Fr. Sosa, walking with young people also means looking at the world from their perspective. Young people, he explained, can help understand the changes in society, to grasp the sense of a new culture. We must therefore "open up spaces for young people, for their creativity", he said, adding they must also learn from the young.

## d. Caring for the Common Home

The fourth preference concerns our common home, this earth. Father Sosa said we must try to participate in urgent actions that can help prevent environmental destruction. Alternative formulas and creative action must also be sought to rediscover the earth as our beloved home, which we need to protect.

Father Sosa said the UAP was unlikely to cover all bases for Jesuits in their myriad missions around the world due to the different "needs of the Church in particular territories with specific conditions." The Jesuit Superior General responded by writing, "we realize that unless we live *The Spiritual Exercises* – if we are not persons who engage in discernment – we cannot help others or contribute to others in discernment. We have to live them deeply."

These priorities were well received by the Indian Jesuits. Fr MK George, Provincial of Kerala maintained that these priorities are "both relevant and timely." Fr Edward Mudavassery, former Provincial of South Asia said: "Personally I am thrilled at the choice of the four UAP by the Society of Jesus. Undoubtedly Pope Francis has been an inspirational figure ever since he began his Pontificate to bring to focus and urgency these four areas to address the burning problems of the world and the Church." Fr BhausahebSansare, Rector, Papal Seminary says the preferences reflect the optimism that the society feels for the world, in spite of the challenges. He added that "we can collectively be part of the solution." Fr George Pattery, President of South Asian Assistancy, reiterates that "UAP the mood and sentiments of our times and holds hope and courage for the youth, especially in viewing secularizaion as 'signs of the time' and a critique of 'religious world'. That our Earth is a common home provides a large frame work for all religions and cultures to work together. the marginalized are part of this common home."[4]

Obviously, we cannot transport these priorities for the India Church. But they can serve as guiding lights in our common discernment for our apostolic priorities. We can learn from the Holy Father and the Superior General of the Society of Jesus to have a guiding vision that includes everyone, including those who do not think, act and hope like ourselves. Our vision will shape the future of not only ourselves, but of the whole world!

## Notes

1. This article is adapted from my article for *The Smart Companion*, March 2019.
2. O'Connell, Gerard. "Pope Francis approves four priorities for the Jesuits' next decade," *America: The Jesuit Review*, February 19, 2019, https://www.americamagazine.org/faith/2019/02/19/pope-francis-approves-four-priorities-jesuits-next-decade. Accessed on February 23, 2019.
3. Lomonaco, Amedeo, "Pope commends Jesuits for being in tune with Church priorities," Vatican News, 19 February 2019, 14:33, https://www.vaticannews.va/en/pope/news/2019-02/pope-francis-letter-jesuit-general-sosa-four-priorities.html. Accessed on February 23, 2019.
4. All these reports are results of personal communication. It may be noted that the Jesuit General is visiting Mumbai, Goa and Pune in March 2019. Fr Selva Rathinam, President, Jnana-Deepa Vidyapeeth is "excited to have the presence of Fr General, who will enlighten us more on these

# Select Bibliography

"Empowerment of Women in the Church and Society". *The Gender Policy for the Catholic Church in India 2009*. New Delhi: CBCI Commission for Women Catholic Bishops' Conference of India, 2010.

Alexander, Anna Vareed. *Biblical Women Our Foremothers. Women's Perspective*. Indore: Satprakashan Sanchar Kendra, 1997.

Bhardwaj, Kritika, and Ashok K. Sharma. *Nobel Peace Prize Winner Malala: The Crusader of Fearless Freedom*.New Delhi: Diamond Pocket Books (P) Ltd, 2015.

Carmichael, Amy Wilson. *Things as They are: Mission Work in Southern India*. London: Morgan and Scott, 1904.

Chakkalackal, Pauline. "Consecrated Life a Prophetic Witness," *Conference of Religious India: CRI New Delhi*. No. 54 (July-August 2014): 10.

Charters Molony, J. *A Book of South India*. London: Methuen & Co. LTD, 1926.

Clark, N Nason. "When Terror Strikes at Home: The Interface between Religion and Domestic Violence". In *Journal for the Scientific Study of Religion*, 42/3, (2004): 303-310.

Crossan, Dominic John. *The Historical Jesus: The Life of a Mediterranean Jewish Peasant*. Edinburgh: T & T Clark, 1991.

Culpepper, Alan. "The Gospel of Luke: Introduction, Commentary, and Reflection". In *The New Interpreter's Bible Commentary*. Vol. IX Luke and John. Nashville: Abingdon Press, 1995.

Deka, Meeta. *Women's Agency and Social Change: Assam and Beyond*. New Delhi: Sage Publication, 2013.

Dungdung, Gladson. *Whose Country is it anyway*? Kolkata: Adivaani, 2013.

Fischler C., 1980, "Food Habits, Social Change and the Nature/Culture Dilemma,"*Social Science Information*, 19(6), 937-953.

Fox, Henry W. *Chapters on Missions in South India*. London: Seeleys, MDCCCXLVIII.

Garriz, D., "Fifty Years of Ahmedabad Diocese," in AMGJS. Ahmedabad, 1984, pp. 4-10.

_______, "The Shrine of Unteshwari Mata," ibid (1988): 384 ff.

_______. "Inculturation: Notes on an Experiment," *Indian Missiological Review* 10 (1988): 371 ff.

_______ "Twenty years of Growth," in Suria (ed.), *History of the Catholic Church in Gujarat.* Anand: GSP, 1990. p. 358 ff.

Ghai, Anita, and Rachana Johri. "Religion, Feminist Politics and Muslim Women's Rights in India". In *Women and Law Critical Feminist Perspectives*, edited by Kalpana Kannabiran, 264-273. New Delhi: SAGE Publication, 2014.,

Goody J., 1982, *Cooking, Cuisine and Class. A Study in Comparative Sociology*, université de Cambridge traduit en française Cuisines, cuisine et classes, collection Alors, Centre Georges Pompidou, 1984.

Gray, John. *Men are from Mars, Women are from Venus*. London: HarperCollins Publishers, 2012.

Hambaye, E. R. *History of Christianity in India* Vol. III. Bangalore: Church History Association of India, 1997.

Heredero J. M., *Education for Development.* New Delhi: Manohar, 1989.

Hull, E. R., *Bombay Mission History, 2* Vols.. Bombay: Examiner Press, 1927-30

Jesurajan, Aloysius C. *An Evaluation of the Communication Apostolate of Andhra Pradesh: A Case Study. Secunderabad: The Catholic Information Center of Andhra Pradesh, 1971.*

John Paul II, *Vita Consecrata, Post Synodal Apostolic Exhortation on the Consecrated Life and its Mission in the Church and in the World.* March 25, 1996.

John, P.R. "Daring to Hope: Challenges to the Church in AP." *Vidyajyoti* 76/9 (2012): 645-63.

John, P.R. "Christ in Telugu Poetry." *Jeevadhara* 37/219 (2007): 214-26.

Kaitholil, George. *Consecrated Life: Challenges and Opportunities.* Mumbai: St. Pauls, 2014.

Kroot, Antony. *History of the Telugu Christians.* Trichinopoly: St. Joseph's printing press, 1909. Reprinted by Fr. Vatti Joji. Krishnapuram: Sri Sanjivanandha Swamy Shrine, 2009.

Kujur, Marianus and SonajhariaMinj (ed.). *Pearls of Indigenous Wisdom*. New Delhi: Indian Social Institute, 2007.

_____ (ed.). *Indigenous People of India: Problems and Prospects*. New Delhi: Indian Social Institute, 2007.

Leonard, Richard. *Beloved Daughters.100 Years of Papal Teaching on Women.* Melbourne Australia: David Lovell Publishing, 1995.

Lewis, Hedwig. *At Home with God.* Anand:Gujarat Sahitya Prakash, 1991.

Lobo, L, "Christians: Challenges, Contributions," *The Times of India,* March 23, 1990, pp. 7-8.

_______, *Religious Conversion and Social Mobility: A Case Study of the Vankars in Central Gujarat.* Surat: CSS, 1991.

Mananzan, Mary John ed..*Women and Religion.* Manila: Women's Studies Series, 1988.

Mattam, J., "Christian Identity: Is Baptism an Element of Separation or of Human Solidarity," in Puthanangady (ed.), *Sharing Worship.* Bangalore: NBCLC, 1988, pp. 430 ff.

_______, "Priestly Training in Gujarat," in AMGJS, 1984, p. 28 ff.

_______, "Specific Problems of Evangelization in Gujarat," *Indian Missiological Review I* (1988): 359 ff.

Maurer D, Sobal J., 1995, *Eating Agendas. Food and Nutrition as Social Problems*, New York, Aldine de Gruyter.

Mauss, Marcel,1977, *Manuel d'ethnographie* Petite bibliotèchèque, Payot, Paris, 1977.

McIntosch A., 1996, *Sociology of food and nutrition*, New-York, Plenium

Mennell S., Murcott A., Van Otterloo A., 1992, *The Sociology of Food: Eating, Diet and Culture*, London, Sage.

Milford, C.S. *South India's New Church.* London: The Cargate Press, 1947.

Minj, Francis. "Mission of the Adivasi Church in the Era of Globalization." *Sevartham* 39, 2014:25-42.

Mullens, Joseph. *Mission in South India.* London: Baptist Mission Press, 1854.

Nachef, Antoine E. *Women in the Eyes of Jesus. Yesterday, Today & Forever*. New York: St. Pauls, 2003.

Natabar, Garada. "Agrarian Distress and farmer suicides in AP." *Social Action* 59/1 (2009):66-78.

O'Day, Gail R. "The Gospel of John, Introduction, Commentary, and Reflections". In *the New Interpreter's Bible Commentary*. Vol. IX Luke and John. Nashville: Abingdon Press, 1995.

Paul, R.C. *History of the Telugu Christians*. Madras: Good Pastor Press, 1929. Reprinted at Secunderabad: Jeevan institute of Printing, 2003.

Perkins, Pheme. "The Gospel According to John". In the *New Jerome Biblical Commentary*, 970. New Jersey: Prentice Hall, 1990.

Prakash, Mallavarapu. "Andhra Telanganalalo Sreesabha Edurkontunna Samskrtulu." *Lokaniki Nene Velugu* 39/3 (July-September, 2016): 31-40.

Puthumana J. *A Brief History of Catholic Church in Andhra Pradesh*. Secunderabad: Jeevan Institute of Printing, 2011.

Raj, Solomon. "Christian Song Tradition in India with Special reference to Telugu." *Exchange* 29/4 (2000): 353-60.

Saldanha, J., *Inculturation.* Bombay: St. Paul's, 1987.

Saminathan, Padmini. "Revisiting the Theme of Women's Empowerment': How Leadership Matters". In *Interrogating Women's Leadership and Empowerment*, ed. Omita Goyal, 13-29. New Delhi: Sage Publication, 2015.

Sankarathil, John. *Towards a Prophetic Spirituality of Religious Life.* Bangalore: Asian Trading Corporation, 1999.

Saunders, Ross. *Outrageous Women. Outrageous God. Women in the First Two Generations of Christianity*. Australia: E.J Dwyer Pvt. Ltd, 1996.

Sebastian, Jose. *The Jesuit Carnatic Mission: A Foundation of Andhra Church.* Secunderabad: Andhra Jesuit Society, 2004.

Sharkey, Peter. *The Essentials of Community Care.* New York: Palgrave Macmillan, 2007.

Soares-Prabhu, George M. *Biblical Spirituality of Liberative Action.Collected Writings of George Soares-Prabhu,* ed. Scaria Kuthirakkattel, vol. 3. Pune: Jnana-Deepa Vidyapeeth, 2003.

Solomon, Thanugundla. *The Structures of the Church in Andhra Pradesh.* Rome: Pontifical Urban University, 1976.

Sudheer, M. "Christian Shanti Asharam: An Indigenous Movement in A.P." *Dharma Deepika* 6/1 (2002):31-6.

Suria, C. (ed.), "Early Churches in Gujarat," in AMGJS, p. 165 ff.

_______ , *History of the Catholic Church in Gujarat.* Anand: GSP (with articles by Garriz and others), 1990.

Swami Bharati, Ageshananda. "Women's predicament as They Encountered Christianity: A Case Study of C.M.S Telugu Mission.' *Indian Church History Review* 35/2 (2001):147-67.

Taneti, James Elisha. "Beginning of Christianity Among Telugus." *Indian Church History Review* 42/2 (2008):118-34.

Taneti, James Elisha. "Empowering mission or Enslaving Enterprise Women Missionaries attitude to Telugu Woman." *Bangalore Theological Forum* 39/1 (2007):161-72.

Taneti, James Elisha. "Reconfiguring Home: Telugu Bible woman, protestant missionaries and Christian marriage." *International Bulletin of Missionary Research* 35/1 (2011): 30-35.

Tirkey, Agapit. *The Liberator of Tribals: Short Biography of Servant of God Father Constant Lievens, SJ.* Ranchi: Ranchi Jesuits, 2014.

Valiamangalam, J., *The Mission Methods of Father Joaquin Vilallonga.* Anand: GSP, 1989.

Varghese Paul (ed.), *Ahmedabad Mission Golden Jubilee Souvenir* (AMGJS). Ahmedabad: Catholic Information Centre, 1984.

Waller, E. H. M. *Church Union in South India: The Story of The Negotiations*. London: Macmillan Company,1929.

Wiebe, Paul D. *Christians in Andhra Pradesh: The Mennonites of Mahabubnagar*. Madras: The Christian Literature Society, 1988.

# Our Contributors

**A. Soosai Nathan (**Jammu-Srinagar Diocese), is presently pursuing his doctoral studies at Angelicum University, Rome. Email: frsoosainathan@gmail.com

**Arjen Tete SJ** (Calcutta Province) has specialized in Systematic Theology and teaches at JDV. Email: arjensj@gmail.com

**D. J. Margaret FMA**, belonging to the Congregation of the Salesian Sisters of Don Bosco, is a systematic theologian. Email: djmagifma@gmail.com

**Denis Rodrigues**, with his background in Philosophy, Theology, Political Science and Science, is a consultant, based in Pune. Email: audden@gmail.com

**Fabian Jose UMI**, teaches at JDV and has specialized in Spirituality of Consecrated Life. Email: fabianaumi@gmail.com

**Francis Gonsalves SJ**, Dean, Faculty of Philosophy, JDV, has specialized in Systematic Theology. He has taken over as President, Jnana-Deepa Vidyapeeth, on July 31, 2020. Email: fragons@gmail.com

**Jacob Manathodath (Rt Rev)** is Bishop of Palghat and the Apostolic Administrator of the Archdiocese of Ernakulam. Email: jmanathodath@gmail.com

**James Charles-Davis** (Jammu-Srinagar Dio) is presently completing his post-doctoral studies (Habilitation) in ethics from Humboldt Foundation, Germany. Email: charlesdavisj76@gmail.com

**Jangkholam Haokip**, Dean of Theology & Ethics Division, is Professor of Union Biblical Seminary, Pune. Email: lamboihaokip@gmail.com

**Jayaraju Ghattamaneni SJ** (Andhra Province) is a research student in Systematic Theology at JDV. Email: jayaraj23sj@gmail.com

**Joaquim Reis** is a practicing advocate in Bombay High Court and in the Supreme Court. Email: dv.jreis@gmail.com

**John Ponnore**, Director of Biblical and Catechetical Commission of the Archdiocese of Raipur, has specialized in Diocesan spirituality. Mob: 84589 88842

**Jose Thayil SJ**, Registrar, JDV, is a moral theologian who obtained his PhD from the University of Innsbruck. He is a Jesuit belonging to Patna Province. Email: josethayilsj@gmail.com

**Joseph Kaipayil MCBS** is Professor of philosophy at Jeevalaya Institute of Philosophy, Bengaluru. Email: josephkaipayil@gmail.com

**Joseph Mattam SJ** (Gujarat Province) is a systematic theologian. Email: joemattam@jesuits.net

**Kuruvilla Pandikattu SJ** (Dumka-Raiganj Prov) is Dean, Faculty of Philosophy, JDV. Email: kuru@jdv.edu.in

**Michael Bansode**, is a Salesian priest, has specialized in the history of the Church in Maharashtra. Email: michaelbansode@gmail.com

**Nishant Alphonse Irudayadason** (Palayamkottai Dio) is a Professor of Philosophy at Jnana-Deepa Vidyapeeth (JDV), Pune, India. Email: nishant@jdv.edu.in

**Paul Thelakat**, Editor "Light of Truth," has specialized in Literature. Email: thelakatpaul@gmail.com

**Prasad Lankappalli SJ** (Andhra Province) is a Jesuit and Professor of Systematic Theology at JDV, Pune. Email: lankaprasad4@gmail.com

**Rony George**, Director, Chaitanya Institute of Mental Health, is a practising social worker. Email: chaitanyaimh@gmail.com

**Sebastian Vazhapilly SJ** (Gujarat Province) is a Jesuit and Professor in the Dept of Indian Studies, JDV, Pune. Email: vvsaby@gmail.com

**Shashi Minz** served in Indian Revenue Service (Indian Customs and Central Excise and Narcotics). Email: shashminz@yahoo.com

**Stephen Chundamthadam SJ** (Emeritus Professor of Philosophy, JDV, Pune) is the Director, Samanvaya Centre for Indian Studies, Kanjirapally. Email: sthadam@gmail.com

**Stephen Jayard** (Trichy Dio) is Professor of Cosmology and Philosophy of Science, JDV, Pune. Email: sjayard@gmail.com

**Subhash Anand** (Udaipur Dio) is Prof (Emeritus) of Indian Philosophy, JDV, Pune. Email: 43subhash@gmail.com

**Thomas Dabre (Rt Rev)** is Bishop of Poona. Email: bishopthomasdabre@gmail.com

**Thomas Karimundackal SJ** staff at JDV, Pune, and Papal Seminary, is author of *A Call to Commitment: An Exegetical and Theological Study of Deut 10,12-11,32* (Forschungzur Bible). Email: tomksj@gmail.com

**Victor Ferrão** (Goa Dio) is Dean of Philosophy at Rachol Seminary, Goa. Email: victorferrao@yahoo.co.uk

**Vishal G. Jadhav** is Associate Professor and Coordinator, Nehru Institute of Social Sciences, at Tilak Maharashtra Vidyapeeth, Pune. Email: vishalsocio@gmail.com